Beyond Therapy

Beyond Therapy

Igniting Life Focus Community Movements

Erving Polster

Transaction Publishers
New Brunswick (U.S.A.) and London (U.K.)

Copyright © 2015 by Transaction Publishers, New Brunswick, New Jersey.

All rights reserved under International and Pan-American Copyright Conventions. No part of this book may be reproduced or transmitted in any form or by any means, electronic or mechanical, including photocopy, recording, or any information storage and retrieval system, without prior permission in writing from the publisher. All inquiries should be addressed to Transaction Publishers, 10 Corporate Place South, Suite 102, Piscataway, New Jersey 08854. www.transactionpub.com

This book is printed on acid-free paper that meets the American National Standard for Permanence of Paper for Printed Library Materials.

Library of Congress Catalog Number: 2015005664
ISBN: 978-1-4128-5689-8 (cloth); 978-1-4128-6262-2 (paper)
eBook: 978-1-4128-5656-0
Printed in the United States of America

Library of Congress Cataloging-in-Publication Data

Polster, Erving.
  Beyond therapy : igniting life focus community movements / by Erving Polster.
    pages cm
  Includes bibliographical references and index.
  ISBN 978-1-4128-5689-8
  1. Self-help groups. 2. Psychotherapy. I. Title.
RC488.8.P65 2016
616.89'14--dc23

2015005664

Contents

Acknowledgements   vii

Section A. The Importance of Life Focus

1   What I Mean By Life Focus   3

2   The Drama of the Split Mind   23

3   Life as Microcosm   33

4   A Focus Revolution   49

Section B. How Life Focus Groups Work

5   Life Focus Community: Design Ideas   69

6   Artful Engagement   85

7   Themes that Mark a Lifetime   97

8   Communal Setting   113

Section C. Social Implications of Life Focus

9   From the Supernatural to the Human: Part 1   127

10   From the Supernatural to the Human: Part 2   143

11   A Psychotherapeutic Morality   163

12   Dependable Identity   175

13	Belonging and Indivisibility	183
14	A Social Trust	193
Bibliography		205
Index		209

Acknowledgements

Writing can be a lonely experience. However, while it is essentially done privately, it is always directed to an imagined otherness: One that is vital to the need we all have to a connectedness with the world outside. Writing is commonly interwoven with other forms of communication, such as those of the teacher, the correspondent and the conversationalist. I want to recognize this largeness of engagement, by naming certain people who have made my writing less lonely and more embedded in my everyday world. I especially point to Joseph Barber, Natasha Josephowitz, Michael Yapko, Paul Pinegar, and Caroline Paltin who have invigorated me with their sage observations about various aspects of this book.

I am also blessed to be a member of a long-time discussion group, which has addressed a few of this book's themes among its many discussion topics. They're my good friends and they make anything I write privately feel as if it's a part of a larger platform of relationship. Their names are John Reis, Rich Hycner, Roy Resnikoff, Milt Richlin, Jean Wiseman, Sharon Grodner, Mark Lewkowicz, Linda Hart, Madeleine Haley, and Rose Lee Polster.

I also want to thank Jean Femia for her early editorial assistance. I have been enabled by my sensitive assistants, Kathryn Conklin and Erika Iacona, who have provided me with a loving presence in managing my communications concerning this manuscript. Furthermore, I am grateful to my wife, Rose Lee, who's connoisseurship of language and organization of ideas have kept me on track.

I am grateful to Brian O'Neill and to Talia Bar-Yoseph Levine for permission to include excerpts from chapters I wrote for the anthologies they authored. The titles of their anthologies are, respectively, *Community, Psychotherapy and Life Focus*, published by Ravenwood Press, 2009 and *Gestalt Therapy: Advances in Theory and Practice*, published by Routledge Press in 2012.

Section A

The Importance of Life Focus

1

What I Mean By Life Focus

Over the ages, many famous thinkers have grappled with the choices people make and how these choices affect their lives. Nowadays, more than ever, in a society enamored of self-determination, the importance of choice-making has become popularized, sometimes reaching sloganized proportions. Jean-Paul Sartre, for example, famously said that we *are* our choices. J.K. Rowling said, "It is our choices, Harry, that show what we truly are, far more than our abilities" (Rowling 2012). Eleanor Roosevelt said that one's philosophy is not best expressed in words; it is expressed in the choices one makes. Indeed, the message is that choices are daring declarations that we are masters of our own fate.

Yes, of course, choosing is an impactful part of our lives. We choose whom to marry, the work we do, whether to go to the theater, where we live. Not so pointedly, we also choose how to raise our children, and whether to celebrate, commiserate, laugh, cheat, rebel, and/or congregate. However, we have to ask whether "choice" is always the best word to apply to these behaviors. What about choices we make that may also subsume future choice? For example, to choose to be married "until death do us part" limits later choice; to choose the life of a scholar builds in a lifetime of reading; and to choose any ideology causes us to prejudge specific issues. In each case, one may continue literally to be free to choose, but the one large choice compromises later specific choices.

A further and more fundamental complication is that while choice is commonly understood to refer to sharply delineated options, that is very different from the options that are part of a perpetual challenge that goes on and on. It is an ever-present selection requirement that calls for responses that go beyond personal awareness, where we involuntarily incorporate our life experiences, much of which becomes inaccessible, resulting in significant loss. We see the poetry of this fate in William Wordsworth's classic message:

> The world is too much with us; late and soon,
> Getting and spending, we lay waste our powers:
> Little we see in Nature that is ours;
> We have given our hearts away, a sordid boon!
> The Sea that bares her bosom to the moon;
> The winds that will be howling at all hours,
> And are up-gathered now like sleeping flowers;
> For this, for everything, we are out of tune.

This lament is still well-known 150 years later. It brings recognition to the very simple fact that the world is, indeed, too much with us. There are so many moments when sharply targeted choices must take their place within a broader process of selection, a process operative in every moment of our lives. Much of this is experienced simply as life's flow as we, for example, rush to work without kissing our kids good-bye.

The Speed of Life

Never can we be aware of all that is going on; our attention skills are overmatched by the continual input from an irrepressible flood of happenings. Think of each twenty-four-hour day as having the startling number of 86,400 seconds, with each moment containing its own detail, then sliding into the next moment. While we cannot begin to describe all the minutiae, we are always more or less attentive. We open our eyes in the morning, suddenly feeling awake. We ponder a dream; hear our neighbors quarrel; eat breakfast bite after bite after bite; listen to our children's pleas, laughter, and battles; get flashes of the day ahead; exchange ideas with a friend at lunch; get stopped by a traffic cop; wrestle with feeling a friend's disapproval; weigh important decisions; and perhaps even philosophize about life purposes. The books and newspapers we read, the multiple sounds and sights of the streets we drive, the gym conversations, the calls we receive, the parties we attend—they all contribute to the superabundance we face as we endlessly move through an insistent continuity. This surfeit of stimulation leaves us with an inventory of the unattended that resides silently in the background of our minds.

We can live very well with that fluid process, making the most of what matters to us, steeped in an effervescent universe. While much of what enters us eludes awareness, it is perhaps never neurologically absent, lying in latent potentiality, as we ride above a dimly realized fluidity of experiences. Everything just keeps on going so speedily forward that we set aside the raw material for a lifetime of personal stories, which remain fallow in an indistinct background. Except for special conversational opportunity, that is where this raw material of life experiences remains, impactful only in the mystical sense that everything matters.

In her recent novel *Flight Behavior*, Barbara Kingsolver opens a window into such sidelined experiences of rural parishioners. Bobby, the minister, in talking to the people in his congregation, encourages them to catch up with what they have left behind. He says, "What I want to ask you right now is: What do you love? What has the good Lord bestowed on your home and family that has brought grace to your life?" A woman named Rachel responds, "My little grandbaby Haylee." The minister spotlights this feeling by saying to his people, "I want everyone here to covenant with sister Rachel." The room does, indeed, warm up to Rachel's story, and then, when she has said what she wanted to say, another person tells about his daughter, Jill, getting over cancer and how he loves her pretty yellow hair. His story of gratitude and Rachel's tears combined to further warm the room. Then it was one surprise after another, as people poured out dear experiences: a new porch deck, with a view of the sunset; the wedding of a disabled cousin; a pure white calf (Kingsolver 2012).

Here is where the psychological professions may enter, offering their forms of communal opportunity for people to catch up to the speed of their lives. Their groups provide a *time-out* from the exacting momentum; a time-out for people to pay attention more pointedly to the choices they have made, thus restoring the nourishment that has been lost through inadequate recognition. Psychotherapy has had a century to prepare for explicitly creating a special place, a special time, a special frame of mind, and a special communal ethos, where it has created a freedom that allows people to surpass habit and seek personal enlightenment. In its therapy sessions, both individual and group, people have been enabled to retrace their lives, by telling the stories that mark their pathway. In expanding from these precedents, I am pointing this book toward the formation of Life Focus Community groups, which are vehicles to help people get off the conveyor belt of worldly insistence so that they may be free to understand and assimilate what is happening in the broad landscape of their minds. These groups enable catch-up opportunities on a continuing basis: they provide designs for people to revisit the life themes that color their journey, and they restore disconnected sources of personal enablement and affirmation.

The Social Setting

These groups are part of a mushrooming movement that is reaching into many corners of modern living. While ignited by the invention of psychotherapy, this social dynamism has gone beyond the language of disturbance to look at the way people live their lives. Huge numbers of people are participating in a large range of social applications. (See chapter 4 for greater detail.) We see this popularity in the "mindfulness" programs that are sweeping the country, in widespread "spiritualistic" practices, in the large variety of self-help groups, and in the prodigious sale of self-help books. We see it in journalistic perspectives appearing in books and magazines. We see life-exploratory conversations in men's and women's groups. We see the life focus need addressed in book clubs, where people identify with the novel's characters, who provide enlarged recognition to obscured aspects of their own lives. Newspapers and magazines respond every day to a public thirst by reporting "human interest" stories.

The beat goes further, into the work-a-day world. We have seen the expansion of life focus practices in commercial organizations, where the formation of in-house groups is flourishing, bringing employees together to learn how their emotions and attitudes affect their work. While these people often begin with the exchange of ideas about solving bottom-line problems, they, more than ever, emphasize their own personal needs and characteristics. They recognize that the diverse personalities of their fellow employees must be coordinated for top-flight productivity. The procedures in their meetings, therefore, range from a sharp attention to decision-making itself to an examination of how the psychological priorities and habits of employees may be modulated to affect organizational effectiveness.

We also see a new level of person-to-person exploration in religious organizations, which have created many relational groups, through which people are augmenting their more familiar worship formats. In these groups people are guided to talk to each other, to tell each other about their concerns, which are reflected in stories about their lives. While God is commonly in the background of their orientation, the participants are, more than ever, directly engaged with each other by examining what they feel, what they think, what they hope, and what they want. They offer expanded understanding and acceptance of each other's feelings, and they are hospitable to whatever their members want to say.

On the cusp of the future, we also see the exercise of life focus in the wildly growing phenomenon of networking. Facebook alone has over six hundred million people registered, and the company's annual revenue was over four billion dollars! (Lee 2011). The total numbers are monumental. The range of purposes is very broad; planning, reporting, requesting, celebrating, complaining—an expansion of opportunity for people to talk about things they might otherwise say to each other face to face, but don't. Through this process Internet correspondence offers an unprecedented opportunity for many people to go beyond ordinary conversational exchange into a personally vital conversation. This provides each person with an enlarged hospitality inviting each other to tell and hear about experiences that mark their lives. These conversations are often very personal: they reveal people's values, their ambitions, their animosities, and their loves. Individuals tell each other about what is happening in their daily lives and how it feels to be talking to each other. Clearly, we are seeing a commanding openness of person-to-person conversation, a social eruption of communal accessibility.

In viewing the baby steps of this network phenomenon, it is too early to know the full story of the benefits and the dangers. We can already see that it can have many negative, as well as positive, consequences: venom intertwined with affirmation, people going through the motions of engagement without empathy or consequentiality. Therefore this expansion of communal attention to how we live our lives calls for vigilance and a range of creative designs to be described in detail in chapter four. However, what is already unequivocally evident is the compelling need for people to join together to focus on how they are living their lives. While that need is being insistently expressed, the most desirable means for influencing the effectiveness and safety of these engagements is unclear. However, electronic communication has opened to society the widest opportunity yet for the expansion of life focus into a communal force for relational connectedness (Weinberg 2014). (See chapter 4 for greater detail.)

In this variety of applications of life focus, we see a large range of purposes. At one extreme, people are searching for the answers to ethereal unknowns, such as life after death, extrasensory communication, or foretelling the future. These are enticing speculations, which inspire people to transcend familiar observational limits. At a more common level, though, there is a clearer ground in direct observation. People at this level explore experiences that more obviously and directly matter to them: their surprises; their fears; their guiding beliefs; their experiences of pleasure, adventure, and dismay; their bodily sensations—the everyday happenings in people's lives. We also see life focus deepened in the poetry and novels that clarify elusive personal themes, such as love, contradiction, tragedy, and survival. We see life focus in the religions that direct behavior and perspective. All of this is part of a human mission: to probe the nature of our existence.

Modernity of Life Focus

With the invention of psychotherapy, now more than a hundred years old, western society reached a milestone in how we attend to the lives we live. It was then that Freud introduced his epochal psychoanalytic method. At its roots the method was simple. It was called the talking cure. However, it was more than just talking. It examined each person's life, evoking stories and providing insights that gave each one's experiences meaning. However, the medical purpose was to improve troubled lives, to correct what had gone wrong. What seemed irrelevant to these corrective purposes was the *enchantment* that many people felt in taking a guided tour of their minds. The patients were raptly attentive when they told stories about the excitement of their first party, breaking their mother's favorite china, stealing money from their father's pocket, or getting their first A on a school test. They would talk about their current anxiety when the boss entered the office and their scorn for the way he curled his lip. They would shake while telling about murderous thoughts, rant about obsessive jealousies, and despair about failure to satisfy grandiose ambitions. In the late nineteenth century, such probing was a sensational innovation, an incision into the privacy of the mind. Psychoanalysts were in a good position to conduct this exploration because of the special license provided by the urgency of medical purpose, and they initiated the most penetrating examination of the individual psyche in all of history.

That is a lofty claim to make, considering the many historical precedents. Among these we include Socratic dialogue, early Christian confessional groups, ancient mystery religions that used psychoactive drugs, religious prayers, shamanic healing, Christian monks' devotions, Zen disciplines, and other forms of exploring the landscape of life. None of these matches the psychotherapist's detailed attention to the ordinary person's *life scenario*, a step-by-step scrolling of the most intimate details of thought, feeling, action, and memory. In this conversational sweep, within the sanctity of the psychotherapist's office, people became impelled to recount long-forgotten stories: some with traumatic implications, some with revelatory self-affirmation, some just reports of everyday living. The commentary on life itself was reflected in the range of stories: about bullying by an older brother, sassy remarks to a visiting aunt, a rescue from drowning, or embarrassment at the loss of bowel control. All of these scenarios serve as the building materials for self-realization.

Remedial purposes notwithstanding, what is crucial to recognize is that, while the psychotherapeutic intention was to dissolve the sources of psychological trouble, it incidentally introduced much more than that. The method not only uncovered the sources of trouble, but also illuminated the markers of a lifetime, of anyone's lifetime. What was masked by the unprecedented medical tracking were societal reverberations that have led to the remarkable ascendance of the psychotherapist as the *cultural agent for a new dimension of life focus.* This broadened implication was grounded in an *innately human need to pay attention to one's life, an indispensable complement to just living it.* To point these revelatory experiences toward the remediation of psychological trouble was a commendable purpose, but it only scratched the surface of its social potentiality.

Now, I propose a *paradigm shift* that would point the healing professions beyond the remediation of psychological disturbance to a larger and more public focus. The original medical purposes and insights still serve well as psychological troubleshooters. However, what is potentiated in the detailing of each person's life experience is a public enchantment, not just with changing people but, more broadly, with a spirited enlightenment. To use the word "enchantment" may seem an extravagance of both language and experience, since therapy has been nothing more manifestly than two people talking to each other. Nevertheless, over the years it has always been apparent in common conversation how important regularly scheduled therapy sessions have been to patients, much more a part of their everyday lives than the need for professional problem-solving consultation. A large part of this attraction, I propose, is the explicit intention, absent in most problem-solving engagements, to enter deeply into the person's lifetime of experience. This is achieved by a highly charged pointedness that is aimed directly at how people live their lives, as well as how life itself is lived. The conversation attends enduringly to ordinary awareness, but it also cuts through to new insights, much as the X-ray picture reveals outwardly invisible parts of the body, as ethereal music and religious ideas tap into an otherwise undecipherable world, or as the imagination of the arts takes us beyond our direct experience. Those forays into the mystery of the mind tap into the enchantment potential of the unfolding unknown.

In transforming this traditionally private experience into the formation of groups, a process I will be elaborating in this book, the enchantment is further enhanced by the multiplicity of minds that converge toward the examination of specific themes. This convergence of minds, all pointed toward the same object, brightens the life experiences upon which people are concentrating. Furthermore, these themes are given an additional exceptionality by their separation from the normal demands of everyday living. Within this Sabbath for personal exploration, these themes are named; they evoke stories waiting to be told, and the conversations create new relationships. Further inspiration for amplified attention is created by a selective inclusion of poetry, music, dancing, and singing—all vehicles for celebrating the life experience. These concentration magnets induce a mélange of surprises and a high level of open-eyed interest, guiding people to reveal an otherwise veiled background of wishes, feelings, memories, and future prospects (Perls 1992). This arousal engenders a hallowed status, as people become transported from the restrictive familiarities of everyday life into a world apart, a world covenanted for personal expansion and meriting the pleasure of ceremonial affirmation.

I will illustrate this awakening to life focus by remembering the spell cast upon me in my first experience of therapy, a step in my graduate student training in psychology. I wasn't looking for a cure, as patients normally would, but, as a student, I wanted to experience the rudiments of psychoanalysis. As I walked into a large apartment, into what served as a waiting room, I didn't know what I was getting into; I felt only a sense of an indeterminate adventure to come. I knew it was going to be about me, but I had only the barest idea what form that would take. The room was dimly lit, with large hangings on the wall, a level of acculturation that added mystique to my naïveté. I knew that there was someone who had preceded me into the inner sanctuary, who, even as I waited, was having a private experience that I judged to be more deeply pertinent to whatever life was about than anything with which I was familiar. My turn would be next. Then I went in—into the strange privacy of the analyst, curtained off from everyday living;

for me it felt like an initiation rite into self-realization. While I knew I was there to talk, there were no assignments. My analyst gently guided my next moments, with little pressure other than in the strivings that were my very own.

A few questions from my analyst conjured monk-like images, and I was on my way to a detailed account of my life, which I never dreamed would merit a devoted listener. My psychoanalyst listened to me not only as any interested person might in everyday life, but for *session after session*, always with a sharpened sense of meaningfulness. What was amazing was how important everything seemed. With his guidance I told him about many experiences: some recent, some placed on the shelf long ago, some about a dimly sensed expectation of the life ahead. The stories just flowed out. Some of it would never have crossed my ordinary attention. I told him about my first athletic experience, throwing rocks at the rats scurrying outside my apartment building when I was three years old. I told him about my awe at seeing a movie screen for the first time. I told him about my first sense of the ominous, which I felt as I heard a radio report about an auto accident. I told him about being lazy, about being quiet, about my Walter Mitty fantasies of being a ballplayer. I told him about a dream in which my hair was the color of flames. This man listened to it all. No matter what I said, he listened. No matter how many times I came back, he still listened. Never had anyone listened to me so enduringly and with such absorption. Furthermore, I could tell by his sensitive responses that he knew what I was talking about, as though he was at home with my mind. This pointedness directed me first into a new respect for what I was already saying and second into a trajectory for saying many things I would never otherwise have thought important enough or safe enough to say.

I am well-aware that my story is my own and that it is hardly the universal story of the psychotherapy experience. In fact, it is far out-of-date compared to the style of therapy prevalent nowadays, and I myself came to do therapy quite differently from this early experience. What has stayed with me prominently—and what I have witnessed in the subsequent sixty-five years of my work as a therapist—is the deep absorption that colored this mysteriously private setting. Even though we were just two people talking about the events of my life, I now realize more clearly than ever that this special environment, with its sharpened attention, was an invitation into a new world filled with "experience" and a heightened sensibility. I had only the most innocent glimpse in those early days of what I see more clearly now: the primary enchantment with the exploration of the life experience. I doubt my medically oriented analyst saw this either. We looked past the enchantment of this engagement and packaged the experience in the wrapping of a professional healing. The *adventure* of my enhanced life focus was overshadowed by a targeted but dimly understood search for *personal improvement*. Instead of realizing clearly that I was in the grip of a biologically driven human need to explore the landscape of living, I saw it as a practical, though humanly rich, medical instrument: a vehicle intended to modify the consequences of my innermost psychological dynamisms. That is to say, my mind was directed by the widely recognized medical purpose—the solution of acute problems and the accompanying need *to change people's lives*.

This medical intention to change lives, valid though it was and still is, *overshadowed* the exploratory excitement that life focus has also aroused in the minds of many of the huge number of people who have flocked to therapy. Driven originally by a sense of personal disability, many have discovered an attraction not unlike those that accompany other biological imperatives. What has become more recognizable nowadays is that life focus is just as natural to our lives as eating, sex, physical movement, talking, or any of the other biological basics that direct us. These are all so crucial to human existence that people are driven to exercise them, irrespective of their biological purpose. We eat because of our appetite, not to make us healthy, *yet that's what makes us healthy*. We have sex because we feel its urge, not because it replenishes the species, *yet, it replenishes the species*. We move physically because muscular activity is a biological necessity, not just because we need to get somewhere, *yet moving gets us there*. So also we engage in life focus because we are biologically geared to pay attention to what is happening, not because we seek the orientation and directedness it provides, yet we come to feel at home with the world inside and outside us and are, indeed, guided in how to live our lives.

Of course, it is true that focusing on one's life may have undesirable effects. Just as we sometimes encounter unsatisfying sex, pathological eating, and poorly directed movement, there are many examples of excesses and distortions in life focus. There has been considerable commentary on the "Me Generation," a literature that rightly gnashes its teeth about self-centered thinking. This is reflected in people becoming so enamored with the self-exploratory process that they lose track of the daily demands of personal purpose, accomplishment, and relationship. We must not, however, let the excesses of life focus overshadow its benefits. The need for a rightful proportion underlines the importance for *guidance* in the enhancement of life focus.

A story about Freud will highlight life focus as a fundamental function. He said that psychoanalysis would never catch on in the United States because Americans, to his dismay, insisted on *improvement*. He was obviously wrong about Americans accepting psychoanalysis, but what a strange put-down about the American need for improvement! It seemed like a bizarre complaint from someone whose whole system of therapy was presumably devoted to helping people whose lives cried out for improvement. But in thinking over what Freud could have meant, I recognized a pivotal message in his observation, one that was bypassed not only by the American public but also, ironically, by Freud himself.

He could have meant, and I would have agreed, that the enormous challenge of curing patients diminished the psychotherapist's contributions to the portrayal of life. His method was, indeed, not only about improvement. It was also about looking to see what was going on in our minds. It is only natural to examine our conflicting purposes, to wonder about our place in our children's lives, to weigh a good balance between work and play, to be alert for connecting with our friends and community. All of these and many other themes of living are often the source of psychotherapeutic attention, but they also are simply part of a continuing personal attention.

I came across a strangely illuminating story that touches on this border between curing people and enlightening them. Daphne Merkin, who is a literary critic, essayist, and novelist, wrote about her experience in psychoanalysis. She spent forty years in it and was searching for clues about what she got out of it. Her story is one of enduring allegiance in spite of a pitiable range of misconnection between Ms. Merkin and some of her analysts. While she had many good experiences, she also ran into examples of the analysts' self-indulgence, impersonality, failure to get the point, and conceptual emptiness. Now, this highly sensitive, intelligent, and motivated person who had participated abidingly all those years, moving from one analyst to another, was trying to understand why she had done it (Merkin 2010).

I am in no position to examine the ins and outs of her "case": neither the wisdom of her choice of therapists, nor the alternative options she might have had for more clearly curative results, nor her own utilization of therapeutic opportunities. For all I know, the long years of her therapy may have led to a considerable healing effect; they may, for all I know, have saved her life. Her report is pertinent here more because it is a perceptive insight into the broad value of life focus, one that stretches beyond the clarity of ordinary standards of cure. Through her experience Ms. Merkin, even under seemingly infertile circumstances, found personal benefit in an increased appreciation of her life, which is no small achievement. Here is what she says about her years of therapy:

> And yet it seems to me that the process itself, in its very commitment to interiority—its attempt to ferret out prime causes and pivotal events from the psychic rubble of the past and the unwieldy conflicts of the present—can be *intriguing enough to stand in as its own reward...*
>
> Therapy, you might say, became a kind of release valve for my life; it gave me a place to say the things I could say nowhere else, express the feelings that would be laughed at or frowned upon in the outside world—and in so doing helped to alleviate the insistent pressure of my darker thoughts. It buffered me as well as prodded me forward; above all, it provided a space for interior examination, an education in disillusioned realism that existed nowhere else on this cacophonous, frantic planet. (Merkin 2010, 47)

We see in Ms. Merkin's report an entry into the interior of her mind; we see a release from the standards and pressures of everyday living; we see disillusionment given realistic, mind-expanding context; we see perspectives that light up her life in the face of her darker thoughts. Of course, the implication of a forty-year duration for her therapy as a shocking excess is based on the traditional medical model of curing specific, acute problems. That is the destination to which her therapy was pointed. However, for many people, perhaps for most people, perhaps even for Ms. Merkin, the exercise of life focus is a more pervasive function, independently important. While therapy was invented as a medical specialty, always primed for corrective results, it is worth noting that the *instrument* may be as compelling as the *product* (Beisser 1970).

While psychotherapy is commonly associated with such office practice, it is only a short step to see that the need for people to focus on their lives, as Ms. Merkin did, is operative every day across the entire landscape of our society. Enter the Life Focus Community group, the formation of which provides an assured continuity of exploration; members meet continuingly, perhaps for a lifetime. These groups serve as a breeding ground for themes that rattle around in people's minds, at first lying dormant, but then, when aroused, are ripe for elaboration into personal stories. The meetings provide a place like none other in everyday life, a place set apart from the daily movement from moment to moment into a stimulating attention to commonly experienced life themes. The dependability of this process releases people from the speed of life, partly because it is an assured process and partly because the design of meetings softens personal pressure. (See chapter 5.)

Furthermore, these groups offer the responses of a *community of people*, a relational opportunity unmatched in private exploration. The members enter together into a guided tour of the mind, a tour mapped out with specific exercises that lead them to discover their own voices. As they tell each other about a lifetime of events, each experience is amplified by sharpened group discussion. This pointedness is achieved through the synchronicity of many people attending to the same theme. The resulting feeling of mutuality is further enhanced by music played, poetry read, and the contagious influence of an assured continuity of meeting. Such a setting will create an unusual combination of respite and stimulation, a place where demands are reduced but the menu of ideas and activities will be invigorating. All of these conditions converge into a collective welcome to every person's mind, enabling all members to more confidently navigate the broad parameters of their existence. To flesh out the cultural imperative for the enhancement of life focus, I will now show how this need already feeds three of society's most widespread and cherished activities: everyday conversation, art, and religion.

Life Focus in Everyday Conversation

Paying attention to how we live our lives is so natural that it is apparent everywhere, not only among seekers of enlightenment. We see it in ordinary conversation when people tell each other about the horrors of moving from one house to another. They tell about the paralysis they feel in talking to lawyers who are handling their divorces. They tell about the pleasure of beating their friends at the golf course, their disappointments about not getting the job they wanted, their survival in a potentially deadly auto accident. They discuss books they have read and movies they have seen. On and on, every day they transmit the workings of their minds to the people around them. However, unless they give enhanced focus to their experience, their casual storytelling, while it is happily engaging and while it creates friendship, often lacks the strong personal registration that key personal themes deserve.

I will illustrate what may happen when, with a slight conversational twist, people consciously explore their lives. A group of my friends recurrently go out to dinner, just an ordinary evening out, joining together for sociable talk. On this particular evening, one of the five men asked the rest of us whether we have *directed* our lives or whether the things we did in our lives *just happened*.

What a fundamental question this was, and it hit the mark for all of us. We talked all night about it, but I'll give you only a couple of examples of what was said. One of the men didn't feel like he directed his life at all; he just tuned into events as they happened. He told us a story about how, long ago, after some years as a successful engineering consultant, he was fired from his job. He was stunned because he had no hint this was coming. Then he picked himself up and started his own company, now a thriving enterprise. For him this was just a serendipitous call to answer this unanticipated challenge.

A second man told a quite different story—of consciously steering his life. He was a young but highly successful physician when he realized that success was not enough for him. What he wanted most was *free time*, for him life's greatest commodity. Not confining this wish to fantasyland, he pointed himself toward an early retirement. Fastening his mind on this goal, he retired in his forties, earlier than anyone else in his position might have imagined. Now in his seventies, he has never "missed" his work, and, more importantly, he has created exciting projects. He told us about some of them: as a surgeon, his agility in the use of his hands led him to play around with metals, forging imaginative constructions, a number of which grace his house; some reflect whimsy, some show complex the relationship of shapes, and some create unusual combinations of colors, but all give him the pleasure of an unexpected and fulfilling activity. At another point in his life, he bought a ranch, where he built a pond and bridges, adding beauty and practicality to his property. He read copiously. He has played an extraordinarily active role in his relationship with family and friends. He has traveled to places he might otherwise have been unable to visit. Always sharply absorbed, he was impressed that in all the years after retiring, he has not had a boring day.

What was true about both of these people is that they told stories that combined the planned and unplanned: the one who felt he lived serendipitously had plenty of planning in his life; the early retiree with a fixed purpose also lived very spontaneously. Whether their lives could be identified as directed or ad lib was not as important as the stories the theme evoked. Each of the others also told us how they perceived *directedness* in their lives, each story adding depth to what we already knew about their lives. Not only did we expand our sense of each other, but the time flew. Though we came to the restaurant early, we were the last to leave, just short of being tossed out at closing time. While we were there only for the pleasure of our company, we, without prior intent, lit up some aspects of life—not only of our specific lives but also about life itself. The targeted conversational theme accentuated what would commonly, in our own private minds, pass through more fleetingly than the experiences deserved.

Life Focus in the Arts

It is hardly news that people flock to the works of artists. The *New York Times* (Book Industry Study Group 2006) reports that 3.1 billion books were sold in the United States in 2005. As mighty as this number is, it is limited to the United States, and it is only a small portion of the public that achieves life focus through the arts. There are also a colossal number of people who are drawn to *other* art opportunities, such as those provided by movies, museums, lectures, and educational classes.

While it is true that the content of these artful productions portrays the lives of people *other* than the consumer, these other people spawn implications for the lives of the consumer. Taking the novel as an exemplary form of life focus, the reader feels a common ground with much of the conceived world. Whether the setting is as foreign as the gulag or the character as far removed as a mountain climber or the theme as bizarre as the theft of a museum painting, the events are accessible to the imagination of the reader. While these experiences are vicarious, for many readers there is a meeting point along two dimensions. One dimension is a similarity between themselves and the characters. The other is the expansion of the reader's landscape of living beyond his or her own, a lesson in the range of life scenarios that are out there to be lived (Polster 1987).

Still, because the reader's experience is so clearly vicarious and because it often serves as entertainment, the personal implications may go unnoticed. Many people are so absorbed in the pleasure of the stories they read that they will not recognize the experiences as having anything to do with their own actual lives. Nevertheless, the characters and circumstances do have large resonance because they represent scenarios that are either approximated in the reader's own life or that accentuate special aspects of the world in which the reader lives. Salinger's *Catcher in the Rye*, for example, awakened a generation to the tribulations of trying to live a life of directness and honesty; *Moby Dick* taught us about struggle and grudges and grandiosity; and Kafka made us aware of the misty inaccessibility of the world we all live in. An observation made about a sixty-year-old teacher, a character in Anne Tyler's novel *Noah's Compass*, accentuates the role of art in calling attention to his depersonalized living. Tyler writes that the teacher "experienced only the most glancing relationship with his own life.... He had dodged the tough issues, avoided the conflicts, gracefully skirted adventure." He finally realizes this as he tells his wife, "It's as if I've never been entirely present in my own life."

Such an amplified reality is apparent in Steven Galloway's novel *The Cellist of Sarajevo*, in which the title character, in the midst of a war zone in Bosnia and in full view of snipers, played his instrument as a memorial to the killing of twenty-two innocent people. He risked his life every day at 4 PM and enthralled those who could hear him, both by his beautiful music and by the hidden meanings behind this heroic transcendence of danger. Two of the book's characters are discussing this man's mission incredulously, trying to understand it from a personal perspective and to guess at his motivation (Galloway 2008). One character, Emina, says, "I don't know the piece he plays, what its name is. It's a sad tune. But it doesn't make me sad.... Is he playing for the people who died? Or is he playing for the people who haven't? What does he hope to accomplish?" The other character, Dragan, responds by saying, "Maybe he is playing for himself. Maybe it's all he knows how to do and he's not doing it to make something happen."

These characters want to know what is going on, as does the reader. In one sense, what they have witnessed is a simple drama. It is composed of a sequence of: *focal event*, playing the cello in the face of snipers; *consequences*, in the cellist's survival and his inspiration to others; and *closure*, sought through the search for meaning and relevance by people who listened to his music and *felt* personally moved by it. The events and circumstances invite the reader, as well as the observing characters, to feel a common humanity with the cellist. His dramatic playing and his resonance with empathic neighbors served to expand the reader beyond his or her own familiar life into an enhanced bonding with the hero's compassion, courage, and survival.

That's what the artist does: evokes the reader's own sensibility about the experience of living. While these experiences are very different from the reader's own experiences, the stretch of the reader's mind transforms the seemingly unachievable into a felt commonality. The *portrayal* of courage creates a vicarious resonance in the reader, who catches a glimpse of what is only potential within himself or herself, and this glimpse affirms his or her membership in the same world as the novel's characters. When Galloway, the author, dramatized the human decency of the cellist, who simply did what he knew how to do, Galloway was going beyond this cellist, highlighting human decency and courage, derived of unaware potentials. Although such extreme heroism does not have to be set as the standard, the reader may well be inspired to stick up for a child abused by a school principal or to bounce back from being disheartened or to take a chance on an unpopular opinion. While these experiences may not measure up to a heroic dimension, the intimacy of face-to-face personal stories, told to an attentive group of people, will provide its own drama. Without such accentuation the vital truth of personal enterprise would often reside silently in diminished awareness, primed to be ignited. As I have previously written:

> Many people appear linguistically sterile, morally neuter, visually plain, or depleted in energy. However, these are all camouflage, intended to deflect from whatever is interesting. . . . In giving up such a dulled image, such persons offer remarkably individualistic, suspenseful, and colorful memories, attitudes, expectations and insights. (Polster 1987)

With the arts as a precedent, the Life Focus Community groups prioritize the portrayal of life experience over the *changing* of people's lives. For the novelist the priority of portrayal is so clear that it hardly needs to be stated. Not so for the psychotherapist, for whom it is almost heretical to step away from solving problems. What I am proposing is to rise *beyond* the natural attraction to creating change—to give enlarged homage to the *portrayal of lives*, itself a humanly compelling process. While the stories people tell each other in the Life Focus Community groups don't reach the quality of artistic portrayal, they don't have to. It may seem like it is the exclusive domain of artistic quality that draws people to these stories, which are unmatched by the stories ordinary folks tell each other. However, ordinary folks have an important advantage over the artist. The intimacy of immediate and live connection often trumps talent in transmitting a message. If, for example, the group theme were to be so common as "dinner table conversations you have had or wish you had," this would trigger personalized stories, the individual importance of which would provide an entrance into the drama of everyday living. As charity begins at home, perhaps drama does also, as it becomes recognized in the *in vivo* importance of our own lives (Polster 1987). (See chapters 5–8).

Life Focus in Religion

The huge number of religious congregations is another familiar ground for the exercise of life focus. According to the Hartford Institute for Religion Research, there are three hundred thirty-five thousand religious congregations in the United States alone. The Hartford Institute also reports that there are approximately fifty-six million weekly Christian worshipers. Other surveys report that anywhere between 20 and 40 percent of people attended church on the previous weekend. The rise of the mega-church is a stunning testament to the popularity of the religious experience. There are more than thirteen hundred such Protestant churches in the United States. Approximately fifty churches on the list have average attendance exceeding ten thousand, with the highest recorded at forty-seven thousand in average attendance (Hadaway and Marler 2005).

What draws all those people? The most simple answer is that they *like* to come. They like to be affirmed; to be part of a community; to deepen their sense of what it is like to be alive, to be entertained, to have cosmic mysteries explained, to hear inspirational music, to follow tradition. Yes, religious leaders do often exhort people to change; goals matter. Yes, religious behavior is institutionally regulated, as in the Ten Commandments; morality matters, guiding people to live well together. Yes, the message of salvation offers a religious parallel to the psychotherapeutic cure or growth; improvement matters; healing is not uncommonly sought in religious congregations. Yes, many people's way of life has been transformed by their religious experience in which one's way of life can be strongly affected.

However, if you ask people why they go to church or synagogue, the therapeutic purpose is missing. A Gallup Poll study in 2007 reported that of 562 adults who attend church at least monthly, only 23 percent said they came for spiritual growth and guidance. The rest came to keep grounded, to feel inspired, to honor their faith, to worship God, to have the fellowship of other members of the community, to support their belief in religion, or to follow in the path in which they were brought up. While this kind of survey only scratches the surface of a complex web of reasons for church-going, its results are harmonious with what people are likely to hear in ordinary conversations about going to church. For churchgoers, the familiar psychotherapeutic intention to "work on" relational issues or overcome behavioral or emotional symptomatology would be an unlikely reason to go to church. While many people do, indeed, benefit psychologically from being a member of a religion, the complexity of reasons does not include getting over a post-traumatic stress disorder or anger management or relief from obsessive thinking. They don't typically evaluate their religious experience on a scale that measures personal change.

What is most apparent to the church-goer is that the combination of absorbing rituals, the music, the history, the ethos of exceptional acceptance, and the good works amplify the positive value of being alive. A touching example of the human scale reward is the report by T. M. Luhrmann that in a study of nearly ninety psychotic women in an urban Chicago neighborhood, half of them went to church at least twice each month and 80 percent of them said God was their *best friend—for some their only friend* (2014).

Furthermore, the Judeo-Christian *story line* is also a great attraction. The story of Christ is said to be "the greatest story ever told." Not only is the story of Jesus compelling but also the stories of Moses and the many other characters who have played a role in the history of these religions. What young person reading the Bible is not enthralled with the drama of the exodus from Egypt, the murder of Abel by Cain, Moses's rise to leadership, Christ's healing of the sick, the drama of the Last Supper, or Joseph's rise to power and his forgiveness of his brothers? These are events that are fascinating simply as spotlights for life experiences, more than as a tutorial for change. The stories give special focus to betrayal, victory over disaster, compassion, and many other humanly compelling themes.

The Life Focus Community groups do not have their own public heroes or defining stories. Perhaps they will, possibly to be taken from literature or history or symbolic current happenings. Personal heroes matter also and may be recognized in the drama of individual story lines. An uncle, a teacher, a neighbor, an athlete—any of these may be registered more indelibly in the communal setting than in the dim periphery of the person's private mind. These personal stories, which give dimension to the individuated life, lift certain people into hero status, a celebration of their importance. (See chapter 3 for more detail.)

Conclusion

In conclusion, it is fair to ask whether the vast popular interest represented in everyday conversation, the arts, and religion is a valid precedent for the formation of Life Focus Community groups. Popularity by itself is hardly a sufficient reason to do so. The errors that accompany popularity range from excessive conformity to tyranny. Yet, there are some processes that are popular because they are insistently human. They go on irrespective of how effectively they are applied or whether they are good for the community. Given the belief that life focus is one of those innate needs, we must create the most promising formats for a beneficial satisfaction of this need. We are only on the cusp of knowing the details of a desirable format, but the "mental health professions" are well-positioned to design them. Because these professions have spearheaded the society-wide spread of life focus with the invention of psychotherapy, it seems timely now for them to stretch their outreach a step further: to create communal opportunity that engages people at large. The Life Focus Community groups build on the same source of enchantment with the life process as is evident in ordinary conversation, the arts, and religion. Participants come together not so much to address what is wrong with them as to explore what their lives are about. The premise of such community-friendly vehicles is therefore grounded in the widespread need for people to *register* their life experience rather than in the targeting of personal troubles.

2

The Drama of the Split Mind

Children laugh about Humpty Dumpty, the fairy tale egg that is a caricature of things falling irretrievably apart. While the anthropomorphic example of the egg's inadequacy is funny, the problem becomes pivotally serious when we as adults recognize that we live every day with splits in our makeup and with the imperative of putting them back together. Fortunately, we live on the cusp of unification, the potential of which provides an undercurrent for life's throb. Two of life's most prominent of these splits are the split between hidden and manifest experience and the split between the observer and the observed. Before elaborating on these splits, let me briefly introduce them.

The manifest aspect of the mind is composed of all the experiences that are on life's surface: the things we do, say, see, and want, such as hearing a dog bark at night, licking an ice cream cone, or rushing to be on time. These are the directly observable happenings that make up our daily life scenarios. More or less split off from this is a background of events, which are no longer part of our awareness but close enough to the surface that they pulsate on the fringe of life's ongoing narrative. Perhaps this disconnect from immediacy would include a friendly message that surprised you yesterday, a lingering wish to visit Yellowstone Park, an old warning from your uncle to go over important decisions with your wife. Also residing close to the surface are stories about your struggle of learning to whistle or a funny twist to your first job interview or a falsely diagnosed illness. I want to show that these split-off experiences remain latent, but they are ready players in the mysterious alchemy that colors a person's intuition of who they are and what their lives are about. This background houses details that are percolating, that are quietly ready to pop up on stage as actors in the ongoing scenario of anyone's life (Polster 1995; Csikszentmihalyi 1991).

The second split, also always present, is the one between the observer and the observed, that is, between the part of the person who examines what he is doing and the part of the person who is doing it. For example, if I am the person who is running a marathon, I just run it. However, I am also the person who takes note of the length of my stride, remembers how I have run the race before, gauges my pace, is distracted because my wife is in the hospital. This split may be well harmonized or not. For optimal function, however, I must have full concentration on what I am doing, while at the same time I tune in to how I do it.

Here are some perspectives that will give life to these splits and provide opportunity for conversational explorations in the Life Focus Community groups.

The Manifest/Hidden Split

From the beginning one of psychotherapy's most evocative observations was that the unconscious, that repository of a personal history, was mysteriously guiding our lives. While that view of the unconscious as a deeply buried region of the mind was an important illumination, it was not user-friendly. It had great psychological and social impact in opening both the patient and the society to a new breadth of the psyche, but for most people this version of the hidden was a drastic disconnect from everyday experience, too far removed to be commonly orienting. In contrast, I shall describe what is a more readily applicable influence, the *accessibly hidden*. This is a user-friendly region of the split mind, only a short step from immediacy into a surprising and easily integrated flow of thoughts.

Here is a simplistic version of the split between the hidden unconscious and the manifest. A five-year-old person is affected for a lifetime by a stunning event, let's say, by two neighborhood bullies beating up a drunken man. Later, as an adult, having long ago forgotten about seeing this, he made a career out of helping the downtrodden. His preoccupation with being a Good Samaritan came at the expense of his own family, who felt disregarded. The family friction got so problematic that he went to therapy, where, under meticulous probing, he remembered his *disconnected* early experience, and this memory revealed the troublesome split between the hidden and the manifest regions of his mind.

To discover that split and to do anything about it would be difficult enough in the private office. It is far too large an ambition for most people and is surely not part of the Life Focus Community group design. Happily, it is not necessary. The deep unconscious, while always with us, need not be the definitive source of enlightenment. What is more pertinent to most of us is the *accessibly hidden* region of the mind. It may seem strange to say that accessible experience is hidden.

Whatever thoughts spring forth out of moment-to-moment sequences are much more familiarly seen as part of a simple continuity, with the sequences taken for granted. Yet, in full truth, everything that happens next wasn't there before it happened. But we only experience it as having been hidden when it is *distinctly* outside the current experience; it comes largely as a surprise.

This is more than splitting hairs about what is or is not hidden because I am proposing that we see beyond the ordinary sense of continuity, of normal and necessary, but not the whole story. I first suggest that, as I shall illustrate, the idea of the accessible hidden adds a dimension of drama to ordinary experience and, second, that it is a key influence in representing a more full dimensionality in one's life. It is the work of the Life Focus Community group to capture this lightning in a bottle, activating the hidden toward an integration with the manifest.

Let's examine this process by looking at an everyday life scenario that will illustrate how this accessibly hidden content sits in the background, irrelevant to immediate purpose. Without awareness of a latent inventory, we normally live with an acceptance that much will be left out when we do what we do. For example, my wife and I, because of my hearing loss, went to a technology store to select and order a wireless headset so that I could more easily hear certain TV programs. The manager spoke to us, then sent someone named Mike over to help us; this was a tiny diversion from our continuity but nothing much, just part of a routine sales sequence. But Mike was an interesting phenomenon in his own right, the source of a lifetime of potential story line. Of course, we did not care about that, though I silently noticed a scar on his jawbone. *What is that about?* I thought for a second, not long enough to draw him out. Surely there was the promise of an interesting story, but Mike was not there to become revealed nor I to explore. That's OK, but that part of Mike remained hidden, though probably accessible. Under the right conditions, even in the store, it could have been the source for a personally interesting story.

Yet, he did begin to tell us about his grandfather's hearing difficulty and how effectively the wireless headset had worked for him. Again, this was a promise of the appearance of the accessibly hidden that was left out of the conversation. We know nothing else about his grandfather, although he may have been the mayor of Peoria. Nor do we care.

There was, of course, more to the conversation. At each step of this matter-of-fact engagement, as you can imagine, there was much more that was not said than was actually said—naturally so. The tiny surprises, the sidestepping of elaboration, the guiding influence of purpose: this is the normal stuff of everyday life. We all ride over the untimely possibility and could not live our daily lives without leaving behind a lot of potential. However, even this routine exchange had a throb from the accessibly hidden, hints of potential information that was bypassed in favor of headset indoctrination and purchase. The pleasure of this unknown background was intriguing because with Mike's intonations and facial expression, there was always the sense of a mysterious underground, even though it had an inauspicious place in the business sequence. We are, likewise, in many normal life situations, likely to be affected by this mysterious potential even though we are unlikely to follow through as it pulses with an unacknowledged influence in the continuing business at hand. This potential for novelty affects our absorption, affording a measure of drama to otherwise routine experiences.

Now, let's look at a nonbusiness scenario, where there is a greater latitude in our conversational choices. When I meet you for lunch, the vista from which the silently imminent may appear is broader. As you speak, you create an anticipatory attention in me. Either because of my history with you or how you speak to me, I feel that, whatever you are saying, there is more to come; an anticipation amplifies my interest. From the accessibly hidden region of your mind, you may have a story about your wife, who may have banged her head this morning and who wouldn't go to the doctor, and you are now wondering whether she had a concussion. Or you may have just signed a new contract to sell an exotic coffee from Brazil. Or you may wonder why I did not respond to your last e-mail message. On and on, the approaching unknown spurs our conversation, and, while much of it may be accessible, its appearance is unassured, to be determined by the way our conversation plays out. This level of suspense ranges from hardly noticeable to highly charged.

Many people are excellent at creating an expectation of impending novelty and need very little help in revealing it. They characteristically convey an unspoken promise of the more that is to come. Perhaps they do it with a breathless tone of voice; perhaps with intriguing ideas; perhaps with stories about a mutual friend; perhaps with their own anticipatory pleasure; perhaps, perhaps (Polster 1995; Csikszentmihalyi 1991).

Igniting the Hidden

For the Life Focus Community group, such spontaneous promise of the appearance of the hidden remains important, but spontaneity is not enough, as the program design must address a community of people.

It names themes that are universally important, and it provides accompanying exercises that ignite the life-defining stories that lie in wait. An example of this arousal is the following verbatim response to the theme of "home." Irene, who was a member of a four-person subgroup conversation, said to the others:

> I hope I can do this without crying, but I don't know if I can. It was really meaningful to me because I came across the ocean fourteen years ago full of excitement to stay here for one year and go back home. It didn't work out that way. I met a man who persuaded me to stay, but I made him promise me two things: that there would always be money in the bank for me to go home and for me to be buried at home. I was panicked at the idea of dying in this country, which says nothing about America or the life I made, but it is a strong longing for me to return home.
>
> And there came a time in my life that it didn't matter so much to me where I was buried, and I thought it was crazy to think of it that way, but now I'm sixty-eight and I do want to be buried at home. I don't know if it is a longing that is overwhelming. Maybe it's as simple as: there, people meet in the cemetery and remember you and they water your flowers. And they talk about you, but it's again a strong, strong longing about going home. So that's what I was feeling and thinking about.

Irene's story was stimulated by several design components. First, there was the naming of the theme of "home"; then a poetry reading exemplifying the idea of home; followed by music that aroused empathy and memory, and by the group's storytelling momentum. Her thoughts had not been a deep, dark secret. Instead, they had resided silently in a corner of her mind, ready to appear only under the right stimulation. The funneling of attention to the theme of "home" sparked her story, but it was propelled further by the conversational hospitality of her subgroup. Telling her story provided her with immediate relational pleasure, but it did more. It actualized a faintly realized internal need, giving it enhanced importance, fleshing out the inclusion of her past with her present.

Countless other themes would tap into a similar readiness. Suppose, in further example, that the group were asked to tell each other about the first time they realized that "life could be *different*." In responding to the question, one person says it was when he stole a candy bar and received no punishment from God. He knew then that the boundaries for his behavior were looser than he had thought, and he tells about two experiences that settled his mind on it. Strangely, he paralleled this naughty freedom with riding his bike with no hands on the handlebars and with realizing how funny he was when he mimicked his teacher. Another person says the first time he felt life could be different was when he happened in on the story of an aboriginal tribe. He saw how strange people could be, and he is now studying Egypt and ancient religions. Another says it was when he got his first A in school and how it gave him a great boost into an unfamiliar feeling of belonging.

More generalized themes would be: how we manage our time, the ups and downs of loyalty, the relationship between love and dependency, the rigors of discipline. The designation of such themes that are broadly relevant humanizes each person's own private experiences and makes it easier to reveal them. While there is no explicit pressure for anyone to tell his or her story, there is a contagion of expressiveness that sets an example and assures a hospitality for the stories.

This targeted concentration on a single theme serves much like the mantra in meditation, sharply pointed to the object of attention, freeing the person from the distraction of extraneous complexity. While the content of these group meetings is much broader than what is sought in meditation, it is nevertheless the beneficiary of a comparable amplification, produced by highly charged, thematically directed concentration (Perls 1992).

Scaling Down

While people in everyday life have some very dramatic stories to tell, few of these tales would stand up to the standards of the novelist. But they don't have to. The embellishments, the mystery, the masterful language are all lessened. What is apparent is the raw immediacy of the live personal exchange. It is widely believed that the work of the novelist places events in high relief, which, if scaled down in drama, would be very recognizable in regular folks, who live out milder versions of novelistic scenarios. The Life Focus Community group does not try to reach the levels of drama or perspective that the novelist creates, but it highlights what everyday people care about in everyday life, raising events from a routine level of interest. While the group members are living in a lower key than the characters in the pages of a book, they are still living through comparable anxiety, disappointments, delights, obsessions, and enchantments.

Dostoevsky, for example, in *Crime and Punishment*, portrays the experience of Raskolnikov, who navigated his way through desperate circumstances. The grand scenario of murdering his landlady is a leap over the gap between his ordinary sense of life's familiarity and the tragic violation by the eruption of his hidden violence. Of course, the readers, only vicariously involved, are safe in the haven of readership. However, though murder is no part of their lives, the murder shines a light indirectly on the much smaller versions of rage and conscience that touch almost everybody. While this is dangerous territory for Raskolnikov, the readers are given the gift of protected involvement.

This safe emergency simultaneously arouses people and supports them, providing each person with an opportunity for an adventure, while being guided safely through it. This combination of risk and safety is basic to psychotherapy, where there has always been a large personal risk in the revelations about aggression, sex, ascendancy, and aggrandizement. Such utilization of the safe emergency became explicit in the exercises of gestalt therapy, which were composed of imagined reenactments of anxiety-inducing circumstances (Polster and Polster 1974). The risks were taken willingly because the exercises promised psychological benefits. However, the largely unnoted truth is that, beyond the anticipated therapeutic benefits, the suspense of the safe emergency was as fascinating as the reading of a compelling novel.

Observer/Observed Split

The second of the splits is between the observer and the observed, another inner duet we all live with. This is a split between the self who acts and the one who looks inside to observe the actor. This double mind, disjunctive though it may sometimes be, is always seeking unity, because the observer and the observed each contribute to the whole person. This process of self-observation is so crucial to people that it has inspired many famous observations.

As Shakespeare's Polonius said, "To thine own self be true. And it must follow, as the night the day, Thou cannot then be false to any man." As a student walking along my university campus, I read words every day, carved into one of the arches, saying, "Know thyself so that thou mayest depart in knowledge, wisdom and love." It is well known that Alexander Pope said that the proper study of mankind is man, that Socrates said that the unexamined life is not worth living, and that Arthur Miller said that attention must be paid. Marcel Proust was one of those who helped usher in the modern age of self-observation when, in his *Swann's Way*, he intoned these haunting words:

> When from a long distant past, nothing subsists, after the people are dead, after the things are broken and scattered, still, alone, more fragile, but with more vitality, more unsubstantial, more persistent,

more faithful, the smell and taste of things remain poised for a long time, like souls, ready to remind us . . . in the tiny and almost impalpable drop of their essence, the vast structure of recollection. (Proust 1934)

Of course, we don't decide to look inward. We just do it, much as we also see, hear, and walk. When the observer and the observed function well together, we not only do what we do but we know how we are doing it, what our motives are for doing it, how it feels, what it portends, how it fits with our morality or our futures. We see such integration on an elemental level in the meticulous attention of the discus thrower, who focuses inwardly on every detail of his or her preparatory movements, oscillating back and forth, before finally swinging into the release of the discus; in this way the thrower provides great leverage for the thrust and great satisfaction in the graceful union of sensation, movement, and purpose.

This high focus by the discus thrower, beautiful though its results, is concentrated on a narrow range of experience in a carefully circumscribed process. However, the grace so fruitfully delivered by such elemental integration also has larger application in the more complex engagements in everyday living, where attention is more easily diffused. I listen intently to what you are saying, then the telephone rings and my attention must shift to address the person on the phone. My concern with you stays on, but my new requirement may reduce the sharpness of my focus; I am still partially engaged with you and perhaps not fully ready for the phone.

Often this shift is disarmingly simple to accomplish, but at other times it is very difficult. Suppose I have to pick up my dog at the groomers, keep a luncheon appointment, consider thoughtfully how to advise my son about a move he is thinking about, and finish reading a book before the book club meeting. I have to integrate my smile in greeting a friend because I feel a pulse of anger toward him, while my love is actually more vital. Or similarly, I have to coordinate my fatigue while swimming with my expectation of getting a second wind. Or I have to integrate listening with talking. Multiply all of these challenges by the daily accumulations of contradictions, uncertain consequences, and slippery value judgments.

The Life Focus Community groups provide practice opportunities for coordinating this multiplex of happenings. The communally directed elaboration of experience serves as an observational callisthenic, cultivating the look inward. Suppose that members of the Life Focus Community are asked to break into groups of three and instructed to tell each other whether they have ever been *burglarized* and what that experience was like. In practicing such self-observational skills, one member of a small subgroup may say he has never experienced such panic as one night when he heard the rattling of his doorknob. He ran for the phone while calling out to his wife, and he heard a person running away. He called the police anyway; they came and said the chances of catching this person were slim. What really surprised this man when he heard the person running away was that, while feeling relief, he was actually shivering uncontrollably, an altogether new experience. His shivering was for him not only incongruous with being relieved, but, strangely, his body felt like it was bathed in a balmy fluid. Furthermore, he felt the closest to his wife that he ever felt—ever. He 'knew" right there as clearly as he could that he would never again take life for granted. Alas, said he, he actually does still take life for granted more often than he wishes. This exercise left him with a new clarity about his experience, and he realized how much he has wanted to tell the story.

A second person may say he and his family came home from a trip away from home and found a door wide open and footprints in the house. Burglars had come in and taken several valuable items, but what got to him more strongly than the loss was the feeling of violation—a sense of something that must be akin to having been raped. He felt miserable about that for a month afterward, and while he knew that rape is in a different class of experience, he got a glimpse of what it could be like.

The third person may say he had never encountered a burglary but has always dreaded that some day he would be faced with that and he was glad to hear these people tell about their anxiety. Their survival reminded him once more that those things we are anxious about turn out to be survivable. Then he tells about his own experience with survival when he turned around a threat of bankruptcy and the desperation of his position.

Such stories and the ensuing conversations not only *provide practice* in looking inward but they also lead to a sense of bondedness. In telling their own stories about strongly felt experiences, the speakers' relationship with the listeners becomes accentuated, and, more clearly than ever, they feel joined with the people in the group. Many people commonly exchange just such experiences of self-examination in their everyday lives, but they usually do so only under special conditions of intimacy. Even then there is often only a passing commentary, with little registration of its importance. What the Life Focus Community contributes is the *assurance* of communal opportunity, guidance through the designation of themes, and an amplification of respect for each person's individual experience. What might commonly be left to either happenstance or intimacy is built into a format that induces concentration on one's own experience.

The Look Outward

Since anything that can be done can also be overdone, we have to recognize that, vital though this look inward may be, it is only part of the story. The person must also face outward. That is evident everyplace: in talking to people, in gardening, in working out in the gym, in applying for a job. Such outward focus is the major function; the look inward is subsidiary, though crucial. The integration of the two is the optimal result. This is evident in the story of one person, Dan, who tells about his trip to the hospital after a member of the hospital staff called to tell him his mother had died. He was sad but was also smoldering; he felt robbed because he was not there when she died. He had left only hours earlier because the staff wanted her to be quiet and asked him and his brother to leave. They must have known she had no chance of survival. He felt that, with even minimal empathy, they would have allowed the family to remain and be present when she died. But the fundamental reality is that his mother had died, and his feelings about her death were later transformed into action. He started a campaign to foster more responsive medical care in his hospital, an action with a future, one that did not leave his feelings out but also allowed him to see an external opportunity.

On a more day-to-day basis, we understand that our children need support for their schoolwork, and we look to ourselves for kindly perspective and appreciation of the struggles. These insights are vitalized, however, by practical actions, like talking to teachers, helping with homework, and having realistic conversations about talents. We see, therefore, that the Life Focus Community groups must be mindful that their meetings are not limited to looking inward but must transpose these understandings into a world from which they are only momentarily extracted. While the content of the meetings evokes careful attention to many of life's challenges, for the lessons of self-realization to work, they must be transposed into the world at large. The group, as a place apart from the pressures of everyday life, must nevertheless serve as an enablement, not a substitution, for that everyday life.

3

Life as Microcosm

In the earliest days of psychoanalysis, the discipline created a key difference from other professional consultations. Beyond any instruction or advice, it introduced the epochal idea of transference, explaining to the patient how the therapy relationship was a restatement of the patient's relationship with his parents. Through this enlargement of the relationship, the therapist entered into the fabric of the patient's lifetime. Through such fusion of the therapist into the life history of the patient, the therapist became the meeting point of past and present, here and there, you and me, all adding deepened dimension to the immediate relationship. This raised the importance of the therapy relationship, which became a mini-world for the patient, sweeping the therapy beyond common conversational exchange into the realm of implication. The therapeutic setting thus became a *microcosm*, bespeaking a lifetime beyond the world in which the therapist and patient were immediately engaged.

Since that time transference has become a controversial concept. Many people thought the transference scenario depersonalized the *actual* relationship with the therapist, who often saw this relationship as a substitute for that with a parent rather than authentic in its own right. Still, we know that in spite of the frequent distractions from whatever-is-happening-now to interpretations of what-happened-long-ago, psychoanalysis engendered the most inspiring relational dynamic in many people's entire lifetime. How could that happen?

There are, of course, a number of reasons why people would have developed a strong relationship with their therapists. They were speaking with an urgent need to solve acute problems. They were speaking to an experienced person who listened seriously and understandingly to everything they said. The intimate subject matter of these conversations and the openness of communication were the breeding ground for strong feelings. They met for a large number of sessions, where the frequency and continuity was assured. All of these practical conditions were pretty obvious reasons to find the relationship unusually important.

However, I believe those reasons must take their place alongside the universal and mysterious experience of microcosm—the familiar search for the meaning of life and for the understanding of a world beyond the one we know. I am hypothesizing that, on a more mundane level, any relationship that represents a world of experience beyond itself heightens attention to the relationship. We see this in what we call role modeling, where a public figure, be it athlete, politician, or actor, is experienced as an exemplar of behavior and therefore often held to a higher standard. We see it in the soldier whose behavior is seen as a representative of his country. We see it in the songs that represent the character of a country. The Life Focus Community group has a number of characteristics that foster its implications of microcosm. Here are five of them:

1. These groups provide access to a special place, a special time, and a special frame of mind: one that guides the participants into an explicit search first to know their own lives but also, indivisibly, to know life itself, the realm within which their experience fits.
2. People feel a brightened sense of the world at large when they join together with other people in a concrete representation of it. When individual people go to bars, theaters, lectures, ballgames, concerts, and conventions, they become part of a larger entity, a fact that amplifies what might otherwise be a private experience. When people see a funny movie in a theater, they laugh more heartily because there is a world of other people laughing with them. A large attendance at a lecture punctuates the importance of the speaker or the ideas. For many people prayer is felt more strongly in church than when expressed alone. Similarly, the aggregate of people in the Life Focus Community groups stimulates the individuals not only to live in the moment but to tell others about living, not only to live but to hallow the living, not only to live but to anticipate the living: all stretching them beyond immediacy.
3. The convergence of minds into a simultaneous attention to a sharply stated theme combines individual and communal experience. While meditation is commonly seen as an elemental amplification of attention, the communal concentration is aimed at a broader content. Each person's stories contribute singularly to a *communal conversational vitality*, a stretch beyond the self. As in activities as broadly different as chanting and voting in a national election, there is a special enrichment in everybody paying attention to the same theme.
4. The content is very broad, highlighting feelings, sensations, memories, fantasies, and perspectives that are important both universally and

in each person's everyday life. This includes wordly *themes* that are relevant to all: experiences, for example, with jealousy, misunderstanding, hilarity, or ambition. The individuality of each story line has its own detail, but such a form of life focus crosses over individual minds into a larger universe of comparable happenings.
5. The group incorporates music, poetry, lectures, film, and real-life stories in order to give lyrical attraction to the universality of the human experience. These vehicles reflect, animate, telescope, and color the substantive themes of life, which not only are intensely personal but are also vital to the world outside the self.

These guidelines tap the need to integrate one's immediate experience, vital in its own right, with its role as a miniature of the world one lives in, much like the nesting of boxes, where each box fits into its larger housing. Such a recognition of the universality underlying human individuality takes on subtle proportion when we address a set of themes commonly associated with life itself. That is, while the resulting stories evoke sharply identified personal experience, other people recognize the commonalities in their own experiences. Among such themes are nonpathological mourning, comparison of self with others, timeliness of sex and aggression, filling in for ignorance by prefixed opinion, and facing the risks of the future. Of further importance would be such developmental concerns as birth, death, puberty, marriage, personal loss, divorce, and geographical displacement. Other themes that are more relational might be forgiveness, conflict, competition, destructive impulses, and happiness. Obviously, the range of human concerns is huge, far greater than addressed by the remedial purposes of office psychotherapy. These concerns are about the small world of the self and the large world of everybody. I believe it is timely to create communal vehicles for this *microcosmic* effect, thus guiding people to a sense of both themselves and the larger world in which they can discover their own idiomatic contribution.

This promise of a cosmic embeddedness has beckoned large numbers of people to religion, philosophy, transpersonal psychology, spiritualistic practices, and psychotherapy itself. The western religions in particular are well-known for providing extremely ambitious answers to mysteries of a supernatural host universe. They point to the certainty of God, to afterlife scenarios, and to a sacred range of moral values. I am proposing that there is a comparable enchantment available in an alternative exemplar for societal relationships, a human scale version of this exotic search. In familiar contemporary language this would be guided by psychological understandings, attention to common life themes, communal conversations about life experiences, the role of mind-shaping conflicts, and the accentuation of purposes that drive behavior and feeling—all leading to a sense of where we belong in this incomprehensible universe. In simple, open-minded style, this humanized context honors the open-ended question we hear over and over: what is this life all about?

From the standpoint of such a perspective, the Life Focus Community group becomes an invitation into the microcosmic precedents of anyone's life, confirming a connection between each person's own experience and a larger class of existence: family, community, nation, and universe, with each offering its own form of hospitality. This reach into the housing for our individual existence has always enthralled the human mind, providing gravitas and dimensionality to direct experience. It incorporates the history of people and their speculations about the meaning, purpose, and future of people. It is important to recognize that this microcosm is directed toward the future as well as the past. That is, if people are currently kind or instructive or dependable in the Life Focus Community group, this augurs an enveloping universe that is, indeed, also kind or instructive or dependable. The trajectory of these engagements would thus be impelled by the lessons learned in this mini-world of their meetings. The affirmation could well provide a new confidence, one that leans the person forward, *transferring the experience with the group beyond itself*, which in turn leads into new communal possibilities that could feel believable and achievable.

On the road to the formation of these groups, there are three historical developments that inform the process: group therapy, the encounter group movement, and professional logistics. All three represent steps in providing impulse and format for the future of a spirited enlightenment.

Group Therapy

At first, a prime condition of psychotherapy was its individual treatment in an office format, far removed from the communal experience. Privacy seemed so important that psychotherapists even arranged the entrances and exits of their offices so that their patients would not know of each other's existence. This seemed like a necessary part of the package, and the hush-hush nature of the therapeutic process became sacrosanct. That isolation excluded two important contributions to anyone's remediation. First was the unsophisticated sensitivity of everyday people, who, after all, have always enlightened each other.

Also missing from private therapy was the heightening of importance provided by communal affirmation.

On the road away from privacy to therapy's populist destination, group therapy was introduced; it was a stepping-stone toward culture-wide applicability. Though these therapy groups still had a unidirectional leadership and were held in the private office, they did incorporate the wisdom and the interpersonal resonance of the group members. This recognition of a nonprofessional sagacity invited peers to be more than patients. One could say a multiple leadership was instituted; this setup was more like real life because people in the group offered each other untrained responsiveness.

I am reminded of a therapy group I led long ago. One summer I was going to leave town for an extended trip. The sessions would normally have been interrupted until my return, but this group asked my permission to meet without me while I was gone. I said OK. When I came back, they teased me about *how much they had been able to accomplish without me*. Such unschooled interpersonal powers are key to the formation of communal groups, where there is an even larger opportunity for people to communicate their psychological wisdom to each other. Not only would ordinary perspicuity be uniquely different from professional perspicuity, but the resonance with others provided the bonus of a feeling of *belonging*. In such peer relationships, more readily than in private therapy, people can get past the idea of pathology and shift their attention to the common issues of an ever-flowing life.

This normalization of personal experience has long been implicit in office psychotherapy. While therapists focused on specific people suffering from individual disturbances, they have also always found their insights to be relevant to the broader vista of people, far removed from the psychotherapy milieu. They recognized, for example, that unconscious processes existed in all people, not only those who were sick; they exposed unrevealed sadness in us all, not only in the bereaved; they described the omnipresence of sexual influence beyond specific arousal; and they recognized that abnormal projection signaled the fact that we all project. The highlighting of the pathological had served much as our art forms do: it has dramatized the mysteries and surprising motives of ordinary living. Still, in spite of such normalization, the abiding humanity of people's lives remained in the background—even in group therapy. Instead, the mission to heal the hurt patient continued to be a purpose that overshadowed psychotherapy's relevance to the way people live every day. Like the surgeon who concentrates on making an incision, the therapist curtains the area of concern, so as to concentrate sharply on those inner workings that influenced the specific resolutions sought. Of only passing interest were the songs people liked, the arguments with friends, the questions their children asked, the hobbies they nurtured, the people they mourned: important only as they may affect the patients' symptom formation.

The Encounter Group

Then, in the mid-twentieth century, another breakthrough came with the arrival of the so-called encounter group. A key contribution to the expanding landscape was that these groups were not part of anyone's private practice, and were thereby less directed by the medical ambience. This infusion of therapy-like processes into the social stream was an epochal extension of the group psychotherapy precedent (Rogers 1970). It lit up a large segment of the therapeutically minded population to a communal option for expanding the vistas of their minds, including a sharpened recognition of sensations, values, choices, and personal story line. These people joined with each other to talk about their careers, their marriages, their frustrations, their concerns with the meanings of life, their sexuality, their anger, their times of despair. While there would be stories of positive experiences, people were still more likely to address those negatives that were barriers to maximized living. Yet, amazingly, much as these meetings were heavily tilted toward personal troubles, they often produced a holiday spirit, lifting people out of their everyday priorities into the realm of an affirming self-examination.

One example is a session my late wife, Miriam, and I reported long ago. Let's call the focal person Hal. Hal was a group participant who had been immobilized into silence by his fearful expectations. He was bear-like in size and Falstaff-like in personal color and intensity. Nevertheless, while his impressive appearance promised much, he had been sphinx-like in his silence, contributing nothing more than his presence. The sideways tilt of his head made him look as though he might be attacked at any moment. When Miriam asked him about his silence, he said he couldn't trust bossy women. He was sitting on the floor, and Miriam got up and stood behind him. By her move into a position standing behind him, she created a spatial and emotional uncertainty, where she, as the identifiable object of his distrust, could be specifically recognized and the relationship played out.

This was a strong entry—not only into his mind but vivid enough so that it raised the attention of the other people. When she asked him how it felt for her to be standing behind him, he responded without words, by crouching. He looked benign, and she felt confident that she could trust him—even though he said he couldn't trust her. She modeled her trust by climbing on top of his back and asking him what he might do with her. He said simply, without anxiety or aggression, "I could ride you around the room." He had chosen his own medicine. Riding her around the room put *him* in control. Even though it looked like the woman was in the dominant position, he had flipped the sense of dominance over to himself. He then proceeded to turn a threatening situation into a playful one, using his strength, delighted with his activity, and feeling a sense of bondedness: with Miriam and with the group, whose laughter confirmed his acceptance.

Hal had unharnessed his energy; he gave up his wariness and said he would surely be heard from during the remainder of our time together. He then became a central player. While the action with Miriam released him from immobilization and broadened his trust, the role of the group was indispensable. They had been drawn in as a supportive and stimulating witness to a personal challenge, during which his success helped to accentuate and confirm his membership among them. They were cheerleaders, offering support, and they were a community, where he felt he could safely belong (Polster and Polster 1974). We can see in this experience a sharply created drama and an accompanying communal participation, as well as a plucky experimentation not uncommon in those days.

It was often true that the encounter group developed story lines one would more likely expect in the theater or novels, where there is a safety of the vicarious. Carl Rogers, offering another example emotional challenge, tells the story of a man who felt strange because he had no friends and did not seem to require them. Then, after witnessing a number of emotional events, his distancing dissolved, and he became distressed by the story of one of the other group participants. When at that point, in empathy with his distress, someone put her arm around him, he erupted into spasms of sobbing. He had discovered a vein of loneliness inside himself that he had been unaware of because he had long ago reconciled himself to self-sufficiency and its safer rewards. Again, this was a powerful and enabling experience, which gave him the opportunity to experience the advantages of joining up and the release from an otherwise isolating frame of mind (Rogers 1970).

However, it must be said in relation to the risk level of these engagements that these were examples of small groups of psychologically searching people led by sensitive and experienced professionals. Though the favorable outcome of this type of experience was common in the old encounter group atmosphere, it was beyond the capacity of many other participants or leadership. Indeed, while these experiences and many others like it were highly resonant with the needs of many, there were some good reasons for the demise of this movement, which has been resurrected in contemporary days by a very different sweep of psychologically influential social developments, which I will illustrate in chapter 4. As we shall see, the allure of interpersonal encounter has been revisited, remodeled, and hugely expanded in contemporary society's psychological trajectory.

Let's look at the lessons provided by the original encounter group movement, not only from its starry illuminations but also from the failures that led to its dissolution. One of the lessons, I believe, is to remodel the zeal for *change* that carried leaders beyond the safety precautions that had been built into both the protocol and the professionalism of the private office. People were aroused to say and think and feel the unsayable and the unthinkable and the inassimilable, a standard that stretched many minds beyond their readiness. In further excess many encounter group leaders sidestepped certain life realities of the group members, such as their prohibitively difficult problems, including: the integration of family loyalty with freedom to roam; the demoralizing pain of failure, as seen in depression and other maladies; and the astounding organizational powers required for synthesizing all the diverse happenings in anyone's life. In spite of the optimistic view that we all create our own lives, the freedom to do so, while philosophically promising, was narrower in the practical world than in the practicalities of human possibility. The role of habit, accommodation to reality, and human scale ambition were all set into the background of a philosophically grounded free enterprise.

These were all steps into an expanding sense of human possibility, and the accompanying optimism led to behavioral excesses. For example, the common encounter group credo, to be honest and direct, resulted in a distorted permission, sometimes encouragement, for some people to make hurtful observations about others. Other people would monopolize time for narcissistic reasons. Still others precipitously left marriages or jobs, expressed anger when a simple complaint would be more proportional, scorned other people's values and personal style, or felt discouraged when they could not reach their awesome standards for a good life. Kurt Back wrote a damning review of these meetings.

He pointed out the absence of social control in a setting where people were excessively aroused to strong emotional experiences. He was troubled by the lack of research and the reliance on anecdotal experience for evaluating the process. He said,

> We are left here with a situation in which people are induced to undergo a strong experience which historically has been controlled and has frequently been part of the sacred aspect of society. (Back 1972)

One of the fundamental starting points I have proposed is a nonoppressive emphasis on the *portrayal* of life, making this function a greater priority than the call for people to *change their lives*. Surely the search for peak experiences, a common ambition in the encounter group arena, would be more like a guiding fable than an experiential ambition. While wishes for higher and higher levels of pleasure, security, and enlightenment are common, they must not be so compelling as to override ordinary individual limits. Life, indeed, is not an all-or-none phenomenon.

As I have said elsewhere,

> People do not need to have peak experiences in order to gain important nourishment. There are many gratifying experiences that fall short of the deepest fulfillment to which our biological nature points us. People are nourished by singing while not able to produce the full tones and rhythms that our biology allows. People have satisfying sexual experience without having the most reverberative orgasms that our biology allows. We can remember our past without remembering all there is to remember. People play baseball at family picnics and they draw pictures in their spare time. Nevertheless, singing, sex, memory, picnics and the arts are significant sources of nourishment, even when they are not complete. (Polster 2006, 32)

For a diverse community, it is important not to succumb to the embarrassment of the average. The pleasures of community, continuity, and life focus are there to be incorporated at whatever level of experience people can accommodate. While frequently falling short of the highest aspiration, the levels of achievement that people actually experience are not only a pleasure in their own right but they also serve as a guiding light toward the possible. To keep aspiration in proportion to real likelihood is something people do every day. Many derive great pleasure in reading history even though they do not require themselves to become historians, they enjoy solving mathematical puzzles while not becoming mathematicians, and they don't have to be archaeologists to visit ancient tombs. People need to experience the fullest measure they can of what they already can do, and they need to welcome the unfolding scenarios this creates. They require no more reward than what is represented in celebration, acknowledgement, understanding, and belonging. To incorporate such a humanity of need would enhance a communal hospitality for people to be as they already are, joining together with each other in addressing the living process, as it already is.

Structural Logistics

Remodeling the risky and unruly character of the encounter group is important, but it is not enough. There has already been a huge increase in the diversity of formats for the exercise of life focus and an accompanying swelling of public interest. (See chapter 4.) Still, there are professional considerations that keep psychotherapists of all theoretical perspectives fixed into their familiar offices. They are positioned there to solve acute problems rather than to address the haunting range of common human dilemmas. Notwithstanding the large communal appetite, old habits die hard, and psychotherapy is still primarily engaged with the requirements of a quasi-medical practice, which blunts psychotherapy's potential for forming Life Focus Communities. Let us examine three of these barriers and how they are already being loosened.

Time-Bound

Therapy became time-bound when it established the ideal of "terminated" therapy, and so fulfilled the medically familiar premise of a finite curative period. There was a quixotic belief in the old days that once he or she was well-grounded through a "completed" psychotherapy, each person could handle whatever psychological challenges he or she might face. Individual neurosis was the trouble, and cure was the goal. However, this ideal fell far short of a broader reality: that we live *permanently* within a huge range of constitutional, situational, or cultural complexities that are always operative and commonly require a helping hand.

Nowadays, even in office therapy, many people who "end" therapy do come back to it when the need recurs. It has become abundantly clear that the need for help is not just a sign of pathology, it is also a healthy coping mandate that is built into the fabric of human existence. Not only do people come back into therapy to deal again with problems that, once resolved, have reappeared but they come back with new problems.

One person came originally because of her son's unwillingness to do the work required in school. With that addressed she came back a year later to deal with her disillusionment with her own work future, because she had been given increased responsibility with no increase in pay, nor any in sight. Much later she came back in fear that she was losing her religious faith. All these segments were part of an enduring relationship for which there was no expectation of a "termination."

In my early years as a therapist, in the mid-twentieth century, one of the common criticisms of psychoanalysis was the length of the therapy, a presumed sign of endlessly marking time. The criticism would have had greater validity if it were directed to any observed stagnancy of the therapy rather than its duration. In addition to flaws in method, there were two other important negatives about the lengthy duration of therapy. First of all, it was prohibitively expensive, thereby excluding many people from using it. With the formation of the large groups I am proposing, this burden would be lightened because the cost per person could be quite small, much as it is for people who attend churches and synagogues or who go to the movies.

Furthermore, mental health practitioners have not been oriented to the role of lifelong guide, a role that the Judeo-Christian religions have dominated in western society. Because he saw a lifetime of religious guidance as complicit in the societal creation of neurosis, Freud was unwilling to follow these religious precedents. The psychotherapy profession followed his lead, wary about the religious implications of lifelong guidance, and then became fixed into the familiar medical style—the long-honored, time-limited, office treatment. However, as we will be reminded throughout this book, the gap between the traditional professional time limits and the lifelong human need for communal guidance has been closing (Polster 2006, 3–6, 61–74).

Space-Bound

The second barrier to communal formats is the medical example of therapists working in their offices. By the mid-twentieth century the psychotherapist was no more familiar with seeing patients in a broader location than he or she was familiar with lifelong guidance. Even the house call was gone from the medical repertoire. I remember the shock of some of my colleagues when, long ago, I developed sessions for youthful customers in coffee houses (Polster 1969). The people who came to these sessions were members of a young culture, and many of them felt alienated from the society: they were critical of its institutions and were trying to find their way in what they felt to be an inhospitable society. In our sessions they wanted to explore their relationship with policemen, the school authorities by whom they felt violated, family standards that shot down their individuality, the high value given to ambition, and other themes that affected their feelings of dissatisfaction. Over the years it has been perfectly normal for psychotherapists in their offices to cushion themselves from such cultural challenges and the societal drama it represents.

What I am saying about the commitment of psychotherapists to the remediation of personal troubles does not apply to the field of psychology as a whole. Psychologists have been exploring community concerns for a long time. Their endeavors as a whole are beyond the scope of this book, but I must point out that they have been addressing a large range of social issues, such as the voice of the citizen, social justice, health policies, education, acceptance of diversity, and productivity. Albert Bandura, to give one example, is the tip of the iceberg in his explorations of the role of vicarious violence in the social learning of children; Bandura has shown that children learn through public vehicles like TV, movies, or books (Bandura 1986). His work is one of many examples from among his psychological brethren, who have set a standard of communal exploration from which psychotherapists may take encouragement to expand the application of their methods.

Such a shift would call for attention to a far broader set of themes, more commonly associated with everyday life, than with the themes that are sharply identified as acute personal problems.

Except for their relevance to the resolution of specific problems, where they are often faced, these themes are absent from the repertoire of psychotherapists. That gap goes all the way back to Freud. What else could he and his followers have done? Already on the edge of medical acceptability, they were pointed sharply toward the pathological. As a physician Freud worked with his natural constituency, patients. *So his therapy became a patient's therapy rather than a people's therapy.* Paradoxically, from Freud's attention to patienthood came his observations about the more widely interesting workings of the mind. While much of what he wrote was clearly relevant for the population at large, medicine had given him the pivotal permission, granted nowhere else, to introduce his explorations of the buried details of any person's life. This fertile ground for a psychic archaeology provided a windfall of revelations. His interest in the dimensions of the neurotic mind was a breeding ground for a string of procedures, including free association, which tried to restore fluidity of mind; interpretation, which tried to make sense of personal experience; and transference, which created a quasi-holy presence of the therapist as an illuminating authority. Just as important as his techniques, however, was his effect on the culture; he brought the examination of the mind to an unprecedented level of popular interest.

Unfortunately, however, Freud also set the stage for psychotherapists, even a hundred years later, to blanch at the term "religion," long the definitive communal instrument for guiding people in how to live their lives. The precedent of religion was there, not to be imitated but to offer lessons about the need the community feels for orientation and guidance. Even up to the present day, psychotheraphy has not utilized inspirational stories and sermons, which awaken people; has seldom regularly practiced self-exploratory procedures, such as we see in prayer, ritual, or meditation; has provided no lifetime continuity of guidance; and has offered no moral perspective. Otto Rank, one of Freud's earliest associates, long ago pointed to the psychoanalytic reverence for individuality and how this ideology counterpoised the communally oriented but fascistically minded political entities of the twentieth century. While the communal emphasis in communism and National Socialism was on the *likeness* among their own people, psychoanalysis focused on the freedom to be individual. Rank saw this as a struggle between the indivisible forces of community and individuality, in which "psychology is the last and youngest offspring of religion" (Rank 1941, 61).

What does it mean to be an offspring of religion? Clearly Freud wanted no part of religion as his heritage and was not moved to leave his office. However, one does not, after all, get to choose one's ancestors. Whether he liked it or didn't like it, wanted to emulate it or didn't want to emulate it, the differentiation between the religious style and the therapeutic is instructive. Psychotherapy's priority for individual life scenarios was a decisive orientation and certainly merited great support. However, to sharply contrast it with religion's priority for commonality is to create a misleading dichotomy. This split helped to throw psychotherapy off the communal track. Inexorably, the qualities of the individual and the community call insistently for reconciliation. While western religions have laid more emphasis on a communal focus than psychotherapy has, that historical precedent is, of course, no acceptable rationale for psychotherapy to shun the communal.

This contrast between religion's communal format and psychotherapy's individual orientation provides key lessons for each. Many years ago I remember addressing this polar difference by joining with a rabbi, Arthur Lelyveld, in leading a group formed in his congregation. The format for the experience called for the rabbi to conduct a religious service in the standard liturgical style. After the service I would explore the individuated experiences of the group members. During the service one of the prayers was rhapsodic about the virtues of gratitude. I then asked the group members to tell each other about their own experiences with gratitude. One was regretful not to have expressed gratitude to an uncle for his kindnesses, another was troubled about having receiving no expression of gratitude for a kind deed he had done, another spoke of the self-consciousness involved in putting gratitude into words, and yet another spoke of gratitude expressed through deeds rather than words. Each person gained a new awareness of how gratitude fit into his or her life and felt the normality and warmth of his or her concern. In sum, what the rabbi and I had done was to marry the generalities about gratitude that were expressed in the communal prayer with the individuality of personalized exploration. The choice between the community or the individual is not cut and dried; on the contrary, there is no community without individuals and no individual without community. It is just such coordination between the communal and individual experience that a populist psychotherapy is well-placed to address.

Career Logistics

This brings us to the third structural barrier that may obscure the communal imperative. It is a practical concern and perhaps the most problematic of all the structural interferences: the logistics of professional careers. Psychotherapists with backgrounds in any of the mental health professions are already well-established in the therapy they do, either in private offices or institutions. This would include psychologists, social workers, psychiatrists, marriage and family counselors, pastoral counselors, coaches, or others who come under the umbrella of professionals who foster personal well-being. The major problems they would face in trying to transform their current work into leadership of a Life Focus Community are fourfold.

First is the need to learn how to apply their knowledge to the communal setting, where a diversity of people must be addressed simultaneously with the focus on individuality. Though the needs of these people are indeed diverse, there is also a broad sweep that applies to everyone. The new requirements for coordinating these contrasting orientations would have to be learned. For one thing, for those groups that are large, the leader must prepare meetings in advance by designing a series of interactive events. This involves building a repertoire of exercises that tap into the diverse backgrounds of group members. This learning process is developmental as the leaders build a repertoire, step by step, based on the fundamentals of a group's needs. While the knowledge gained from a vast psychological background would have to be translated into a new form of education, the therapists may have no more difficulty than they had in moving from individual therapy to group therapy. The rest of this book will offer many illustrations lighting the way to this transition.

The second barrier is unfamiliarity with the executive enterprise required for forming the groups. There would be a less clear picture of how to attract the people than we now have in the familiar referral system. One important source would be institutions that provide psychological services for their many clients. That would include welfare agencies, universities, hospitals, religious organizations, commercial organizations, and retirement communities. Each of these has its own needs for developing a communal spirit and improved personal motivations among its people. It is especially noteworthy that many agencies that provide psychological services to people on an individual, face-to-face basis have no process through which these clients may connect with other people visiting the same agency. These agencies work with a large number of people but in a vertical relationship of client to counselor rather than the horizontal relationship of clients to clients. An additionally clear advantage for the agencies of the large-group option would also be the larger number of clients who would receive the benefits of psychological services.

Another potential source for membership in such groups is the clients who are already in office therapy, who would augment their office sessions with a communally oriented psychological exploration. This would be especially important in the light of current limits set on much psychotherapy, either by insurance companies or the attractions of brief therapy. Membership in one of these ongoing groups would offer people continuing opportunity for new awareness, affirmation and generative community. These groups could easily become complementary to the existing therapeutic format.

Still another source is the Internet. There are already Internet relationships established by innovative psychologists, especially those of Martin Seligman, Donald Meichenbaum, Haim Weinberg, and Michael

Yapko. There is an especially large potential for people who want to communicate with each other via the Internet about their relationships and other personal needs. This movement is largely without leadership, often chaotic. How this grassroots movement will end up is unclear, but there is no doubt about its vitality and its representation of a cultural need. The future of these possibilities for communal formats is unformed, but the population is there to be met, including retirement residential settings and Buddhist retreats.

The third barrier is the financial aspect. How would therapists who want to work privately be paid? How many groups would they have to lead to have the income they need? How large would the groups be, and how often would they meet? Could this be an auxiliary professional activity, combined with the more familiar roles they already play either in private practice or in working with an institution? Whether this format for groups would lead to a drastic change of careers would be quite individual. Probably most therapists who were interested would continue their office work, adding some leadership of large groups to their repertoire. Those who would choose this new direction would have a chance to grow with the advancing sweep of societal interest.

The fourth barrier is the absence of sufficient evidence that these groups are valuable. A common-sense attention to consequences is natural and indispensable. It is the basis for scientific examination of both the process and the effects that are already fixed into the psychological professions. Whether any social movement is good for an individual or for the society calls for careful assessment. Yet, culturally insistent social change does not wait for scientific proof. Psychotherapy itself, practiced by professionals in their offices, originated before there was any clear evidence that it worked. Of course, there have subsequently been an enormous number of scientifically accepted research projects, many of which have provided evidence showing the beneficial effects of psychotherapy. While such evidence is highly desirable, there would have been nothing to research if the method had not advanced first on the steam of cultural intuition. It is surely true that the profession will want to explore the value of these groups, fleshing out what procedures, what form of leadership, what content, and what forms of communication would be the most effective. There is no doubt that when these groups form in larger numbers, there will be more studies, a welcome addition to understanding the formation of these groups.

4

A Focus Revolution

Psychotherapy's social impact has gone far beyond helping those people who need psychological treatment: it now has a large influence on everyday people's lives. By its advocacy of individuality, its accentuation of relational bonding, its emphasis on free expression, and its description of common states of mind, it has provided an encyclopedic range of writings and lectures that populate our libraries, bookstores, and universities. For more than a hundred years, these communications have multiplied, evoking a community-wide interest in self-examination and moving society into the age of the psyche. When there is a mass shooting, we ask why the mental health system can't prevent this and we seek public commentary by psychologists. When a marriage goes bad, we talk of suppressed anger or excessive dependency or self-centeredness. When someone gets fired from a job, we may say he or she was too bossy or too rebellious or too meek. Hardly anything we do these days is free of speculation about our motives, our conflicts, or our identities.

But this influence is not just about problems. People analyze movies to find the psychological message. They form groups of like-minded people, including such categories as single mothers or ornithologists or even those with the name of Smith. A large body of empathy is publicly and privately expressed for the downtrodden or the misunderstood; it is recorded in books, magazines, newspapers, and television. There is a considerable consciousness about people trying to become the best people they can become.

The volume of such energy, which is devoted to the nature of living and the directions we take in our lives, has become so large that it merits recognition as a major cultural force. The pervasiveness of this cultural advance into popular importance is evident in three social currents. One is the extension of psychotherapy's own professional contributions beyond the therapy office. The second is the increased attention to the psychological considerations in worldly vehicles, such as industry, government, social networks, and self-help groups. The third is the growth in popularity of relational groups in churches and synagogues.

Psychotherapy Beyond the Office

I will include here only a sample of psychotherapy's many contributions to the popularization of life focus, illustrating it with selections from gestalt therapy, Martin Seligman's positive psychology, the mindfulness movement, and Ericksonian hypnosis.

Gestalt Therapy

While psychoanalysis was the historical marker for enhanced focus on a lifetime of personal experience, it originally placed greater emphasis on *understanding* the meaning of these events than on focusing on the events themselves. This understanding was called insight, the primary goal of psychoanalysis. When gestalt therapy came along in the mid-twentieth century, it elevated *concentration* and its accompanying *awareness* of life experiences into primary importance. Frederick Perls showed that sharply honed concentration not only brightened personal experience but pointed psychotherapy beyond pathology into increased absorption with the detailed actuality of being alive. Perls said,

> Correct concentration is best described by the word fascination; here the object occupies the foreground without any effort, the rest of the world disappears, time and surroundings cease to exist; no internal conflict or protest against the concentration arises. Such concentration is easily found in children, and often adults when engaged in some interesting work or hobby. (1947)

A pivotal benefit of such sharpened focus was its simplicity; *anybody could do it if he or she wanted to.* To pay attention to one's breathing or one's sadness was a human scale task that did *not* require the more complex integrations of insight. This simplicity moved psychotherapy from the intermittent and often abstruse enlightenment of insight, into a more innocent attunement to what is continually going on in one's life—large or small, intellectual or primitive, inferential or direct. Here is an example. In a psychology class students were given assigned exercises. They were asked to pay attention to any concrete object that would normally not draw high focus. One student said the following:

> Today I concentrated on a friend's Cadillac, which he has owned and been tremendously proud of for over a year and which I have

frequently ridden in. I had always been a trifle scornful of his great pride of ownership. For the first time I really noticed the beautiful lines and curves of its construction, and its magnificent functional capabilities. I received an esthetic emotion that I never would have expected a car would arouse. My pleasure from this was exceeded by my friend's when I made a sincere and spontaneous comment on the car's beauty. A small incident, perhaps, but I found it indicative of the new areas of experience that true awareness can open for me. (Perls, Hefferline, and Goodman 1951)

We see here a simple, though sharply pointed, focus that offered both esthetic and relational pleasure. From this position, he could see beauty where his routine vision passed it by; then, equally important, he could join his friend in enthusiasm. He had thus expanded his vista from casual recognition of the car into a perceptual bonanza, in which he was surprised at its beauty, a step beyond the routine experience for which he would otherwise have settled. This was insight, in a way, but not as much about causation as it was about the *phenomena* of beauty and relationship.

While the beauty of this car emerged from an otherwise routine experience, the salutary effects of sharp focus are also evident in a deeper and more complex emotionality. One illustration is the story told by a member of a small Life Focus Community group.

This member is a woman whose fifty-year-old son had been diagnosed with a life-threatening illness. There was no bromidic slippage from her feelings of desperation and helplessness in telling her story to these people. They were fully concentrated listeners in conversational resonance. They were not looking for a solution, because they were engaged with what seemed like a necessary suffering, an inextinguishable one. The words they spoke accented them as a world of people who would continue to be available in intimacy and dependability. Nobody needed to exactly say that. The bonding permeated the group atmosphere. But there was more than bonding.

This mother came to make a major distinction between what she *could do* and what she *could not do*. She was able to realize that *her powers were limited*. Though that may seem like a practical reality, for her it had felt like a defeat. Now, in this highly focused atmosphere, it represented a pivotal reshaping of her mind. The combination of the group conversation and the *aura of the group continuity* was a heartening reminder, beyond resignation or defeat, of the palpable reality of her continuing existence. This opened the lens of her awareness to receive the hint of a world broader than her pain—a world that included so much that she still valued.

Seligman

A seminal contribution to a communal application of psychotherapy is the work of Martin Seligman, whose concepts have attracted large numbers of psychotherapy professionals (Seligman 2002). However, what is more relevant here is the wide outreach of his work into lay circles. Using the Internet as an enlarged classroom for empowerment for daily living, he has created questionnaires, exercises, and advisory opportunities for people to expand their awareness of everyday personal needs. Into this public constituency he has entered as a voice from the center of psychological practice, injecting clinical expertise into the examination of everyday living. This range of common personal themes includes optimism, satisfaction, virtues, listening, loving, validation, raising children, and dreaming. Not only is he making good on such teachings, he is doing it on a very large scale. As of this writing, more than seven hundred thousand people have registered at his website, a phenomenon that promises to have great impact because of its size and because the themes addressed by his exercises tune into the language and customs of the society at large. His exercises, though calling for individual personal exploration, also may serve as a rallying point for uniting the healing professions with the population at large (Hendrix and Hunt 2013).

Stretching this communal agenda still further, Seligman and his team have created a vital new passage into populist importance by designing a Comprehensive Soldier Fitness program for the military establishment. This program is oriented not toward the cure of psychological disability but toward the creation of psychological *resiliency* among the soldiers. Again, this process, though altogether harmonious with therapeutically grounded understandings of human experience, goes beyond addressing pathology. It attends, instead, to the normal needs of huge numbers of soldiers, whose continued psychological well-being is the core purpose of these educational methods. A preliminary reading of the results tells us that those participating in the Comprehensive Soldier Fitness programs showed greater emotional fitness, were more adaptable, and thought in less catastrophic terms when faced with adversity than those in a control group (Seligman 2011).

In one of their other programs, the Seligman group applied the Penn Resiliency Program in training to noncommissioned officers, who would teach resilience skills to their soldiers. The farming-out of leadership is an important innovation, reminiscent of peer counseling. It creates an expanded leadership potential to accommodate the need of a huge public. Seligman's team instructs military personnel, teaching them to help develop soldiers' competence in self-awareness, self-regulation, optimism, mental agility, identifying character strengths, and connectedness in relationships. While results are still preliminary, the extent of coverage of life-defining themes was large, and the reactions of the students are promising. (Reivich, Seligman, and McBride 2011). This is a prodigious enterprise, and while the final results are not in, it is an important response to an urgent social need. It pioneers a populist venture into the state of mind of our military personnel, people drawn from the population at large.

Though this opportunity was created by military crisis and targets the needs of people who must employ life's most demanding survival skills, it promises more. The potential for positive unintended consequences has been activated, providing a bright signpost toward expansion into a culture-wide application of psychotherapeutic understandings and methods. As Seligman et al. say,

> Traditional psychology addresses the issue of how to treat pathology, but it has little to offer with respect to how to improve the performance of large numbers of people. This confluence of need (high PTSD, suicide rates, and divorce), the emerging paradigm of positive psychology, and the Army's holistic view of soldier fitness has created a unique opportunity to demonstrate how psychology can effect significant positive change in large organizations. We believe that the CSF program may ultimately be a model for psychological fitness in other large organizations. (Seligman, Matthews, and Corman 2011)

Mindfulness

A further contribution to the focus revolution is the mindfulness movement, which has grown immeasurably in recent years, spreading its influence beyond its origins in eastern religious practice and influencing a range of medical explorations and grassroots meditation. One indicator of the widespread interest is a report by the National Center for Complementary and Alternative Medicine, an arm of the National Institutes of Health (www.nccam.nih.gov), which tells us that 9.4 percent of respondents in their study, which surveyed more than twenty million people, used meditation in 2007 for health purposes. That is a huge number of people devoted to focusing on their personal experience. That number is especially impressive when we take into account the larger number of people who use meditation for reasons other than medical ones and also the much larger numbers of people outside the United States who practice meditation.

These numbers are only a hint of the general impact of mindfulness as a guide in living our lives. There is a host of widely read authors whose perspectives have been vital in the mindfulness movement. This includes, among others, the writings of Daniel Goleman, Jean Houston, Deepak Chopra, Donald Meichenbaum, Ken Wilbur, and Mihalyi Csikszentmihalyi. Bookshelves are also filled with self-help orientations for people at large who want to expand relational skills and the regulation of their everyday lives. Most of these writings are currently directed toward individual readers, many of whom have no communal format for the endeavor but who are personally stimulated to experience the spiritual side of living and are enlightened by the writers' exercises and guidelines. The multitude of people who are trying to understand their lives and achieve higher levels of personal satisfaction is everywhere apparent in the extensive interest in these writings.

The term "mindfulness" is closely related to "life focus," the term that I am using in this book to designate the process of people paying attention to the lives they are living. While there is considerable overlap between the idea of mindfulness and life focus, mindfulness conjures up interiority while life focus points to life in both its interior and exterior dimensions. That means, for example, that mindfulness points me to the details of my breathing, bodily sensation, and movement. It may also target my pleasure over my promotion at work. Even more broadly, it may attend to the role of this pleasure within my sense of my life and purposes. Life focus, however, commonly calls attention to a broader range of content, including conversations I have every day, a car accident, or a family quarrel. These are recounted in stories addressing a range of emotions and aspirations that have marked my life—expectations for the continuing sweep of my life. In any case, definitions notwithstanding, mindfulness and life focus have a sibling relationship.

While the eastern practices of meditation have been influential in arousing western society to the simplicity and the power of self-observation, the contemporary mindfulness movement has moved beyond that image to incorporate more broad aspects of personal experience than are represented in the meditator who concentrates in solitude. Of course, an extraordinary number of people use it in just this solitary way, setting aside a time of privacy when they are free to focus on nothing else but their internal experiences. So compelling has this practice become that huge numbers of people do it, often devotedly. Still, while the primary image of mindfulness is in this role—that of directing sharply delineated attention to a mantra or other narrow focal point—it also addresses the broader human concerns such as anger, ambition, cooperation, and other commonly perceived human challenges.

One of the primary examples of such an organized and externalized mindfulness is the work of Jon Kabat-Zinn. He provides a mindfulness process in his work at the University of Massachusetts Medical School, where he has led the Center of Mindfulness, operative for thirty years. Under his leadership it has trained eighteen thousand people in the MindBody Stress Reduction program. Kabat-Zinn sees the idea of mindfulness as an offshoot of Buddhist practice, which guides people to "wake up and live in harmony with oneself and with the world" (Kabat-Zinn 2004). This wake-up call goes beyond the Buddhist ethos, as many professionals in the mindfulness arena have come to their own unique application of mindfulness.

Kabat-Zinn emphasizes that the fullest application of meditation does, indeed, influence worldly action and relationship. In addressing the importance of generosity, for example, he says people should start their meditations with a look at how generous they may be with themselves. But he makes it clear that one can't stop there, that the state of self-realization is insufficient in and of itself, as we are all biologically created to act in the social world and to develop relationships. As he proceeds to remind his readers, this self-awareness and self-generosity must be shared also with the family and the world. There are widely varying processes for helping people to navigate these personal issues in order to reach that level of communal relevance.

One example of this relational objective is the work of Ronald Alexander, another teacher of mindfulness, who says,

> You establish a practice of meditation in order to develop the habit of mindfulness so that your awareness remains engaged when you leave the meditation cushion and go out into the world. Developing mindfulness allows you to quickly and naturally become aware of what's really going on in any situation. (Alexander 2008)

Alexander gives substance to this relational need by advocating a "wisdom council of support." This calls for individuals to augment private mindfulness practice by inviting consultation from a group of people with whom they have had a prior relationship. While this is a private selection process, requiring individual enterprise and opportunity, it accentuates the benefits of connecting with other people.

Hypnosis Theory

Current hypnosis theory contains a variety of theoretical perspectives, even including the idea that there is no such thing as hypnosis. The complex question of what is hypnosis and how do you exercise it is far beyond either my expertise or my purpose. However, what is relevant here is the role of hypnosis in the societal attraction to heightening life-clarifying awareness. In this respect, the increased societal interest in hypnosis takes its place right alongside meditation, self-help groups, and Life Focus Community groups as a vehicle for the exploration of personal experience. Hypnosis does this through many forms of induction, each of which, when successful, alters the life focus of the person being hypnotized. Instead of remaining preoccupied with the troublesome problem, whether it be physical pain or psychological suffering, the induction of an unfettered mind—concentrated on benignly felt awareness—replaces the pain or suffering, which becomes diminished.

On the face of it, the Life Focus Community functions quite differently from hypnosis in its targeting of attention. It thrives on conversational engagement, which is quite recognizable in its familiar forms of everyday relationships. However, in its own way, it also pointedly directs the mind's attention by pointing the group toward assuredly important themes. What is, therefore, intriguing is the fine line to be drawn between the hypnotic experience and the more familiar personal interactions of psychotherapy technique.

Michael Yapko is one of the writers who describe the interface between the sharply directed attention in traditional hypnosis and the relational component of his own style of hypnotic work. Yapko believes that the strict induction procedures often associated with hypnosis are unnecessary for hypnosis to occur, as the phenomena may very well happen spontaneously (Yapko 2003). Accordingly, procedures that are commonly identified with hypnosis—counting; concentrating on an object; speaking in special cadence; and the suggestion of odd physical consequences, like the inability to move an arm, or mental phenomena like amnesia—are unnecessary. Perhaps people wrongly attribute the drama of hypnosis to these exotic phenomena rather than to the more proportional drama of therapy. Here is an example that shows the more conversational flavor of one of Yapko's induction processes:

> You're describing to me how uncomfortably tense you feel much of the time and I guess it isn't often . . . or often enough . . . that you take the time to relax . . . and I'd like to tell you about a client I worked with not long ago . . . a woman who is not unlike yourself . . . with many responsibilities . . . and she came to me feeling so tense . . . so unsure of herself . . . uncertain how she could continue to function on too little sleep with too much to do. . . . (320)

Yapko goes on speaking in a measured but intent tone, while creating a conversational continuity about this person's importance. His cadenced voice gets a poetic flavor that induces a single-minded attention to his words, a concentrated focus remindful of meditation's mantra. While effecting a mantra-like focus, he is, nevertheless, broadening the content of her attention by intoning a story of her life. These details are the vitalizing force of life focus, irrespective of whether she is hypnotized or just contemplative in listening carefully to Yapko's affirmation of her life. The relationship itself is always operative, as Yapko, while pointing her attention inward, toward her own experience, is also always personally supportive, intent on her safety and her progress.

These relational and attentional processes converge to register the experience, which is felt with lowered pressure about any responsibility for personal accomplishment. In listening with such narrowly targeted absorption, the listening person experiences this quiet drama so pointedly as to become less aware of her previous mindset. Free of that mindset, she is also free to engage freshly in the evolving conversational story line. This willing openness would, when successful, move her beyond fruitless preoccupation into undistracted concentration on the actual challenges that she faces. And, most dramatically, it blurs the distinction between hypnosis and deeply engaged conversation. Instead, this process dramatizes the value of enhanced attention and serves as a contributor to the social embrace of life focus.

The Landscape of Everyday Living

There is an important arc to be drawn between the psychotherapy setting and the everyday life situation. I will now proceed to show some of the psychotherapeutic influence as it has become embedded into the everyday cultural activity.

Commercial Organizations

Psychologists have long worked as consultants to commercial organizations. A major threshold of their influence was crossed in mid-twentieth century, when sensitivity training dramatized the role of human relationships in creating effective organizations. An eye-opener into the importance of personal awareness was the discovery that when participants in training heard tape recordings of their meetings, they became heavily impacted by listening to themselves, a fact that added considerable importance to their original experience. This accentuation of their experience was a surprising phenomenon. It created an amplification of the experience, and these people proceeded to systematically reproduce such heightened personal awareness into what they called sensitivity training groups. Some of these groups were clearly wedded to organizational function, with many hardly distinguishable from the encounter group. In fact, many of the practitioners leading the sensitivity training groups had one foot in the psychotherapeutic community.

Overlap notwithstanding, the role of personal explorations in the organizational context presented a new challenge for organizations. Psychotherapy, in its emphasis on privacy, had been the inner sanctum of life exploration. The patient entered the therapist's realm, a world with its own expanded expressive opportunity. That special atmosphere was taken for granted, but in organizations the conditions were decidedly different. The leader was working in the world of the organizational client, a territory that had its own history, relational standards, purposes, and styles. Though the leader's approach would include his own professional understandings, he had to recognize that, as a consultant, he was in a large system with many working people, some of whom may have had no interest in receiving his messages. These people were far from uniform in either motivation or habits. The world of the organization was a lot closer to the real world than was the world of office psychotherapy.

In psychotherapy the client has typically come of his own volition and, indistinct though his wishes may sometimes be, he is commonly motivated toward participation. In organizations the needs and purposes of many participants are often opaque. In fact, in some cases, the benefits to one person may be contrary to the interests of others. The participants also differ greatly: in levels of awareness, in the barriers they put up against effective relationship, in skills for listening, and in dedication to applying what they learn. Some are excessively conforming while others may be chronically rebellious. Some are at the edge of anger, envy, domination, or ambition. Some are full of energy; others have great lassitude. The multiplicity of needs demands a special coordination between addressing common needs and those needs that are altogether individuated.

Still, complexity notwithstanding, organizations these days commonly recognize that employee productivity is related to the psychological state of their workers and to their relationships with each other. Therefore, the challenge of coordinating individual and corporate need is fundamental to them. One example, illustrative of a large number of organizational groups, can be seen in the case of Donald Zauderer, who in his Key Executive Leadership program guided a group of mid-career managers in developing effective relationships (Zauderer 2009). A key goal was to reduce a general negativity among managers. When he started to work with them, almost every commentary by the participants about each other's work was negative; each person showed his or her own perspicuity by diminishing the accomplishments of others. The managers had no idea that this negativity was so prominent because they were more task-oriented than relationship-oriented.

Zauderer set out to create a more enabling relationship among these people, where growth could happen jointly rather than at the cost of others. The kindliness of leadership, the pointed questions, the conversational opportunity, the perspective about living well—all were incorporated into the engagement with his students, as well as into their engagement with each other. In targeting their actual feelings, with no corporate pressures for the right answer, Zauderer found that, in spite of their competitive habits, every group member preferred a communally minded path over a competitive path. That is not to say that they shunned competition. They liked it. But they realized that in their complex reality they also wanted mutuality. They believed that this mutuality would not only make them more effective but also more happy. For these people, who were steeped in a competitive history, the idea of competition became modified by the surprising-to-them recognition that they wanted more out of their work and out of their lives than competitive victory. This should take the form, they said, of confidence in relationship, fruitful coordination, and emotional satisfaction.

Accordingly, these employees were placed into small groups and were asked to identify the behaviors that would brighten their professional experience. The qualities that stood out were respectful dialogue, careful listening, helping others to succeed, showing up fully prepared, and organizing study sessions. The discussions went beyond learning skills. They included attention to future goals, personal characteristics, cooperation with others, meaningfulness in living, and the importance of learning. Clearly, their concerns fleshed out their career perspectives and led them to consider how these would fit into the way they wanted to live their lives. Of course, this example does not represent the whole of the organizational world, which is a complex system of conflicting motivations, the examination of which goes far beyond the purposes of this book. However, it illustrates an important set of desires widely felt in organizations and basic to a humanistically grounded way of life, one that has been influenced by the injection of psychotherapy principles and procedures.

America Speaks

While this kind of psychological perspective is widely recognized and highly developed in commercial circles, Carolyn Lukensmeyer, an organizational consultant with a background in gestalt therapy, has entered a broader public vista. She heads America Speaks, which has designed programs for the public to participate in governmental decision-making. It has created a rigorous, technically advanced, and humanely directed system of group meetings that feeds the personal perspectives and needs of everyday people into governmental decision-making. This democracy-in-action process has task-oriented objectives: to create conversational opportunity and stimulate individual expression. When these groups come together, the participants focus on designated legislative themes, tapping into those aspects that people most care about. They want to know the whole story about the problems they have come to address; they pose questions such as: "What is going on here?"; "How is this going to affect my life?"; "How do I coordinate with other people?"; and "How do we make this work?"

One example of this process is the role of America Speaks in reconstructing New Orleans after the catastrophic flooding of 2005. The organization brought together four thousand people to help create a blueprint for the city's recovery, a plan for a wide range of civic actions (Lukensmeyer 2007 and 2013). In these discussions people gathered in groups of eight to ten and talked to each other about their communal and personal values and how these could be satisfied in the city's reconstruction. These people, accustomed only to a role as consumers, said they wanted not only to choose among already established options, as voters usually do, but also to *shape* the process in moving toward the consequences they were going to be living with. Throughout the conversations these people felt heard by the others in their group, and they felt like they "belonged" in a mindful and enterprising community.

While the relational openness was crucial, these conversations were more than evanescent personal exchanges. The highlights were registered and assessed by a team of analysts who collated the strongest themes. The registration of this subgroup process was a key vehicle because it made each person's contributions more likely to count. Small groups of people can talk to each other freely and intimately, but the content of the discussion can disappear if not recorded. Instead, the administration of the groups got across its concrete wishes by collecting and evaluating everyone's responses.

All of this helped to create and support plans for a huge civic restoration project. Normally, voters have the relatively empty experience of voting on issues for which they have insufficient information and no chance to thrash out the multiplicity of communal priorities. In these discussions the depth of participation was radically different. People discussed such issues as how to "ensure safety from future flooding, empower residents to rebuild safe and stable neighborhoods, provide incentives and housing so people could return, and establish sustainable, equitable public services." Lukensmeyer observes that the time is now for such citizen participation in a "deliberative democracy." Buttressed by breakthroughs in information and expressive technology, citizens have expanded access to a working dialogue with governance (Lukensmeyer 2007 and 2013).

By 2012, seven years after the flooding, Andy Koppelin, chief administrative officer for the city of New Orleans, said that the plan had a magnitude so large that it was commonly agreed that there would never be sufficient legislative action to implement it fully, but that the city very much has remained faithful to the themes and priorities. Plainly, the full extent of America Speaks' purposes has not been satisfied because of the wide range of financial, political, and cultural forces operative in such a huge civic enterprise. What is manifestly clear, however, is that pointed attention to the individual needs of the citizens of a large city helped it to reach a new level of clarity and significance. The quality of life of these people was so deeply explored that America Speaks moved into common ground with the focus revolution (Paltin 2014).

Self-Help Groups

Alcoholics Anonymous (AA) is the most famous example of a grassroots version of a psychotherapeutic ethos. Introduced in 1935, AA mushroomed into a society-wide haven for people to address problems with alcohol. According to an estimate by the United States General Service Office, in 2012 there were over one million members in the United States alone. The membership goes far beyond this number, as the group operates in 170 countries. Its twelve-step program has spread even further, serving as a model for groups of people with other forms of personal suffering, such as codependents, debtors, gamblers, drug addicts, adult children of alcoholics, and other groups of troubled people. Expanding much further, there has been the more general mushrooming of self-help groups. In 2007, the United Way claimed to have answered ten million calls on its 2-1-1 services line. As long ago as 1991, Yalom was already reporting that 40 percent of all Americans eighteen years of age and over were involved in a small group that met regularly to support their members. He says,

> In 1991, forty percent of all Americans eighteen years of age and over are involved in "a small group that meets regularly and provides caring and support for those who participate in it. . . Forty percent of adults—that means seventy-five million Americans at the time of the survey were currently involved in a small group! And that breaks down to approximately three million small groups! Furthermore the majority of the participants attended a group meeting at least once weekly and had been participating for at least three years! (Yalom 1995)

By 2012 the research firm Marketdata Enterprises estimated the "self-improvement" market in the United States was worth more than eleven billion dollars—including infomercials, mail-order catalogs, holistic institutes, books, audio cassettes, motivational speaker seminars, the personal coaching market, and weight loss and stress management programs. It is likely this number will continue to grow, with global figures echoing American leadership (marketdata.com).

Networking

There has been little recognition given to the connection between the expanding life focus ethos, on the one hand, and the recent eruption of relational networking on the other. Relational networking has now grown so large and diffuse that it is widely seen as a technological extravaganza. "Networking" is nouveau language for computer communities. Historically, "networking" was a term used to establish relationships intended to advance work purposes. To be a good salesperson, for example, one tries to establish a web of relationships one can count on. The same is true for any politician, whose web of influence is a key instrument for getting elected or getting anything done.

The current networking process is much more broadly conceived; it does not just satisfy practical needs but serves as a response to the need for people to "get together" and "talk" to each other, often about very personal matters. This technological terrain has widened eyes to a new level of relational aspiration, increasing the number of opportunities to become part of an enormous, populist connectedness. Such vehicles as Facebook, Twitter, blogging, Mixx, MySpace, Yahoo!Buzz, and Permalink have swelled the accessibility of people to each other. One report on the Internet says there are sixty-five networking sites that have reached over one million registered users. Five of these networks have over one hundred million registered users (Donald 2009). Facebook alone says it had six hundred million people registered in 2011, and the company's annual revenue was over four billion dollars (Lee 2011).

These numbers dramatize the human need for relational connectedness. However, the Internet conversations show drastically mixed results. Some report large relational benefits, created through the ease of a communal engagement and an increased sense of belonging. Others report abusive, even vicious, personal attacks, including group bullying and violation of personal privacy. These networking groups have no single design, congregational geography, procedural guidance, or orienting principles. Nor do they have leadership. Enabled by their remarkable technology, they are a spontaneous gravitation of people to each other, people who exercise their innate need for life focus. This flourishing instrumentality has been mind-boggling, but the eventual shape of these groups' communications and their potential for organizational inventiveness are unknown.

However, irrespective of the network phenomenon's unformed future, what is transparent is that it taps fundamental nerve endings, releasing people for new parameters of relationship. Its eruption into the social atmosphere makes the expanded formation of groups like the Life Focus Community ever more timely because the phenomenon's Topsy-like growth, anarchically diffuse, calls for a more grounded, purposive, and guided prospect. Such administered formations of groups do not contradict the current network spontaneity, but offer a countervailing option for leadership, continuity, and skin-to-skin community. They hold the promise of a responsible hospitality to a land-based incorporation of the zest that is spilling out into cyberspace.

These network outpourings of people talking to each other have a momentum of their own, and they are a natural vehicle for people to "talk" to each other, more openly perhaps than they have previously talked to their neighbors, friends, and families. The network phenomenon offers greater invitation for strongly felt personal exchanges, which harmonize with the contemporary cultural mores that foster self-revelation. The land-based groups, however, add to this flourishing spontaneity by providing design and leadership. They have clear boundaries of purpose, emphasizing mutuality of interest, communal examination of commonly important themes, and exercises to keep the focus on target. The design options offer a dependably continuous, sharply targeted opportunity for people to explore their sense of what it is like to be alive—a step along the road to a solid grounding for the life focus momentum.

Religion

Religion shines a light on personal behavior and purposes. It does this through biblical readings, liturgy, sermons, symbolic story line, and ethereal music. Recently, it has instituted a small-group experience modeled after psychotherapy groups. They are called relational groups and have been described by Bill Donahue of the Willow Creek Community Church to be no longer an *addition* to the ministry of the church; they are "the church in its smallest unit" (1996). He cites ancient precedent in observing that the small group was part of the earliest Jewish community and became fundamental also to the early Christians. As he says, "It was natural, therefore, for Jesus to develop a community of followers and for Paul, Peter, and other church planters to start new communities wherever they went as they proclaimed the gospel" (26).

Donahue's view fits those of others who also report that the recent development of relational groups is not a novel approach but a return to early Christianity. O. H. Mowrer (1964) portrays the early Christian groups as similar to the contemporary small-group movement and the spontaneously emerging self-help therapeutic groups. Mike Mack (1992) tells us that in those early days, the relational was an informal and individuated process, with people meeting daily. He quotes Hebrews 10:25: "And let us consider how we may spur one another on toward love and good deeds. Let us not give up meeting together, as some are in the habit of doing, but let us encourage one another and all the more as you see the Day approaching." Then in the year 313, with the advent of Constantine and the legitimization of the Christian Church, the people were able to meet publicly. They proceeded to erect basilicas, which transformed the church into a place-based, meeting-centered religion. That is what we still have today. Although this move led to a significant degree of formalization, it also brought people together in larger groups, tapping into the exhilaration of mass meeting.

Now, in more recent years, Yalom (1995) tells us that in 1995 there were already 1.7 million church-sponsored groups fashioned after the precedents of group psychotherapy. He says they were remarkably similar to secular support groups and that what they featured was fluid interpersonal opportunities, including members offering encouragement (86%), hearing other members share their views (85%), feeling they were no longer alone (82%), and seeing love and caring in the group (80%). He says that protocols of groups sponsored by churches indicate they are often remarkably similar to secular support groups, and that whatever name we might assign to these groups, the instrument of engagement is the conversational exchange among the members of the group: the invitation for people to look at their lives together.

The religious restoration of the relational group provides a new proportion between a vertical mindset, represented in obeisance to the formidable churchly structures and hierarchy, and a growing acceptance of the horizontal mindset of peer perspective and peer counseling. That is, in addition to the relationship of each person to religious leaders, to God, or to abstract principles, the relational group feeds on what its members say to each other. For example, a sermon in church that advocates fairness in competition may serve as a guideline for general instruction. The relational group becomes more individualized; it pays attention to each member's own life experiences. Through such conversations with peers, we humanize and proportionalize people's concerns. We enrich them with back-and-forth stimulation. When people talk to other people, they move away from abstractions about their lives to a personal story line, a concrete answer to the pointing fingers of liturgy and its formulaic communal worship.

Examples of Religious Relational Groups

One example of the relational transformations dotting the landscape of church function is the work of the Willow Creek Community Church. In the Willow Creek groups, common questions are asked: do you talk too much; are possessions controlling you; are you too worried about what others think? They also ask: what do you miss most about your childhood; what is one of the greatest adventures you have ever been on; what were the circumstances that surrounded your first kiss? Following closer to familiar religious themes is Willow Creek's attention to questions of solitude, silence, fasting, frugality, chastity, secrecy, and sacrifice. The belief systems of the religious and psychotherapeutic relational groups are differently conceived and worded, but they are both dedicated to the enhancement of people's skills for paying attention to their lives (Donahue 1996, 51).

Another example of such a churchly ethos is the work of the African Methodist Episcopal Church. In its formation of a Connectional Lay Organization, this church also created a recognition of the bottom-up value of relational groups, a value that stretches beyond general religious perspectives to enter into the individual life experience. The church wants its leaders to develop ways to enhance expression, using role-playing, simulations, and other experiential techniques familiar to psychotherapists (Connectional Lay Organization 2004, 71).

In the past the major emphasis of western religion was to inculcate communally desirable orientations, but nowadays we see increased attention to the lives of specific people. Generalized rules, such as the Ten Commandments and the Golden Rule, have long been embedded into the Judeo-Christian mind. However, the increase in small-group interaction represents a flowering of individual circumstance in the midst of the more familiar congregational and liturgical orientations. This transforms generalized behavioral standards by targeting specific life experiences. In these groups people can walk the walk of everyday life and see how it fits the talk about general religious guidelines.

Conclusion

These three therapeutically affiliated communal settings—an expanded psychotherapy outreach, the everyday landscape of life, and religious groups—house a staggering number of people who practice life focus. Dispersed as this movement is along several professional and cultural lines, it is embedded in psychological understandings, particularly as they relate to personal awareness, effective communication, and dependable and stimulating community. The activities of these diverse groups are largely independent of each other; they are scattered at various points within the broad range of purposes. The contributions of these groups have served a countless number of people. The groups guide their participants in paying attention to their lives in pointedly expressed detail, which gives more direct homage to the requirements of the human psyche. The soaring numbers of people who are exploring their individual personhood punctuate a human search that has reached such magnitude as to qualify it as a focus revolution.

Section B

How Life Focus Groups Work

5

Life Focus Community: Design Ideas

The shift from private therapy to large-group meetings calls for a departure from the familiarly unstructured format. In the private office the therapist, faced with the uniquely troubled individual, does not know in advance which personal themes will be crucial in dissolving this person's troubles. Because of the patient's singular life, the pathway to remediation gets lit only through the therapist and patient talking to each other.

Not so in the Life Focus Community group, where the aim of resolving a specific presenting complaint is replaced by the purpose of addressing more general human concerns. These concerns are represented by a large range of themes that demarcate those challenges of living that are faced by most people in the group, albeit by each in his or her own individualized ways. The group members face challenges created by their own experiences with friendship, humor, and loyalty. They are vulnerable to failure. They are faced with family interrelationships; with prospects and consequences of guilt about greed, neglect, and cheating; with worry about ambitions they can't satisfy; with pressure about duties they feel they should perform.

These are only a few among the many themes with which people live. These issues are selected from the entire menu of human experiences and become the arousal source for personal stories that flesh out people's lives. The design of these meetings taps into these stories, which are responses to the vital human interests represented in the themes. The stories may be further stimulated, as I shall show, by instructional exercises, abetted by music, poetry, or film. In telling these stories to each other, people laugh about familiar idiosyncrasies, identify heroes and villains, cry when sad, reveal prideful and shameful experiences, and give and receive praise: each person's stories provide both individuality and a sense of common humanity.

While there are many possible designs for these meetings, the example I will present here has a five-step sequence. I will illustrate this process by describing a session conducted at a psychotherapy conference, where there were approximately one hundred people in the group. The following account will show details of the group experience, augmented by my observations and by verbatim commentary by the group members.

Step One: Introduction

The first step was to introduce the theme of "home." As part of the introduction, I read a passage about my own sense of "primal familiarity" taken from one of my previous writings. These words were not exactly about "home," but my thoughts about familiarity were close enough in meaning. This looseness represented an idiomatic rather than routinized response to the idea of "home." A part of what I said was:

> I may get it [primal familiarity] with a stranger on an airplane; it may appear in an awesome physical setting such as the place where the Mediterranean and the Alps meet. It may happen when breaking into second wind while swimming. I felt it when I was making butter in the kindergarten or on the roller coaster or during a holiday in the synagogue or when I first touched a girl's breast or meeting my brother in Little Rock. I felt it seeing my sister married; driving to the hospital knowing my mother had just died; seeing my wife rolled out of the delivery room or even just seeing her as I walked into the house. (Polster 1972)

Then I invited four volunteers to serve as an opening panel. This was done to provide an example to the plenary group of a conversation about the idea of "home." The plenary group subsequently would be dividing into subgroups, where the members would soon have a chance to hold their own individuated conversations. Witnessing the demonstration would further warm up their minds, giving them quicker entry into their own individuated conversations.

Step Two: Subgroup Demonstration

After forming the demonstration panel, I said, "So, that's what 'home' calls forth in my mind, and I'm sure it will be very different for each of you. I wonder what comes to your mind?" Then I listened to the group conversation and joined in occasionally with remarks that would help the flow of conversation.

Person A started by telling the others about the smell of cooking and how his aunt, who was like a second mother to him, would teach him how to cut an onion. He could experience himself at her feet in the kitchen. He told of sitting on her lap and remembering the warmth of the room. He then spoke of his love for her and at the same time of his awareness of how much she loved cooking. This story was told wistfully and received attentively.

The next person to speak, *Person B*, told a very different story. He started out by saying that the concept of home was not pleasant at all for him. Then, after a few remarks about these unpleasant experiences, he went on to tell us where he did find home—in the smell of prairie grass in Illinois and in the remembrance of the land and sunset in the summer time, when the dust was in the air, all red and golden. He said that he was much more at home there than with any people. Though the words were a testament to nature in the raw—not people—his tone was quite warmhearted and warmly received.

Person C then spoke, expressing little sentimentality but impressed with the creativity that he saw in making a home. He had an interesting twist, though: he flipped the experience over from being the finder of a home to the idea that he was "discovered." While this may sound like a passive experience, even vague, it came across more as his way of yielding to a providential world that welcomed him and from which he received a bountiful harvest.

Person D started out by telling us he had not had a church for many years and missed the sacred quality of that experience. Now he was feeling that quality—by being part of this community. He observed that everyone is looking for a home and for connection with others and that such experience is "sacred." He went on to say that speaking this way was scary for him, but he felt it was going to be OK. Furthermore, he said that I reminded him of a good preacher—I emphasized good, said he, and I was not narcissistic but accepting. Then there was a thoughtful moment, and he wanted me to know how much he experienced me as a good father. After I jokingly asked him whether he would write a letter of reference to my son, we ended this part of the meeting with laughter and a strong feeling of mutuality.

Observations

My introducing the session by reading my own words might well raise alarm bells for some. Would not my own thoughts about "home" stack the deck against people speaking their own thoughts? The possibility of inappropriate influence has plagued psychotherapists always, beginning with Freud's insistence on the psychoanalyst as an ambiguous figure.

Still, neutrality has its drawbacks. The fear of undue influence can have a depersonalizing effect if it forecloses influence itself. The therapist must, after all, accept responsibility for the timeliness and proportionality of his or her influence, exercising humility about the limits of his or her powers to know what is best. Full neutrality is an excessive requirement, however, as a guide must guide, with full responsibility in order to be well tuned in.

The range of possible introductions is large, certainly not limited to the writings of the leader. It might include some orienting thoughts of the leader or poetry or music or philosophical gems. What matters most is that the tone of both the words and the delivery should model a heightened sensibility for the role of "home" in the group members' life experiences, both ordinary and extraordinary ones. This introduction is pointed toward the stimulation of a deeper-than-casual examination of the theme, going beyond abstraction into individual events. While starting this particular group process with my own experience could have had a skewing effect, we did not discuss this, and it did not seem to diminish the group's idiomatic sense of "home." As we shall see, the participants each spoke of experiences quite different from mine in both content and style. Perhaps the example did help them reach the deep-feeling tone that they reached more quickly than one might expect of people who were telling their story for the first time in front of a large group of strangers. We do not know whether the emotional tone of the introduction influenced the quick emotional reactivity, but if it did, that would have served the purpose—as stimulation rather than domination.

Though the individuality of each person in the introductory group became apparent, it is important to add that communal convergence was also apparent. For one thing, these four people, who did not previously know each other, seemed very glad to be together and got across a strong sense of mutuality and acceptance. Furthermore, they played off each other, developing an undercurrent sweep of mind in which each story elicited the next, creating an organically felt sweep of mind. While the sequence of stories did not follow any mandated direction, the detail of each speaker's life swelled the group story line, with each expanding the next, like metaphorical yeast, toward a group statement. While the last member's concluding statement that the experience felt hallowed may or may not have been exactly the way everyone felt, it served as punctuation for a strongly felt conversation.

Still, the arbitrary ending, because of time limits, must have created unfinished business because, surely, each person would have had more to say about "home" and about the group experience. They could do so in the subgroup formations that were about to come, or in later sessions of what could, in an ongoing group, become an extended, perhaps lifelong, process. Or they could follow through on this stimulation in their daily lives, having now been invited to incorporate the role of "home." Some people would come to value their homes more, others would want to create some new form of home, others would do just as they are already doing but feel more affirmed in doing it. The leadership must be careful to introduce themes that are broadly important and therefore merit mutual attention, without the group members being pressured by excessive demand to do anything about it. As would be true in many public-learning situations, the audience takes from the experience what fits into their lives. Still, some form of unfinished business is a natural part of any large-group phenomenon, where the independent advance of people's lives continues spontaneously and the unfolding wishes of the group will also continue to give guidance in future group meetings.

Step Three: Subgroups

The next step was to move from the plenary group to subgroups of three or four people, where each person would have a chance to speak. In introducing this phase of the meeting, I added a key stimulus: an evocative song that would further accentuate the idea of "home." Here is what I said:

> OK, I'd like you to divide into groups of three or four now. I'm going to play a song that's written by a woman who also sings it. Beautiful voice. She is the daughter of a missionary and grew up in Tanzania. The song is a story about her experience growing up there. What I'd like you to do is listen closely to the music, just letting it sink into you, and as you drink it in, it will find some place in you. [Aside to reader: Alas, I cannot replicate the beauty of this song and voice, but assuredly their beauty played a role in creating a poignant feeling about home and about the community in which this music was heard.]
>
> Then when the song is over I would like you to tell each other what the song evoked in you. We'll take some time for this—more time than we took for the demonstration. The idea is just to talk to each other; not to do any therapy with each other but just to talk and to let each other know your experience of what the song evoked in you (Johnson 1995).
>
> OK, shall we start? Would you play the music, please?

Step Four: Report to the Plenary Group

After the music played and the small groups had talked to each other for about twenty minutes, I asked people in the subgroup to report to the plenary group about the conversations in their subgroups. I will offer only a few of the many summations given by representatives of the subgroups. Of course, these are brief summations of engaging conversations and can only hint at the full extent of what was said. Still, what is especially noteworthy even in these succinct reports is the rapt attention to the theme, the openness of people in talking to each other, and the quick development of a communal spirit. The following verbatim remarks go a long away toward portraying the communal bond that this conversational bazaar created:

Person 1: "I had a warm feeling, of being *met*. Also to hear from others was touching. One spoke literally of home—the home he's going back to; another spoke of all the different feelings of family and places and people that it evoked for him. This notion of home—what he felt with the music. We also noticed that none of us had an ordinary home, that we all had a lot of longing."

Person 2: "My experience listening to the music—as soon as she hit the refrain of I want to go home to wherever she was going, I just started weeping—not much content (that came later); it's just grief, appreciation—not unhappy but sad."

Person 3: "I'm just aware of how fast my heart is beating right now. So I know that I've been very touched by this experience and very appreciative to you and my small group and the large group as well. I don't know why I'm always so amazed by the power of group, but I don't ever want to become not amazed by that. In the beginning I was 'current' when the song started to play, and I started thinking about how many bodies of water and ponds and oceans and rivers we all cross to get here. Then I started very quickly to think about my parents, not so much in a sad way but in a longing way. I won't have my mother's loving arms around me ever again because she's dead. I'm so thankful that I have had this and that I've created other ways to have that in my life. There is something wonderful about the fact that we are in the room together."

Person 4: "I had nine years of psychoanalysis—a waste of time! I had an experience sitting here that I've never had before. That song, this whole environment, gave me something to think about and feel that I've never experienced before in all my eighty-six years of life. Thank you very much."

Person 5: "I had two really significant associations. First was my mom. She's ninety, and I was home just a couple of months ago to throw a ninetieth birthday party for her, so there were a lot of things about us. Have I done enough for my mom? With what little time that's left is there time to do what's left for her? So it was a mixture of feeling good that I sort of celebrated her just a couple of months ago, but also some regret at the time that's left or whatever there might be there for the two of us, because we've had problems in our past and in the last ten years or so have tried to repair some of the feelings and problems."

Observations

For the members of this group, the idea of "home" hit home. That is, the theme mattered greatly to them, tapping into feelings of belonging, devotion, and gratitude, as well as longing and unfinished business. Their level of concentration was remindful of the meditation process, especially in the depth inspired by the evocative music. This created an amplification of experience, but it had a broader range of content and relationship than one gets in meditation. This high focus created strong feelings of comradeship and community. What is especially noteworthy for me was that people seemed altogether accepting of their own contributions, each with its own validity, with no pressure to do anything better than the way they were doing it.

Step Five: Consolidation of Theme

The discussion that followed the reports from the subgroups went beyond their current experience. Some people spoke about their interest in all the other theme possibilities that could be designed for future meetings. For example, the feelings evoked about "home" brought up other themes, such as courage, generosity, family, and gratitude. For example, one person said, "I was thinking about courage because in that song there was something about going across the sea and leaving. There was such an echo in me that it spoke to me in a very personal way about courage."

Other people observed that society's well-being depends on personal well-being and people caring about each other. Furthermore, someone else added that courage applies to everyday challenges, not only to heroic scenarios. Still another person spoke of a dear friend who died a month ago, and he just wanted to bring his memory into the room. Finally, in summation the last person to speak said,

> When I think of religious institutions, a lot of people go there to confess their sins or feel that they can acknowledge their weaknesses and that they are less than perfect and I also think about the role that

"shame" plays in our society. I'd like to see these groups address those topics because I think that what you are doing structurally is great. You are looking structurally to give people a place to go to connect with family and society and values that are no longer being given by the institutions that used to do this.

The group then came to a close.

In summation, this exercise is one example of a range of exercises, many of which I shall further describe throughout this book. They elicit a sharpened attention to a designated theme, but at the same time, the generality of a thematically engaged life introduces a broad landscape of personal experience. The group members tell each other about the places where they have lived; the people they have cared about; the struggles, hopes and, beliefs that have filled their lives. Communal togetherness, enhanced awareness of key themes of living, rising beyond ordinary social norms—these all create the high interest and self-acceptance so evident in the reports. This form of congregation optimizes the power of directed concentration to refresh people's lives and give luster to the stories of which they are composed. The drama thus experienced points poignantly to a common human desire to tap into the *accessible hidden*, a concept described earlier (see chapter 2).

More Design Options

I shall now describe five other possible design components.

1. Individual Therapy in the Presence of the Group

Conducting an individual therapy session in front of the plenary group addresses both individual and communal needs. On the face of it, a personal session may seem too private to be conducted in front of a community of people. However, I have found that the presence of an audience has been more of a support for the person than a hindrance. The live attention of a friendly audience and its empathic presence create both safety and stimulation. While one person's therapeutic work is the center of attention, the witnessing group is resonating with what they see, vicariously receiving personal illumination of their own lives.

Every therapy session contains within it some common human threads, so the themes of one person come alive for many other people. After witnessing the therapy the group members respond with their own stories. These stories usually reveal a group empathy for the observed person and a lesson for all. Indeed, to know we are all in the same boat, while we are also distinctly different, saves us from the isolation that differences might otherwise create. One such unifying experience is the following:

Oliver is a member of a twelve-person Life Focus Community group, one that has been meeting for about twenty years. He is artful, kind, and effective in his work, and he lives a satisfying life. Nevertheless, he was bothered that he was not using his full abilities. What he meant by that is that he is too careful: in the way he speaks, in the goals he sets for himself, and in using his imagination. However, there was a major exception. He loves to improvise music on his piano, and when he does that he is quite free, playing fully in the spirit of the moment. However, in his reckoning this freedom didn't count because it was private, not something he would never do in front of other people. As the conversation warmed up, though, I thought he might be ready to play the piano in front of us, improvising his way. We were meeting in the house of one of the members, and, happily, there was a piano in the room; and, more happily, he consented to play.

The music he played went beyond any of my expectations: exquisitely melodic and free-flowing, with no sign of uncertainty. The people listening to him were spellbound. For him there was a shy thrill, but more importantly a new insight. He had *lost himself in the music, as though he would dissolve.* The pleasure of it was a great surprise. He had always dreaded this feeling, which represented a troublesome weakness; the softness was a scary contrast to the secure stiffness he usually feels. It took a few conversational exchanges before he could see that his softening, as he put it, was not a muscular softening but a heart softening, in which he opened himself to the feel of the music.

Now, in thinking back to his everyday life, he remembered that the thought of "dissolving" has been on his mind recently. He realized that: "Everything I am doing these days that I most value is slowing down, softening; the way I am with my clients, my poetry, my relationship with my wife; everything that involves slowing down." I asked whether this softening made him feel weaker. He said, "No, actually I feel larger, warmer, and more alive and more capable and competent, now that you ask. . . . It's delicious."

Such a surprise is a curious phenomenon, one that I have witnessed over and over in the years of my therapeutic work. That is, people bring up a problem as though they were just starting to think about it when actually they have already, by themselves, started to solve it. Perhaps the glimmerings of improvement, unacknowledged, have made them bolder in bringing it up and taking a next step toward dependable improvement. Thus, Oliver's sudden willingness to play the piano in front of us was not so much a novelty as a continuity and punctuation for what he had already begun.

Of course, this was an important experience for Oliver. But what about the group? Not surprisingly, Oliver's experience tapped into the lives of others, and we discussed what his story meant to them. One spoke about her own love for singing and how she could not let her voice soar unless she had a friendly environment. Now that Oliver's experience was so moving, she saw more clearly what she could do to focus on what she herself was doing rather than being preoccupied about what others were thinking about her. Another spoke about his lectures and how he has learned that if someone leaves the room, that person may only be going to the bathroom. Another spoke of her role in giving psychological testimony in court and how she got over being intimidated and how she achieved a victory over a bullying lawyer just by sticking to what she knew.

The discussion highlighted two things. First came the *enhanced realization* that Oliver's experience applied also to the other members' own lives. It also sparked an increased pleasure in a renewed connection they now felt with others in the group. The experience not only helped them to name and spell out their own struggles but it lubricated their kinship with each other.

2. Films

Another design component is the utilization of films that represent themes of living, such as sibling rivalry, recovery from trauma, acceptance of diverse styles of life, or the ups and downs of success. Films make human issues come alive in replicating situational and relational realities, which in their vividness serve as springboards for subgroup discussions.

One example is *Flying without Wings*, an absorbing and inspirational account of a life turned around by personal trauma. The film portrays the life of Arnold Beisser, a psychiatrist and Olympic-level tennis player who became a paraplegic victim of polio. The film is a treasure of wisdom, courage, despair, heroism, and ordinary decency. Beisser was unlucky enough to be in the pathway of tragic fate but enterprising and grounded enough to transform this uninvited reality into a transcendence of circumstance. The story line itself is poignant. But it also ignites the viewers' minds about the nature of their lives and how one may navigate through inevitable difficulties. The design for the group meeting would invite people to divide into subgroups to tell each other about the implications of Beisser's experience for their own lives (Estrup 2010).

3. Practice

Two famous forms of practice that have a cousinly relationship to the Life Focus Community groups are prayer and meditation. They are part of the daily regimen of many people and an intermittent activity of many more. While these two practices are different from each other, each induces high concentration and rapt personal involvement.

Prayer, in its role as a communication with God, warms people up not only to their relationship with God but, by extrapolation, to their relationships with other people. Over and over again, one can say either predetermined words that come from religious liturgy or individualized words that are spontaneously spoken by the person praying. When people get good at doing this, they come to feel their sacred words to have been *heard* in the one-way conversation that prayer represents. For those who practice well, this reception by a supernatural otherness promises an eternal relationship, where deep feelings can be dependably expressed outside the stream of social complexity.

Meditation, on the other hand, usually includes little conversational content. It is directed toward transcendence of the everyday happenings of life and, when successfully practiced, impels the mind into a raw sense of life itself. This is a life beyond wants, conflicts, and thoughts; a life that joins each person with a universal energy. Meditation can thus provide a message of internal unity for all those who can transcend the fragmenting experiences that often populate our lives. Both prayer and meditation are the products of antiquity, and thus pass the test of time in establishing themselves as major instruments of life focus.

The fullest dedication required for repeated practice of either prayer or meditation is difficult to achieve, and of course there is considerable variation in the success of its practitioners. Our purpose in the design of the Life Focus Community groups is less ambitious than prayer and meditation in the sharpness of concentration required. It is more ambitious, however, in extending the practice to a socially interactive process—one that is less controlled by the practicing person, who is addressing the diversity of other people's personal experience. The continuity and repetition called for in these groups enhances the person's skill. Such practice programs might include activities as simple as addressing someone by name. But, mostly, they include more complex practice, such as expanding friendship, enriching the time spent with children, or reading more extensively. The options for practice are vast. As Miriam Polster and I have written,

> A few hours are hardly enough time for growth. A few weekend workshops a year, although certainly capable of powerful mobilization, are hardly enough for growth. Something has to reach beyond the guided therapeutic tour to assure a potent level of impactfulness.

How would the Life Focus Community group enter into this process? Suppose, for example, that a group theme is the experience of kindness. The group orientation about kindness and the exercises evoking stories about kindness would be only a starting point for practicing kindness. The subgroups might explore what each person in the group could do in his or her everyday world to practice kindness. Perhaps this would include writing an old teacher who had been helpful. Perhaps it would involve bringing home a special gift for a spouse. Perhaps one would want to make a donation to a cause he or she likes.

Of course, there is a large of range of specific things people can do, and there are differences in personal style. Therefore, people would be free to choose their own particular forms of kindness. Perhaps some forms would feel sappy or too late or too contrived. The members would never be urged to do anything other than what they feel is fitting for them or the recipient. For many people there would be a preference for kind acts rather than kind words. Other people may feel kindness in being softly confronting; others would be altogether supportive. All people would have the opportunity to practice their own forms of kindness and report back to the group about the effects of their actions. The specifics of how any individual might practice or the effects of the practice would be addressed in subgroup discussions, with opportunities for personal enlightenment. Thus, members become more aware of the role of kindness in their lives and perhaps more open to expressing it.

This process of conversation and practice would be applicable to a large range of themes, such as expanding the members' social engagements or recording comical experiences. Or if the theme of "novelty" were to be addressed, people might be asked to write down two or three examples of experiences that they saw in a fresh light. Perhaps they noticed the color of their spouse's eyes more clearly than they normally do. Or perhaps they noticed a friend's smile more consciously than before or heard a song more pleasurably or read a newspaper article they may previously have passed up. The same would be true of the more negative experiences, such as envy or anger. Each person might be asked to notice his or her envy or anger more freshly and write down whether this attention made any difference.

Practice is frequently associated with homework and has connotations of fulfilling authoritarian requirements, often without obvious relevance to the person's life. Some of these examples may represent aspects of a person's life that are too small to care about or too difficult to accomplish, or about which the person is too self-conscious to be graceful. But in the Life Focus Community group, practice will not be required. Those who do practice will be self-selected and will have a hand in modifying the instructions or fleshing them out with individualized action. These practice ideas will be offered to the group at large, a process that expands on the themes presented at the meetings, or they may be based on people's conversations in the subgroups. For some people such simple practice will significantly enhance their life focus; others will have a good opportunity to express their individuality by not doing what others are doing.

4. Music

Many forms of music serve life focus purposes—from the reverence of a Bach concerto to the ethereal sounds of John Adams to the heartening hopes of "We Are The World" or the warning that "The Times They Are a-Changin." The broad range of folk music, rediscovered in the 1960s, is remarkably rich in human spirit, highly entertaining, and largely disregarded nowadays. A renewal of the folk repertoire has a large range of evocative social and psychological relevance and calls out for personal response. Among other musical options meditation music is a common vehicle for enhancing the look inward and registering a sense of calm and acceptance. Still other music might be selected or even composed directly for its value in framing specific themes.

All of these musical options—the inspiration of the rhythms and melodies, accompanied by content-rich lyrics—arouse people to examine many themes that mark our lives. Optimism, generosity, despair, dread, love, celebration, mystery, and other life focus subjects are widely examined in musical compositions. The range of music available to the Life Focus Community group would depend on the leaders' and members' repertoire and stylistic preference. We have already seen, above, how the musical rendition of the theme of "home" affected the conversational tone of a meeting. While musical accessibility is understandably limited in private therapy, it would be easily available for Life Focus Community groups. An obvious precedent is the historically vital music in religious services, which creates both an arousing and a calming effect, inviting people into an increased awareness of the prayers they recite and a devotedness to life itself. Such musical vehicles have been almost entirely absent in psychotherapy circles. Psychotherapists have commonly been wary of the inspirational because of its potential as a means for dominating people. But it is also quite evident that dancing, singing, and chanting serve to incorporate color, feeling, and a union of minds into people's lives.

5. Life Orientation

Verbal presentations by leaders are a familiar form of guidance. To call these "lectures" gives them an academic accent that I do not intend. To call them "sermons" would imply a greater level of moral insistence than I intend. However, the leader's perspective can offer careful orientation about the themes to be examined, themes that create two broad forms of illumination. The first is to provide an educational experience that widens the group's understanding of whatever life theme the group is addressing. The second is to offer the leader's experience, understanding, and inspirational skills to get across the importance of these themes. Among the many possible themes to be highlighted are: competition, sacrifice, generosity, vacations, family activities, politics, optimism, tragedy, and standing up for one's self. The professional literature is vast, and popular lessons about life are everywhere apparent in the cultural extravaganza of information and instruction. What is emotional intelligence; how should we treat those who cannot fend adequately for themselves; what do we emphasize in raising our children; when is divorce desirable and what is the optimal way to handle it; how does adoption fit into our lives—all these questions are illuminated in the popular media and are good candidates for lecture themes.

It would be useful to augment the orientation format by having concrete illustrations to flesh out the theme. If, for example, spending time with your family were to be the theme, a specific family could be invited to talk about its experiences. This exploration of a particular family's life would have illustrative impact for the entire community. The discussion afterward, either in the plenary group or in subgroups, would show both the contrasts and commonality between one person's concerns and those of the membership. As they come forward, people almost invariably discover great harmony with the audience, and they seem emboldened by this to enter deeply into their own psyches.

Conclusion

The above suggestions do no more than to illustrate the range of possible design elements. Some exercises could take on a repetitive role, much as we see key liturgical content appearing over and over again in our familiar religions. The range that exists and the creations that might evolve are enormous, and the content of these themes would evolve over years of experience. One group with whom I meet starts its meetings with drumbeats and ends with arms around each other, singing the song "Bye, Bye, Blackbird." The drumbeats remind people they are about to enter a new region of relationship. Nobody knows how the singing ritual began, but it denotes an end to the meeting and invites them to transfer attention to the everyday lives to which they return. Many groups will happen into rituals, unexpectedly and with a sense of the dearness of the experience.

Underlying whatever design specifics are created, there are two fundamental constants that will support the variety of possible designs. One is the goal of transforming important themes from an abstraction into a concrete complex of events. Abstractions are convenient summations of experience, a condensed view that invites an unfolding detail. They are empty, however, when the story line underlying these titles is either missing or diluted. We seek, therefore, to restore story line. The other constant is the stimulation created by the communal ethos. There is special power in the simultaneous entry of a single theme into many minds. This converging attention amplifies the substance of what many people live with only dimly, providing testament to a vibrant reality residing just outside everyday familiarity.

6

Artful Engagement

With their skill at lighting up experience, artists serve as human microscopes, pointing people beyond the dimmed understandings that dominate our lives. We read their books, look at their paintings, watch their plays, listen to their music, and reside in their designed environments. They transport us into a cryptic reality, inviting us to witness novel versions of a world of events and feelings, filling in missing pieces in the landscape of living. They convey us into softened boundaries: where fact and fantasy may be indistinguishable, where anger and kindness may interweave with each other, where tragedy and happiness can alternate in a flick of an eye, where the comforts of familiarity are joined with open-ended novelty.

These contributions to the cultural climate and to individual people often provide profound insights, but for many consumers of the arts, such depth is not sought. For them the arts are just good entertainment. After walking through a museum or reading a novel or hearing a concert, many people come out happy with their experience, *entertained* by seeing a world portrayed so compellingly. But they are more drawn by the drama or the beauty than by any of the many subtle influences on their own lives.

Many artists would blanch at such a description of their work. Entertainment is less than they intend, but, if this is how they feel, I believe they are underestimating the importance of entertainment. The raw truth is that most people do read novels, look at paintings, hear music, and go to the movies primarily because they like to do so. However, it should be understood that this so-called entertainment is not necessarily lighthearted. It is not a casual experience to be entertained by a Bartok concerto, or to read a novel portraying the struggle between India and Pakistan, or to be appalled in seeing Picasso's *Guernica*. Has anyone seen a Charlie Chaplin movie without being touched with empathy for the honest underdog? Clearly, artistic experience is a pleasure that is not just incidental. It is part of the reward built into the innate function of life focus, the artist's fundamental instrument.

That's true of psychotherapy too. People commonly experience an anticipatory excitement, even though the prospect of the session may also be ringed with anxiety. Trouble notwithstanding, there is a great attraction for many people in being safely guided to address their personal motives, to tell intimate stories, to explore their dreams and fantasies, to expand their versatility of behavior and clarity of feeling: to know life in an expanded range, beyond the ordinarily reachable. You don't need to be "cured" to derive these pleasures. I am reminded of one woman I worked with who had made important strides in her therapy, but she continued coming. I sensed that she was now making up problems because she liked therapy so much she wanted to stay in it. We talked about the fact that if she wanted to come, that was OK as long as she felt it best for herself. But she did not need a problem as a ticket for entry. Furthermore, it was important that she accept the reality of her pleasure, so that she could more clearly accept the pleasures also available to her in her everyday life.

That conversation was a great relief to her, taking her outside the realm of pathology. It was plain to her that her pleasures in therapy were not flimsy pleasures. They were the pleasures of honest communication, of appreciating her life, of putting troublesome feelings into context, of freedom from the judgmental. Moreover, these pleasures, entertaining though they were, were also the seeds of major change. Entertainment notwithstanding, therapy is serious business.

To illustrate the convergence of the serious with entertainment, here is a session of a Life Focus Community that has been meeting for many years. Nancy was complaining about her mate, Angie, who was not as expressive as Nancy wanted her to be. We talked about the problems for a while; Nancy told me how troubled she was that Angie would not say how she felt about things, and that Angie was always task-oriented, not sympathetic, not introspective. This couple had been together for many years. They live well by most standards. As we continued talking it became evident that they always "got over" their frustrating differences. I asked why not just continue to "get over" it each time there is a hassle, instead of insisting on a change in personality.

It was a surprise to Nancy to realize that getting over it could be a livable option on its own—as much so as changing Angie's verbal habits. Not only did both Nancy and the group meet this prospect with interest, but the tone of the conversation took a sharp turn into *comedy*. Nancy began to tell the group how things go when she and Angie get popcorn, either at home or in a movie. The scene became hilarious when the group lobbed in their own experiences, each with its own humorous twists, helping to reset Nancy's rheostat for anxiety. I couldn't tell whether the humor normalized the frustration or whether the acceptance of frustration opened the group members up to humor. In either case, they all became free to see the larger context of relationship, undaunted by relatively minor trouble.

Here is a verbatim account that will show that the resulting entertainment did not sidestep Nancy's complaint. Rather, it lit it up, lubricating and humanizing it by a surrender to the unchangeable habits of a mate. It also drew Nancy closer to everyone in the group, all of whom caught the new spirit. They saw that the joke was on all of us, providing a laugh track for Nancy's version of her world. We shall see the transposition of a somber problem into vibrant camaraderie. Nancy set the tone with this spoof:

> *Nancy:* We have such a history with popcorn; it's so ridiculous. Our whole dynamic can be explained by popcorn. It's like a game almost. Last night we went to the movies with some friends, and I wanted popcorn because I hadn't had dinner, and I asked her if she would like some, and she said, yes, she would. So I got a lot. And so we were sitting in the movies, and I was holding the bag like this [holding it into herself], and she was reaching into it, which was fine, and then she leaned over and said, "Did you get that all for yourself?"
> (LAUGHTER)
> *Nancy:* And my first instinct was to say, "Fuck you! We just had this conversation in the lobby and I bought some for you because you asked me for it." So instead of doing that I said, "What are you trying to say?"
> *Erv:* Well, let me tell you, the most healing thing that I have seen in what you are saying is your humor about it. [Nancy had been making facial movements that were a subtle combination of a grimace and a mischievous smile.]
> *Nancy:* Yes, I think it is very funny when I stand back from it and I see that it started when I started realizing that I really only needed to eat two meals a day, and I'm a lot happier when I do that. Often then I would get a mix of popcorn in the evening as a snack. Then Angie started wanting it, so she would dip into my bowl, and because she is a doctor I'd have to eat fast. She eats three times faster than I do—I mean—her plate will be empty before I take my first bite.
> (LAUGHTER)

Another group member now came in, feeling a kinship with Nancy, by saying, "Did you hear that? I can tell the stories of marriage by way of popcorn."
(LAUGHTER)
Nancy: Good, well, now it's become a universal issue.

At this point, the others in the group told their own popcorn stories, each as funny as the next. One of them said she was absolutely incapable of sharing popcorn with her mate, which she saw as totally ridiculous. She said, "I have taken the blood out of my veins for her, but I would not share my popcorn."

Comedy notwithstanding, the stories threw the spotlight on childishness, greed, much ado about nothing, and the way the trivial can become a monster. Paralleling art, the unfolding of the story line sketched a relational scenario, revealed an unexpected meaning, and joined people in the group together as a Greek chorus, made up of witness and participant. The experience was a commentary on life, *hallowing* the new reality and its surprising development.

As a post script, Nancy expanded the context by telling about the fun she and Angie have with the grandchildren: reading books and discussing them, going to concerts together, and making resolutions together.

The Big Difference

In spite of a fundamental convergence between the arts and psychotherapy, there is also a big difference between them. Therapists must be more attentive than artists to the immediate risks of being misinterpreted, disproportionately influential, or just wrong in what they say to their patients. The idea of therapy as an artistic experience raises alarm, therefore, about the risks of extravagance and self-indulgence. Art is commonly thought to be a place for freewheeling creativity where anything goes, because the audience is more a witness than a participant. Spectators might become outraged, bored, misguided, or seduced, but nobody is directly injured. While the arts do have important social consequences, it is always clear to individual people that they are not themselves the ones at immediate risk. To place therapy in the same category as art may mistakenly seem to give license to therapists to say whatever they want.

However, it should be said that even artists, who are freer in expressive options, don't have that luxury. John Irving, the well-known novelist, once told a story about a reader who scolded him for putting her into a painful position not warranted by the novel's events. She felt this unfaithfulness to be a violation of her. He agreed with this responsibility of the author to be trustworthy: not to sugarcoat, but nevertheless to be tuned into the authentic flow of events; not to be merely cavalier, self-indulgent, or gratuitous in shocking the reader. However, he did not feel that what he himself had written was unfaithful to that responsibility.

For the therapist this responsibility for the well-being of the person is more obvious than it is for the artist. If the therapist says about a patient that the patient's posture reminds the therapist of a goose looking for its gaggle, that may be a funny, even apt way of portraying this patient, but the words "goose" and "gaggle" may feel scornful. To call a person a desert flower may favorably heighten a person's self-identity, perhaps as a picture of growth within arid conditions or strength without environmental support or a surprising colorfulness. But it might also be mistakenly received as a statement of someone doomed to isolation. Much like the artist does, the Life Focus Community recognizes an unspoken invitation to go beyond the routine observation. There is always some risk attached to the novel experience, but, unlike the art forms, the Life Focus Community is commissioned to provide opportunity for a benign experience. I will say more about the safety factors in chapter 8.

Common Ground

In paralleling the role of art, the Life Focus Community incorporates three major functions:

1) Recreating reality
2) Amplifying reality
3) Critiquing reality

Recreating Reality

How would we ever recreate a picture of an old series of events, a once-in-a-lifetime happening? Not exactly, of course. Jorge Luis Borges's poetry addressed the ambition for just such reconstruction in his portrayal of the "other tiger" (Borges 1963). He wanted to portray the actual tiger in the jungle in its full flavor. He wanted this "other" tiger, created by his artistry, to be as alive as the original. As I observed about him long ago,

> He thinks of a tiger, one which actually lives in the jungle—his movements and the tracks he makes, his sniffing of deer. In describing the tiger, conjured, there is a weakening in the reality of the words but

he knows the futility he faces. Nevertheless, an indomitable need compels him to seek out the third tiger, the one that comes to life in his dream. (Polster 1987)

Since there are no carbon copies in the universe, the re-creation, at best, can only be an approximation of the original. For those of us less demanding than the great artist, this is enough: the satisfaction of portraying such verisimilitude. What a great artist like Borges might see as "almost" on target can for most people be a happy success story. Therefore, whatever standard one may have for a reconstruction should be an inspiration and a guiding example rather than an absolute standard (Polster 2006, 32–33). That does not seem like a large concession to make in this Rubik's Cube of a universe.

Let us suppose, for example, that you and I are talking. I have come back from a conference, and I tell you that I was happy to have seen a number of our colleagues. One of them was an old *nemesis*, a word that is key to the tone of the conversation. Is "nemesis" quite the right word? You say a few things about the idea of "nemesis," and you want to know more about what I mean, so I explain. I tell you he undercut a program I proposed long ago and how defeated I felt when the program was rejected. You ask a few questions about the program, and in going further about our meeting, I tell you I was surprised to find that he now seemed only the palest threat.

This shift in the story's basic theme creates a new version of an old picture, one that opens me to a new look. Then, after examining the idea of him as "nemesis," I realize that he never really was a nemesis. I had reacted mistakenly to what I thought was a personal attack. We had just disagreed on some things. He was opposed to the basic premise of my proposed program, but he was not really involved in the decision, which went against me. The word "nemesis," the tip-off on my distortion, was an invitation to a new look. The word had stuck in my mind, but it was an inaccurate portrayal of the reality. Now free of that word, I experienced the old reality in a new key, one in which I saw simple disagreement, with no animosity involved.

Individual therapy is filled with such experiences of the re-creation of reality. I remember a patient who was an attentive, generous, inventive woman, but whose mother's obsessive criticism had blurred the dearness that was evident to others. She was disconsolately telling me about the ceaseless scolding thrown at her and how easily she could now feel put down. I have come to know her honesty and intelligence. I see her color, strong facial contours, sharp choice of language. I see in her what she cannot see, and because I am so confident about the accuracy of what I see, I bypass her discouragement. I tell her that 98 percent of the mothers in this world would feel blessed to have her as a daughter. That is my own image, simple words pointing this disheartened woman to a re-created view of herself, dimly recognized by her but recently getting so close to realization. I know my re-creation of her reality has registered when she lights up, looks right at me, and blushingly says, "You bet they would." I had hit it just right, and we laugh together. She feels the truth of *my* portrait and makes it her own.

In the Life Focus Community, one exercise would be to invite people to an open-minded view of their own reality through a two-step exercise. In the first step people are asked to *name an old and important aspect of their lives.* Examples would be if, in the past, they had been a professional musician or suffered as the youngest of five children or been suspended from school for two weeks. They may have seen themselves as obedient, ambitious, comical, or vindictive. They may have adventurously visited Nigeria or grown up in a foster home or won a spelling contest. Then they are to tell the others in their subgroup how this old part of their identity has contributed to make them what they are. While they are unlikely to be certain about how these experiences affected their lives, their imaginative guesses would accentuate the importance of these experiences.

Then, in the second step, after the first discussion has been completed, they will be asked to turn the kaleidoscope around and *speculate about how their lives might have been affected by having had some experience they never had.* Perhaps it would be a perfect record of As in the fourth grade, or wealthy parents, or a special skill in dancing. To see the world in the light of a new premise opens them to the fluid nature of a lifetime.

Amplifying Reality

Artists are supreme amplifiers of human experiences. Vladimir Nabokov once said about storytelling:

> ... to portray ordinary objects as they will be reflected in the kindly mirrors of future time; to find in the objects around us the fragrant tenderness that only posterity will discern and appreciate in far-off times when every trifle of our plain everyday life will become exquisite and festive in its own right: the times when a man who might put on the most ordinary jacket of today will be dressed up for an elegant masquerade. (McCann 2009)

We also see amplification created when Charles Dickens enlarges the reader's awareness of the exploitation of children. Salvador Dalí amplifies perceptual imagination, stretching it through the exaggerated fluidity of shape and line. Joseph Heller accentuates common absurdity by his comic burlesques of how people talk to each other. Rebecca Goldstein, in her novel *36 Arguments for the Existence of God*, introduces one of her characters, Roz, with this bigger-than-life description, underscoring that she is unforgettable:

> Once you really looked at her, it was hard to look away. She had a high-bridged nose and clear blue eyes, and her upper lip looked sweetened by all the laughter it had laughed, it looked generous to share that laughter with others, and it looked, despite all its fun, noble. Her whole bearing had something noble about it. (Goldstein 2009)

I am reminded of a patient of mine who was the opposite of Roz: who faded into the background. He told me a story one day about his abusive father, who would become vicious when drunk. When the father was "out on the town," drinking, his mother would keep the young boy awake late into the night because his father was less likely to "kill" *her* when he was awake. He told the story matter-of-factly, saying it was a "typical" experience, nothing to make any noise about. Telling the story to me was already an amplification of his familiar dismissal of it. But my stunned exclamation about this ghastly childhood responsibility further raised the ante, making the reality so unavoidable that he told me a fuller story about this part of his life, telling it with a more fitting combination of anger and sadness.

Important as such easily recognizable recovery of the disregarded is, it is only a hint of the role of amplification in our lives. It is easy to see how magnified a home run is when fifty thousand spectators witness it or when a theater audience reacts, as one, with laughter, applause, a groan, a gasp. However, it is easy to overlook the magnification that happens spontaneously in everyday living—the brightness of just walking into your house when you are returning from a long trip or just standing in the lobby of a theater when the bell rings and you walk into that auditorium. Even less noticeable is the most continuing source of amplification: the you-and-me intimacy of people who say a colorful word or smile appreciatively or ask a probing question or cry about something sad.

For the Life Focus Community, this power to amplify is represented by naming life-defining themes, an action that punctuates their importance. In further amplification the converging of concentration by many people in the group assures that the themes receive more than casual or intellectual attention. People may be asked to tell each other about a memorable celebration, or to tell each other about the first time during puberty that they realized something different was happening in their lives, or to tell about a surprise they experienced during the past week. We also see this need for amplification satisfied by many familiar communal acts, such as saying grace at mealtime, arranging a birthday party, honoring a lifetime of service, or giving vows at a marriage ceremony. All of these accentuate people's lives, and they are the antidote to taking life for granted.

On a cautionary note, there are two primary points to be made. First, it is obvious that an infinite number of ordinary events should, indeed, be passed through with little notice or articulation. We necessarily give only the most fleeting attention to most of life's events. The awareness of them must remain unacknowledged or they would stop the music of life's step-by-step movement. Such self-consciousness all too often distracts people from living simply, actively, and confidently.

Second, amplification of specifics, such as a person's intellectual prowess, lovability, or stinginess, may take on undue significance, making it more important than it should be. The downside of high focus is that it is the enemy of contextualization, a process that provides proportion and understanding to the sharpness of immediate focus. For example, the idea of togetherness in the ethos of the Life Focus Community may foster an uncritical acceptance of the group as it is, or it may create an unsupportable optimism. To place an exclusively positive value on togetherness highlights it. But it must also face its potential clash with the opposition of others. Yes, the message of togetherness is an important one, but it is not sacrosanct. The requirement for a clear truth must be softened in a community where no message, valid though it may be, stands inviolate.

Critiquing Reality

One of the most obvious contributions of the arts is to critique some aspect of society. One of the multitude of examples is Kazuo Ishiguro's novel *Remains of the Day*. The novel portrays a robotic English butler in the 1930s who has an obsessive reverence for both his profession and his lordly employer, as he lives a life of servile homage to both. Through this narrowing he fails to see Hitler's influence in his master's life. He ignores his dying father. He overlooks an important love option. He lives a life of empty role-playing. Literature is filled with lessons about life, communicated through stories of fixed characteristics that poison people's lives.

The same function of critique is operative in the Life Focus Community. In its explorations much that is taken for granted won't retain its original standing when put under the light of freshened perception. Bullying, for one example, is a serious personal problem, but it also has broad implications for the society at large. A hundred years ago bullying was largely taken for granted. That's what people grew up with, and they either learned to handle it or suffered the consequences. Nowadays it is a source of public dismay. Suppose a Life Focus Community meeting were to ask whether one of the members would like to discuss his experience with a bully. Travis, a forty-year-old man, comes forward. He tells us that a bully terrorized him in his childhood neighborhood. It becomes apparent that he has been left with a *view of himself as a coward*. This image is so strong that it persists in spite of many subsequently daring intellectual positions he has taken as the historian he has become.

At a key point in the session, the leader guides him in an "empty chair" dialogue. Speaking to the imagined bully, Travis tells him about how terrorized he had been. The bully, role-played by Travis, sneers back at him. Where Travis would have been cowed in his earlier life, he now lashes out, spelling out examples of the bully's grossness, meanness, and exploitation of those who couldn't fight back. The bully is there only in Travis's imagination; he is not really there, but the drama is strongly felt, as though he were there. Travis, having fired off his reaction, is surprised to feel a new sensation, warm and red. For the moment he knows what it is like to have no trace of cowardice. He even begins to feel sorry for the bully, hoping he too has found his way past the ugly beginning.

Such a demonstration is a form of theater, a designed experience that dramatizes aspects of life that have been set aside, an experience that banks on the induction of awareness. Thus does the experience achieve its full significance as it fleshes out an organically fit story line. It is easy to see Travis's release from feelings of cowardice as an individual accomplishment, but it is also a social critique, coloring the suppressive force of bullying for people at large. The symbolic quality of the conversation of one person gives it public relevance, building a fire under cool understanding.

Artful Authenticity

Art is often seen as a tool of authenticity, but it is a paradoxical form of authenticity, housed in fabricated formats. It is not real life even though it dramatizes real life. Each format, whether it be a novel or a painting or a song, provides special conditions for achieving clear vision. Whether the artist is creating a conversation on the stoop of a New York tenement or the machinations of a corporate board meeting, he or she is providing his or her projection of a real-life phenomenon. The Life Focus Community, likewise, is also a departure from the everyday world, framed to offer that world a clarified dimension. It gives people a fresh opportunity, not available in ordinary interpersonal exchange, to see life not as a passing event impelled by its own momentum but as one that invites a new look.

How authentic can the feelings and observations be when the circumstances have been so explicitly arranged? From its beginnings the psychotherapy experience depended on framed hospitality for deep personal engagement. The therapist was commissioned to be absorbed in the relationship itself, knowing that his or her personal investment was only temporary, nowhere near the level of investment he had in family, friends, and business associates. Still, the relationship, in its artful parameters, felt altogether authentic, having its own demarcated reality, evoking feelings and revelations ordinarily reserved for familiarly intimate relationships. The natural question to ask is whether such absorption can be genuine and honest or whether it is merely skillful pretense.

Perhaps the answer to the question of the authenticity of this engagement would become clearer if we look at the theatrical experience. One philosophy of acting is that if the actor is playing Othello, he is not just pretending to be jealous; he *is* jealous during the period of the play. Then, when the play is over, he sets it aside and goes on with his own life. For this to be a valid perspective, a surprising thing must happen to the actor. Because of his openness to the hidden regions of his experiences and because of the stimulation of the play's content, he discovers a jealousy in himself, which does not normally rise to the surface. The theatergoers, who are affected by his reach into this buried emotion, will also be moved by the jealousy, feeling its authenticity and inspiring them to empathize with jealousy. Through this artistic extraction the actor and the audience are enabled to discover the veins of jealousy right underneath their skins, thereby broadening their minds about the nature of jealousy, tuning incisively into this emotion.

Comparably, the Life Focus Community group also permits an extraordinary level of relational interest among people who may never see each other outside the arranged format. They are not intimates in their everyday living, although in contrast to the theatrical experience, they could be. The special expansion of boundaries of the group, which releases people from their familiar barriers, enables them to care for each other, even though they are not a part of each other's everyday lives. To receive this pointed attention and its special conversational opportunity expands the artistic precedent into the realm of actual people talking to each other about their actual lives. What they might normally pass over, they, in a theatrical parallel, are now invited to accentuate in a format that is free of the pressures of everyday living.

Thus, we see that the Life Focus Community group emulates the art forms by pointed words that resonate with a highly aware receptivity. The conversational tone is more ordinary than what we expect of art, and it surely does not require that level of dedication and skill. Yet, we see a brightening of the shadow of experiences that pass through our everyday lives, just short of awareness. To have such a special expressive format advances the chances that this new awareness will happen at all and that it will address psychologically important themes. Many people are already good at doing this. They already find ways to deepen the feeling of being alive. They already gravitate to one or another form of conversational interplay. The artfully fabricated setting is the assurance of continuity in what they already love doing, and it becomes contagious for others.

7

Themes that Mark a Lifetime

Providing content for the Life Focus Community group experience, here is an illustrative look at just a few of the major themes that people are likely to want to explore together. They are examples from a large range of experiences that form the substance of people's psychological existence.

Listening

Listening is a silent, commonly unnoticed force in relationship. Nevertheless, it is a springboard for continuity, assuring that what I say will faithfully connect with what you say. This provides grace to conversation, union between otherwise separated people, and understanding of what is being said. Still, as with other basic functions, there are roadblocks to listening. The urgency to speak may cause me to be more occupied with waiting my turn than with listening. Or I may be afraid of what I hear, of what it might stimulate in me, such as anger or submission or opposition. Or I may become confused about the meaning of what I hear. Or I might feel put down or feel accused or feel invited to something I don't want. In the distracting silence of partial listening, continuity is interrupted, and life becomes choppier than it would be in a more harmonious listening.

Here is an example from a Life Focus Community meeting in which listening was the subject of discussion:

Person number one in a subgroup spoke about the intrusions he felt in everyday life, bemoaning the fact that intimacy of conversation was so rare in his everyday life that he became most aware of its absence only after the electricity went out in a power blackout. The absence of electricity created a metaphorical blank space, making him more clearly aware of listening as a phenomenon of its own, as well as calling out for response. While this accentuation of his listening led him to the practical effect of conversing more intimately, the contrast with his normal experience made him all the more appreciative of the vitality of listening. Then he said, "This is so cozy, and it's romantic and wonderful. But why must we wait until the electricity goes out."

While listening intently to these observations, *person number 2*, influenced by the way he *heard* the observation about electricity, responded with his own experience of intimacy by telling about a personal memory. It was just an ordinary story, but in the high focus of this meeting, it had strong emotional tones. He said, "I was remembering when my two sons were smaller, we'd go into the bedroom at night just when they were going to bed, turn out the light, and they would say, 'Tell us a makeup story, Daddy.' They listened, and then I would just start spinning this story. It's the phrase that the story always started out with: 'Once upon a time, in a place far, far away.' You know, we would just journey to this far away place, you know, like all these stories do. They just listened. It was just incredible. The absolute greatest of pleasures."

He felt deeply about this because he had been more than ordinarily moved by what he *heard* from person number one. The immersion he felt upon *hearing* the first person's candlelight experience impelled him into his own, idiomatic pathway: memory tapped, love for his children registered. When he *listened* to the teller of the electricity outage, he felt the spirit of the story, and it reminded him of his fairyland of pleasure and the marvel of his children listening to him, enraptured as they listen, listen, listen. The same words, heard with a more common half-hearted listening, might have passed by with little effect. Instead, each person in this conversation experienced an affirming mutuality—amplified, incidentally, by the entire plenary group addressing the same issue.

A prime example of the relational leverage created by listening is the work of the actor. For the actor listening is a basic instrument that steers him or her into the believability of his or her own words. To listen well and be authentically affected by what the actor hears contrasts with the pretense commonly attributed to acting. *The actor is inspirited by having heard the other character and also to have the other character as a listener* to what the first actor will be saying. It is probably true that some actors can "pretend" that they are listening to the other actor and speak their lines from memory more skillfully than others, but it is widely believed that acting is not mere pretense. Alan Alda refers to this perspective when he says,

> When I started out as an actor, I thought, "*Here's what I have to say; how shall I say it?*" On M*A*S*H, I began to understand that what I do in the scene is not as important as what happens between me and the

other person. *And listening is what lets it happen* [emphasis mine]. It's almost always the other person who causes you to say what you say next. You don't have to figure out how you'll say it. You have to listen so simply; so innocently, that the other person brings about a change in you that *makes* you say it and informs the way you say it. (Alda 2006)

The same relational reverberation happens in the "real" world, where what is fed into us by the people around us is what arouses us and nourishes us. While the most obvious perception is that we are all separate from each other, such separateness, in some mysterious neuronal dynamic, is not the whole story. The impulse to union goes on, often silently, unnoticed by many because they live in a world where the most evident reality is that self and others are distinctly separate. The boundaries between disparate people become blurred only in special circumstances, such as in the instruments in a great orchestra playing together or in an audience entranced with an orator or a conversation where each remark builds seamlessly on the preceding. In the search for such union, it is restorative for the Life Focus Community group to provide exercises that invite people to pay attention to the experience of listening and how it affects the mutuality of their conversational relationship.

Nevertheless, it must also be said that no matter how strongly people want unity, they don't *have* to have it. Even while listening, humans have a huge capacity for dissonance, which has its own majesty, and is functional in its own right. Sometimes dissonance comes as a relief from union, sometimes as a veiled opportunity to create new harmonies, sometimes as rebellion, sometimes as a challenge to address a puzzle to be solved, and sometimes because it is just there, a part of the natural unruliness of events. That is surely another theme worthy of exploration.

Empathy

Empathy is another vehicle for union with other people. Normally we think we can know how another person feels because of the information we get. That is, if they tell us they are sad, we know they are sad, or if they look like they are sad, they are sad. But empathy takes a more inferential route. We know other people because we know, for one, what it is like to be human and, for another, we know what it is like to be ourselves. It is a short psychological trip to cross the bridge from our own experience of sadness to assumptions about the other person's experience. We have all been children, so we know a child's impatience. We have all made mistakes, so we know the embarrassment that goes with it. We have all suffered injury, so we know the pain of it.

Still, most of us also are sophisticated enough to recognize that we cannot know the full truth about what it is like to be another person. In fact, there is so much difference among people that when we guess about the supposedly mutually understood experience, it is no news that we may well be wrong. If I empathetically say that I am sorry you lost your job, you may tell me that you are glad to have lost it because it gives you new opportunities. Given such ups and downs of accuracy, it helps to talk to each other to discover a clearer truth than our independent imagination provides.

Carl Rogers tells about a man who was speaking negatively about his father. The therapist observed that he seemed angry with his father. The man said no, that was not it. The therapist said, "Possibly you are dissatisfied." The man felt that to be closer to his experience. Then the therapist said it might be more like disappointment, and the man said, "Yes!" Disappointment was exactly it. He then felt met and inspired to spell out how his father had been a disappointment to him. Empathy joined with exploration hit the resonant mark with the discovery of just the right word (Rogers 1980).

The Life Focus Community is made to order for just such a move into empathy. In one exercise people in subgroups may explore their own empathic skills by telling each other about someone whose behavior they simply cannot "understand." Through the subgroup conversations they may discover that they did not "understand" because they felt threatened by the other person's behavior or feelings. Or perhaps they did not "understand" because the behavior was so very different from their own. Or they did not "understand" because they thought only in generalities, believing, for one example, that all people are devastated by the need to move to another city.

Another Life Focus Community group exercise would be for the leader to tell a story that features complications about empathy and to ask for reactions to the story. Here is an example of such a story:

A lesbian woman had rescued a very religious Christian person from a state of despair and destitution. She had a mobile home on her property and invited him to stay there in exchange for some chores he would do. In addition to providing this living space, she befriended him, counseled him, and gave him extra money that he might use for a down payment for a house of his own. He knew she was a lesbian, and as long as this never came up, they got along fine. But then he came face-to-face with her relationship with a specific woman, and he began to shun her. She sensed this for a period of time, and then she would no longer set the issue aside. When she brought up the change in his behavior, at first he denied it, but as the conversation went on, he told her he thought she was a sinner—that we were all sinners, after all.

When she became indignant about being called a sinner, he was dumbstruck by her reaction. He thought that his belief that we are *all* sinners would exonerate him from having been offensive. He could not empathize with her feelings about the difference between the generic human sinner he felt himself to be and his designation of her as a lesbian sinner. And that was that, the end of the relationship.

Most people would think it obvious to empathize with the woman whose surpassing generosity was answered by being called a sinner. Still, there might be some people who might believe that her indignation lacked empathy for the man, who, through his own life circumstances, had gotten fixed into this form of morality. The subgroups discussing this scenario would tell each other not only their view of this scenario but what it calls forth in their own experiences of empathy or lack of it. The individual stories would fertilize their minds, carrying the idea of empathy into the actual relational complexities people live with. Empathy, after all, important as it is, must be coordinated with each person differentiating himself from others. One may "understand," for example, why someone might dominate other people while nevertheless being outraged by it, perhaps even cutting that person out of his or her life. In the Life Focus Community group, the opportunity is provided for opening people's minds to their own sense of empathy and exploring how it may idiomatically fit into their own complex lives.

Humor

Humor helps give an idiomatic flavor to the way people talk to each other, making conversation personal and free-spirited. Still, when somebody is talking intensely about painful problems, there may, of course, be limited opportunity for humor. To offer humor to a suffering person may distract him or her from what really matters. However, to think of humor as an evasion of the serious overlooks the enrichment of relationship opened by perspective. Indeed, it is often more of a lubricant than a distraction, and sets an enjoyable precedent for feelings themselves. Laughter may well be a down payment on future emotions, as we see when people who can laugh together are also people who can cry together.

I am reminded of a recent therapy session where laughing and crying were both key experiences. Conducted in front of a large audience, perhaps a thousand people, the opening interactions included ordinary banter and lightheartedness, a lubricant for warmth and trust. I asked this person what her name was, and she said Michelle, to which I said, "That's a big name nowadays," an allusion to Michelle Obama. In quick rejoinder she said, "It was big in 1969 also" (the year of her birth). To which I replied, "Let me count." She laughingly saved me the trouble by saying she was forty. I replied that I was more than twice her age, and she said, "And still fabulous," at which the audience applauded in approval. I said, "Thank you very much. That takes care of my therapy, now let's see to yours." The audience roared. This humor is no competition for the professional comic, but it was timely and it set a tone, I believe, that paid off in deeper emotionality.

Getting down to business, Michelle told me that she had been very troubled that she was not able to love. I asked whether she felt unable to love some particular person or whether this was a general feeling. She said it was general, that she had no love in her life; then she demurred by saying this did not apply to her kids, that she can love them well. But she was clearly treating that love as irrelevant to her supposed life without love. Actually, it was most relevant even though it did not represent the romantic love she may have had in mind.

Then she went on to tell me more of her story. She had been married for thirteen years, but only two years ago she came out of the closet as a lesbian. She joked about how that did not help the marriage or relieve her of guilt. Since her basic priority was to take care of people, she now felt guilty about satisfying her own needs at the expense of others, especially her husband. Nevertheless, she observed that she has recently been learning to enjoy being what she calls selfish. I asked whether we might celebrate this new pleasure. The idea of celebrating lit her up, making her laugh wholeheartedly, as though she was mischievously getting away with something. Her laughter was so surprisingly free that it was contagious for both the audience and me. I asked her to tell us about what her laughter was like for her, and she was surprised actually to notice what she would normally overlook: that she was feeling her laughter more deeply inside her body than she would have expected.

Then, encouraged by this light heartedness, she asked whether I would like to do a little dance—a rumba or something. I said that would be OK with me but that I wasn't sure I could do it. In the meantime both she and the audience were laughing about her turnaround from the presumably guarded person who had said she was unable to love and who was now behaving so openly and warmly. I said that her laughter had turned her into a new person; that she had previously looked like she was in danger, but now she looked like the world was hers. Well, we did not dance because she went on to other things that were on her mind.

Principal among these was her difficulty in distinguishing between wanting sex and wanting love. Though coming out of the closet two years ago, she has, surprisingly, not had any sexual relationship. She said she cannot separate her need for sex from a pressure to take care of people. Since she does not want to take care of people, to have sex would be prohibitive. She was joking about all this and then said her laughter is a cover-up. I said that her laughter looked to me like a real pleasure—not merely a cover-up. I asked her to notice, furthermore, whether this pleasure committed her to me or anyone else.

She felt no commitment to me. Then, just as real as the pleasure, came thoughts about her husband, and tears came. She was surprised at how deeply these feelings went. She told me how good a person her husband is and how very badly she hurt him and, yet, how well they do together with the children. He loved her so much. Here we have a significant change from her original concern: that she is unable to have love in her life. I thought, *What a waste*. I asked her how many people can say they are loved as you are loved, to know the love, as you do, even in the face of its unhappy aspects. I asked her to try to absorb this feeling of being loved. She paid close attention and said that a familiar tightness in her chest had loosened. Then I asked her to talk to me about something she loves. She started by telling me about her eleven-year-old son, who climbs up on her lap, and she is going to let him do it as long as he wants to.

Then she told me about loving "minimum" days at school, where she is a counselor. And she went on to tell about her love of exercising. Then another turning point! She would love to make connections with people at the conference. She had been afraid she would be rejected, and her eyes became moist at realizing that people might actually accept her. There was a long pause while she pondered the possibility, and I asked whether she would like to put it to a test by just standing and saying, "Here I am standing in front of you." When she did it, the audience applauded wildly. She gasped, "Oh, my," and giggled, saying "There are a lot of you out there." I asked her to let her feelings of embarrassment soak in and to think whether she has a right to be loved. At this point she started to sob deeply for about thirty seconds. When she came back into engagement, she talked about how she feels small and vulnerable and how hard she has striven to be strong. I told her she doesn't have to try to be strong: that she *is* strong, that she has great character. When we ended the session, with pleasure and love in the foreground, she left without any sense of the irredeemable obligation so familiar to her.

In examining the role of humor in this session, we see that light-heartedness and laughter became a fundamental part of our engagement. Many would wonder whether such humor does not serve as a distraction from the person's "serious" needs, or even whether it serves a seductive purpose by drawing the person into a soft and misleading friendliness—a distraction from engagement rather than a substantive engagement. The differentiation is one that is important but it is not an on/off phenomenon. We must understand this person and this therapist to have had serious purpose built into them and that this purpose, not easily taken off track, can be lubricated by humor. Humorous interplay that is heartfelt must be differentiated from avoidance, and of course that is a judgment call. The validity of each emotion must be understood within the continuity of what happens—in this case, whether the humor helped her to face what needs to be faced or distracted her from it.

The climax came with her standing before the audience and receiving the sweeping affirmation that flooded her mind, erupting in a wrenching cry, so deep as to endear her further to both the audience and me. This moment was not only crucial as an authentication of her enhanced hospitality to love but it was also a testament to the power of a large group of witnesses to induce palpable experience. Furthermore, the humor that appeared recurrently set an ordinarily human tone and served as a warm-up to an increased openness to expression and feeling. Having originally seen herself as fated to diminished relationship, she was able with the public affirmation to, at least on this occasion, reset the rheostat for communal accessibility.

Smelling the Roses

Smelling the roses is about savoring experience: getting the essence of it and enjoying it distinctly. That is hard to do when the press of daily events upstages the good experiences people actually do have. For the Life Focus Community group to explore this theme, a statement from the leadership about the way we bypass simple pleasures would be one starting point, followed perhaps by a poem, a paragraph from a novel, a public interview, an observation from a psychological book, or a group discussion.

One exercise might begin with the reading of a poem by William Blake. People divide into groups of three. The leader distributes a printed version of the poem and then reads it:

> When the green woods laugh with the voice of joy,
> And the dimpling stream runs laughing by;
> When the air does laugh with a merry wit,
> And the green hill laughs with the noise of it;
>
> When the meadows laugh with lively green,
> And the grasshopper laughs at the merry scene,
> When Mary and Susan and Emily
> With their sweet round mouths sing "Ha, ha, he!"
>
> When the painted birds laugh in the shade,
> Where our table with cherries and nuts is spread,
> Come live and be merry, and join with me,
> To sing the sweet chorus of "Ha, ha, he!"
> (Blake 1946)

In the subgroups people respond by telling what the poem evokes in them. It might remind them of their own children jumping onto their laps, comical scenarios in their lives, the calming effect of beautiful trees, the family feeling they felt at a recent party, the exhilaration of getting promoted at work, the joy of picking up a favorite uncle at the airport, or the feeling of not wanting a novel to end. The discussion is intended not to be an evaluation of the poetry but rather to guide the group members in the telling of their own stories. The intention is to recapture the abundance that lies in wait, ready to be felt; to recover the nourishment that has slipped away into the neutrality of the mundane.

One cannot work twelve hours a day, continue to think about unfinished work, and still savor the pleasures of family. Enter the concept of the Sabbath, which is individualized for people to get off the conveyor belt of life for needed retooling. The driven passage through time must not be all there is. The duty, the ambition, and the rush of events must all be interwoven with the seemingly irrelevant details of life: the feeling of drinking when thirsty, the casual conversation, the wandering mind. People take vacations. They meet with accepting friends. They arrange family entertainment. They create hobbies. They celebrate a birthday or an anniversary. They engage in sports activities. They go to the movies. For many people, however, these options are not enough.

The institutionalization of life focus assures that smelling the roses will be raised to an acknowledged and dependable level of attention that provides opportunity for the registration of life's experiences.

Sacrifice

Sacrifice usually refers to people giving up something they value. Workers may keep their mouths shut so they can maintain their jobs. People marry the wrong person to satisfy their parents. Women unquestioningly put their careers aside to raise their children when they could do both. There are many such examples of possibly unwarranted deprivation and empty conformity that are associated with sacrifice.

Nevertheless, there are many sacrifices that are quite worth the cost. Hard study instead of play does not have to cost a neutered, boring, or unrequited existence; on the contrary, the knowledge might make you more interesting. Limiting your career for the sake of your children may create greater happiness than your career would. Yielding to your wife in an argument in order to maintain a happy duet may increase happiness, as well as a sense of generosity. The major requirement is for people to make good bargains. There are good bargains to be made, such as waking up in the middle of the night to feed your baby or helping a friend even when you are swamped with other responsibilities.

It is important to recognize that the level of sacrifice is personally determined, laced as it is with many possible meanings. How, for example, do we distinguish between a sacrifice and a gift? To buy my son a set of golf clubs when I don't feel I can afford one for myself is an act of generosity as well as a sacrifice. Alternatively, when people are maneuvered into doing what they don't want to do, that is a defeat. In the Life Focus Community group, people may be asked to discuss the meanings they have given to the idea of sacrifice. They may be asked to tell the group about a particular sacrifice and whether they are glad to have done it. For example, if you agreed to go on vacation to a place your spouse wanted to go even though you were dubious, did it turn out to be as pleasurable as the choice you would have made? Or were your worst fears realized, confirming not only your sense of sacrifice but perhaps poor judgment in making the sacrifice?

Then, after a discussion of this theme in the plenary group, people are asked to move into subgroups and to think of a sacrifice someone has made for them and talk about its effects. Did it help or not? What feelings did you have about the sacrifice? Did it make you feel obligated?

Did it bring you closer to the person who made the sacrifice or make you more distant? Did you feel grateful or neutral or even violated?

The Unsung Hero

For many people, it may be unclear who their benefactors have been, because they may have been operating from the sidelines of one's life. There are many easily dismissible, off-center experiences that, upon closer examination, have been important. I think of Randolph, a person in a Life Focus Community group, whose family was irredeemably insensitive, unsupportive, humorless, and, at times, viciously cruel. He thought of his parents and brothers as psychotic and was unaware of any significant kindness in his family life. Yet, he is a kind man, successful in his business and his marriage, and everyone marveled at how he had pulled himself up by his bootstraps. Nobody can reliably say he or she knows how such an incongruity could happen, but it is clear that painful experiences can shut out many otherwise important experiences. So, I wondered whether there had been benefactors of whom he was unaware. Surely, at some point in his life, he must have encountered someone who contrasted with what he experienced at home.

He then remembered a neighbor of his and began to tell us about this man. This neighbor was a reclusive person who was not much known in the neighborhood, but Randolph had often visited him. Neither one of them seemed to take much account of their relationship. They just took their engagement as it came; it was built upon easygoing conversation about things he doesn't even remember. These experiences had just passed right through Randolph's mind.

When it was pointed out to him that this was an exceptional relationship, he looked surprised, but he began saying more about the ease and casualness of their conversations. Then, somehow, this man disappeared, both from his neighborhood and from his mind. At the thought of his disappearance, Randolph began to cry, saying this person may have saved his life. Bypassing something vital had been a relational style for both of them, and Randolph simply had taken this relationship for granted, overshadowed as it was by the more pervasive family horrors. There may be many more benevolent experiences in Randolph's past that have been overshadowed by the main event of his family life.

This experience represents an extreme contrast with his overall sense of growing up, and we have no clear way to know the actual role it played. It is nevertheless a striking example of what happens all too frequently: the helpful experiences that make their mark with little notice. I remember when a sixth-grade teacher of mine asked me at recess time to go across the street to buy her a candy bar. What a sign of trust and responsibility! To be singled out that way is something I still remember. There is no way to measure any specific help it gave me in my schooling, but it was a validating moment for a very quiet boy, selected by his teacher as a trusted member of his class.

It is quite evident that many of us have experiences that we just pass through without knowing how they benefited us, only to discover later how they made a difference: for example, parents who were painfully heavy in discipline but who prepared us well for the future to come, a playmate who was wise and funny and free-spirited, or a public figure who modeled courage. We are all accumulative beings, who live with one thing building on another, like the incremental nourishment that comes from healthy eating, one bite at a time. Some of these experiences have only the most temporary role, as tidbits. Others have affected us for a lifetime, even when unremarked.

One exploratory exercise in the Life Focus Community is for people to name one person from their family and one outside the family who have been important to them and what benefits the group members derived from the relationship. They may remember people they have forgotten, celebrate people they have only silently recognized, or affirm those with whom they feel a clear sense of belonging.

In still another exercise, all the group members individually create a fantasy in which they *add* a person to their lives. They add a person who would have contributed something they have missed, something that would have made a difference in their lives. For example, they might add an older brother, or a certain kind of teacher, or a career benefactor. They then tell the group their fantasy about the difference such a character might have made.

Recovering What One Already Has

Surprisingly, people often already have what they are seeking—and they don't know it. The woman described earlier in this chapter was troubled because she had no love in her life. Actually, she had two children whom she adored and who adored her. That is not to say that this love would be sufficient and that she should make a life out of it. But having that love says much about her capability to have other forms of love. One should start a journey supported by whatever relevant assets one actually has rather than dismissing them as irrelevant.

Furthermore, the existence of one asset may make up for the absence of another. Though a young boy might be inept physically, his verbal strength may be more than enough to make up for it. If he were interested, for example, in snakes or in music or in Egyptology or in computers, he could find a universe of life-affirming options. A troubled child who discovers something special that he or she can do well, like drawing or dancing or scholarship, has a stepping stone into building relationships and accomplishment. One of my most rewarding experiences in doing therapy has been hearing revelations about overshadowed assets that are sitting right there but are unrecognized. This should not be mistaken as a positive-thinking psychological trick for people to just look at the bright side of things. Rather, it comes with the evocation of what is validly waiting in the background, ready to appear. It requires a keen eye that sees through a lifetime of camouflage into a reality that has substantive backing. This recaptured reality resets the dial, going beyond a preset standard for what counts.

One exercise would be to ask people to tell each other about any favorable quality of theirs that they might be undervaluing. One person might say, for example, that he is very *dependable* but that quality doesn't measure up as much as being *interesting*. In telling stories about his dependability, he will commonly show a range of other characteristics, lost in the glare of dependability. In being dependable, he may also show sensitivity to other people's needs. Or he may reveal his generosity. Or he may show high intelligence. Or he may represent consistency. Because of a lifetime of preset impressions about dependability, these accompanying characteristics may have become overshadowed, but they are his and they are real.

He may now remember how, as a ten-year-old child, he took care of his mother when she was dying. Or he may tell how he fled from a sexual invitation when he was delivering pizza at sixteen. Or he may tell how people who think of him as dependable would be surprised to know he writes poetry when he is alone at home. Suddenly, not only do these many characteristics rise into awareness but what he is saying also turns out to be *interesting*. Through an unfolding story line, many people become awakened to the inclusion of the previously dismissed. As I have previously written,

> People often squander their authorship. They don't grant the same importance to experiences in their own lives as they do to those of the characters in romantic novels or popular television soap operas.

Instead, they set high standards for interesting experiences, sifting life's waters with a large-holed fishing net, letting a lot go through untouched. (Polster 1987)

Aspiration

Happiness, the ultimate goal for many people, is often influenced by the gap between aspiration and actuality. If I aspire to take a backpack trip with experienced friends, that may not be as daring as going it alone on a dangerous mountain climbing trip, but if that fits my aspirations, I may be quite happy with it. On the other hand, if my aspirations are set at too high a standard—to have five children, or to get the top award my company offers or the approval of my father—then failure to satisfy those aspirations may well be the source of unhappiness, irrespective of any actual accomplishment. Therefore, a key question to ask is whether aspirations are flexible enough to be harmonious with one's own actuality, rather than other people's standards or one's own skewed standards.

The Life Focus Community conversations provide opportunities to recognize the gaps. In the plenary group and the subgroups, some of the questions to be asked are: What are your aspirations? How strong is the need? What are you willing to do to satisfy it? How confident are you about reaching it? What part of the aspiration have you already achieved? Can you see any advantage to changing either the content or extent of your aspiration? Who are the people who have affected your aspiration? How does the cultural affect your aspirations?

Freedom

"Freedom" is one of the most hallowed words in our society. I am reminded of a colleague who took a sabbatical from the life she was living. She wanted *freedom* from the excessive pressure she felt from her everyday commitments. She wanted romance and drama, and so she moved to Spain, to live there for many months. When she came back home, she described many pleasurable experiences, but there was one experience that was surprisingly troublesome, and incongruous with her original purpose. When she woke up in the morning, she was often miserable to know she had zero obligations and zero routines. She had become a poster child for the old adage "Be careful what you wish for, because you might get it." She yearned for the feeling of being swept into her next experience by the givens rather than having the freedom to decide every day what she would do next. The freedom she fantasied was not what she had believed it would be.

Freedom, along with many other human functions, coexists with seemingly incompatible qualities, like dedication, security, and continuity. These contrasts, which might wrongfully be seen as incompatible, can very happily live together. I am reminded of a violinist who practiced the same phrases over and over all day long. When asked why she did that, she said she was incessantly repeating the basics so that they would be so deeply embedded in her that when she was performing she would be *free* to let her feelings guide the music, trusting that her repetitious practice built the fundamentals indelibly into her playing. She had interwoven her repetition and discipline with a seemingly incompatible artful freedom, and she discovered that the two qualities coexisted.

In the group meetings the subgroup members may be asked to tell each other how their freedom and their discipline vie with each other. When do they favor one or the other? When discipline is required to reach a goal, can it become interesting in its own right? Give examples. Do you feel freedom most clearly when doing something familiar, or do you need novelty? Is freedom dangerous? How so? Is there a good rhythm between discipline and spontaneity in your life? Who are the people with whom it feels good to be disciplined? When you are disciplined, are your purposes clear?

Gratitude

Gratitude is an important source of both personal affirmation and the affirmation of others. Though gratitude is commonly seen to be pointing to specific happenings, such as a promotion at work, a successful surgery, or someone returning a lost wallet, it can also be thought of more generally. One can feel and express gratitude for more general pleasures, such as having a loving family, a job one likes, high social status, or good health. In the subgroups people might tell each other how gratitude plays out in their lives, both specifically and generally. Do you think gratitude needs to be expressed, or can it just be felt? How are you affected when people do or don't express gratitude? Do you miss it? Do you feel satisfied when it comes? To whom would you like to express gratitude, or from whom would you like to receive it? Is it important to you as a giver for your gift to be explicitly appreciated, or can it be sufficient to assume the appreciation through the pleasures of the ongoing relationship?

Conclusion

It is important to recognize that the above themes are only an introduction to a huge range of options. A further sample would include other ordinary life processes, such as developing friendship, listening to music, managing time, falling in love, and planning a trip. These common themes—only a hint of the possible—are the building blocks of life. People navigate through them every day, and they are often spoken of in ordinary conversation. But the raw fact is that people need greater opportunity to address these themes than day-to-day habits and pressures allow. The arranged *assurances* of a special place and special procedures help develop the necessary trust in fleshing out these markers of a lifetime.

8

Communal Setting

There are three enabling concepts that will color the Life Focus Community groups, each of which contributes to transforming the distance of strangers into a comradely connectedness. They are congregation, ethos, and guidance.

Congregation

"Congregation" is a venerable word, used to identify religious assemblages. Through religion's historic role in tending lives, the concept of congregation offers lessons to the Life Focus Community. The first lesson is that the congregation provides a primary place for many people to come together to solemnize their lives and give these lives purpose and meaning. Second, the religious congregation is usually larger than the therapy group, which gives it a more distinctly communal flavor. Third, in contrast to the therapy group, the congregational continuity is long and dependable. This enduring assurance of relationship and exploratory opportunity enables the members to immerse themselves more fully in the ongoing process.

However, I am not using the term "congregation" in the portrayal of the Life Focus Community because it is so closely identified with religious messages that are so different from those of psychotherapy that such a designation would have misleading implications. An alternative designation, the "group," is more familiar to the history of psychotherapy, but it too has implications that contrast with my portrayal of the Life Focus Community. The "group" designation is so closely associated with the "therapy group" that it has too much curative implication. That is, if you are in a therapy group, you are likely to be there because you think something is wrong with you and you want to correct it. To emphasize such a need overshadows the equally fundamental need for a look at what our lives are like.

"Community" is also an imperfect choice because the designation "community" refers to a range of entities, like neighborhood, profession, or nation, which are much broader in their purposes than what is intended in the Life Focus Community groups. But the idea of community contains much of the primary meaning I intend. It emphasizes the importance of bringing people together to satisfy a mutually felt need for enlightenment, and it names life focus as the defining vehicle.

Still, the Life Focus Community groups do parallel both the congregation and the therapy group by creating a special atmosphere of heartfelt and open-eyed interest in examining the landscape of living. As I have already indicated, the Life Focus Community is a place for release from the pressures of the secular world, while receiving guidance in understanding and participating in that world. It provides a combination of respite and stimulation: a communally based time-out for marking pivotal life experiences. People can, for example, tell each other what is like to have a new baby or about their frustration about surprise visitors when they are dead-tired or the sadness of nursing a sick mother. In a climate of mutuality, people are enabled to satisfy both the need to be individualistically heard while, at the same time, feeling that they *belong among each other.* As I have previously written, "People may wipe the slate clean in the unprejudiced atmosphere of special expressive opportunity" (Polster 2006).

The prospects for creating such communal harmony may sound utopian when viewed in the light of all the problems that plague communal living. Yes, indeed. In spite of the intention to incorporate both unity and diversity, it may not be enchanting to hear about the ins and outs of desperation about someone's baby crying last night. The benefits of a common ground with this person are thwarted by the equally powerful need for people to be individuals, whose diverse self-interests can tear the group apart. The design and purposes of these meetings will always be challenged to overcome these incompatibilities. The process will be made easier by exploring universally important themes, in which people's minds are already set to feel a meeting point. Each person's stories are his or her very own, while these stories join together with the overlaps in human experience. The stories may be funny or wise or appalling, but in the brightened aura of life exploration, they take on the character of being just human.

This prospect for the merger of minds does not seem unwarranted when I think of my eleven-year-old granddaughter's dance groups. The dancers really enjoy not only their own individual dance talents but also the coordination of their movements with those of all the others in the ensemble. Some of these children do this better than others, but all are intent on coordinating, and it is exciting for them to do so. Richard Dawkins, when examining evolution, sees a comparable predisposition in the communal behavior of birds (Dawkins 2009). He tells us about a flock of starlings that demonstrate what seems to humans to be a miraculous communal synchronicity. These flocks may be composed of thousands of individual birds flying at great speeds, and yet they never collide with each other. He says, "Often the whole block seems to behave as a single individual, wheeling and turning as one.... What is remarkable about the starlings' behavior is that, despite all appearances, there is no choreographer and, as far as we know, no leader. Each individual bird is just following local rules."

While human beings in their choice-making complexity face a more difficult chemical mutuality, the inclination to join up is, nevertheless, a compelling phenomenon. We see it even at the tiniest cellular level, where the organizational imperative silently commands people to create a whole organ or a whole organism out of a diversity of minute cellular beginnings. At a higher level of this organizational reflex, we see that humans are gregarious beings, joining together because of the innate pleasure of doing so as well as for strategy. Neurological studies more and more recognize the phenomenon of mutuality. High among these is the recognition of mirror neurons, which fire up when people have vicarious reactions to other people's experiences. While the research is in the early stages, there seems to be a neuronal web that spurs common understanding and interrelational mutuality. On a behavioral level this empathic resonance reminds me of a two-year-old child whose reflex, upon seeing another toddler crying because his mother was absent, was to take the second child's hand and lead him to the first child's own mother.

Limbic resonance is another of those neurological basics that are said to draw people to the experience of unity. Lewis et al. (2000), for example, elaborate the role of the limbic system in its hospitality for an empathic harmony that tunes one's own inner states to those of another. This undercurrent responsiveness between people serves as grounding for our social context, a housing for feelings of mutuality. This need for unity is often crushed by the cultural and interrelational clashes of incompatible interests, including parental and societal insistence on successful competitiveness. While these are clearly powerful forces in human existence, they are opposed by an equally natural interdependence. Lewis et al. ask of psychotherapists:

> Shall we tell them again that no one can find an arm to lean on, that each alone must work to ease a private sorrow? Then we shall repeat an experiment already conducted; many know its results only too well. If patient and therapist are to proceed together down a curative path, they must allow limbic regulation and its companion moon, dependence, to make their revolutionary magic. (2000, 171)

To further this sense of people building on each other's experiences, it helps to recognize that this option contrasts harshly with the risks of incompatible diversity. In reaction to the paralysis of conformity, our society is coming out of centuries of literary and philosophical entrancement with individualism. It may be timely now to accentuate the enabling powers of the communal need. A personal illustration of this union between individual expression and a communal grounding is the report of Daniel, a member of a long-standing Life Focus Community. When he was asked to tell about his experience of his own individuality within the group's experience of communal connectedness, he said,

> When I am here, I can dig a hole and pull things out, and I'm saying, "Oh my god, look at this," and you are all just sitting there looking and saying, "Oh my god, look at that" [laughter] ... you are with me. And so over time I have come to feel at home here amidst you. And that feeling of being at home here and having you look at something that I have brought out about myself that I didn't even know if I could look at. It's like there is a ground to put that into and it takes hold, and it's real, and so when I leave here, I carry a sense of substance of those ideas, that they've planted themselves, they've taken root.
> I then feel the substance of that way of being, outside here. I'd have this big buffer around me of my experience here. The storms would still blow in about my imagined "judgment-by-other-people," but I am buffered here. This is so profoundly important to me. And it has something to do with us and how we have known each other for a long time. Let's just go deeper; it's really the way we treat one another.

While there is no sure formula for such resonance between individual and communal behavior, what is clear in Daniel's account is that he was able to say what he individualistically needed to say, and he found his group to be a place where these stories belonged. He went on then to compare his experience with that of his father's religious group, which he once attended. He said the members of that group did not take anywhere near the chances he did, but whatever they said, people paid attention and they received recognition from the others in the group.

Some groups are broader than others in the range of their worldview or their expressive priorities. So, while Daniel saw his group as exceptional in its enlarged openness, his father's group, narrower in its vista, was nevertheless also open to its members' individual needs. Whichever level of originality or depth is operative, the design of specific meetings must create optimal functioning for the existing level of group interests. Some of the guidelines are: to address themes that are of *mutual* concern, to create the assured feeling of being part of a continuing community that exercises its own individuality, to relieve people of the pressure to change, and to create an aura of "live and let live." It is most apparent that the search for self-actualization, a familiar goal of individuality, is not just a cold enterprise; it flourishes in the relational hospitality of the engaged people, with one hand washing the other. This is no casual phenomenon. It is the foundation for belonging and for the accompanying pleasure of feeling at one with the world.

Ethos

Closely interwoven with the enabling powers of congregation is the mandate for a benign ethos. This has not always been a standard for religious congregations, which have varied greatly in their benevolence toward dissident members. For the therapist, however, it has been fundamental to assure safety, even in the face of troublesome eruptions. Such a safety, assured in privacy, must be transposed into the enlarged membership of the Life Focus Community. Among these people some may dislike others, some may compete for centrality, some may take up too much time, and some may become too easily defensive. While members of the Life Focus Community vary in both readiness and skill for maintaining safety, this is, nevertheless, an important condition because only in safe situations will people at large speak openly to each other. Therefore, the benign ethos must survive differences in perspective, one-upsmanship, and other adversarial challenges.

Many would see the adversarial component as an important *spur* for growth. I am reminded of some trainees in our gestalt therapy training programs who, wary of conformity, felt that there was not enough anger in the groups. For them the absence of anger was a sign of inauthenticity, a surrender to the communal ethos. However valid such vigilance against conformity may be, it is just as important to recognize when a benign atmosphere may also be authentic. In an environment where each person's concerns are honored, there is less reason to be angry with each other than in a competitive or otherwise pressured atmosphere. While my experiences are only anecdotal, in the Life Focus Community groups I have either led or witnessed, the people have been decidedly respectful of each other's reactions, without sacrificing their own well-being. Furthermore, they are quite open to expressing strong feelings, clear self-interest, and novelty of story line, all of which color their lives. Nevertheless, such successes notwithstanding, there is no assurance of a benign ethos, and here are some elaborations of the conditions that soften the adversarial pressures:

1. Piggybacking Conversation

People in these groups play off each other; each person's participation is stimulated by the other's. One person says, for example, "I left home a long time ago, left a country that I lived in, that doesn't even exist anymore."

A second member wanted to know what country that was, so the first person went on to say, "Yugoslavia, and it doesn't exist in a political sense. It just exists in memories, and it's an interesting experience, very painful and very joyful at times. It's a gypsy experience, in the best sense. There is a song in Yugoslavia by one of my favorite poets about what would happen if gypsies took him away."

That was the beginning of a tale about his relationship with gypsies, elaborating his sense of the romance of gypsy life. He spoke about the range of their pain and joy, about the lyricism of their songs, a contrast with his expectation of kidnapping and thievery. At the same time, influential though his story was, it was just one statement in the continuing group conversation, with no requirement that he further unravel his thoughts.

Instead, a third person, building on the stimulation of the story, took it a next step, saying,

> This is a coincidence; my friends and I were just talking, last night, about how I feel like a gypsy. At this point in my life, I am almost homeless, I would say. I have moved around a lot in my life. I went to school in California, but I am now in the process of finding home, where I'm going to plant my feet, and I'm moving to England, to London, in a week. My mother and my sister live there. But I felt so at home in California that I'm in this in-between stage. So I feel like

in a way, I don't really have a country. I have an ethnic background which I feel somewhat connected to, but as a home, in and of itself, I don't feel like I have one.

In this overlap of gypsy allusions, these people had joined up while each tapped into each other's own individual life of wandering, schooling, transition, and the potential isolation of having no country. The payoff came because the common ground of the stories added to the sense of personal affirmation, which was registered into their humanity by the meeting of minds. Many of the Life Focus Community exchanges could very well be part of ordinary conversation, held at dinner or while on a walk in the park or with someone just met on an airplane. However, the *communal* stamp of recognition raises the experience beyond ordinariness; it sharpens the reality, with the union of minds giving it added importance, a tipping point for self-affirmation.

2. Language of Positivity

Another way to nurture a benign ethos is to use language and ideas that accentuate positive feelings that might otherwise be overlooked. That is not to say that we pretend to be positive when the negative is the truth. But I do say that many positive feelings are taken for granted when the right word would give them a more fitting registration. For example, at one point in a Life Focus Community meeting, I was impressed with the solemnity of the group's exchanges, and did not want this quality to be overlooked. I could have remarked about the solemnity and, that in itself would amplify the quality of the experience, but it would not have signified the hushed dearness of their exchanges. When I said, "What I've heard feels like a personalized version of prayer," this caught on and the group members rode with it, one of them saying, "It feels like a heart connection. Yeah. I never really thought of it being a prayer. I really like that thought."

Another said, "Yes, I liked the idea that it was a prayer, because there was a loving genuineness that happened really quickly; it was beautiful."

The use of the word "prayer" not only gave positive perspective but also implications of a cosmic depth to what might otherwise have felt like a more transient experience.

3. Individual Pacing

The option for people to speak at their own pace also contributes to a benign ethos. As one person said in reporting his subgroup experience,

> I noticed that one person in our group didn't talk until the very end, and I started to feel uncomfortable. I was wondering, *Is this person too shy to say something?* What happened was when she spoke at the end, it was really a great and interesting thing that she said, and we just need to figure out how to go with the pace and wait until they can come out with what it is they have, at the pace they need.

Indeed so. The atmosphere of permission requires an acceptance of variations in timing. Nobody knows exactly how to assess another person's pace. Though the community is oriented toward a laissez-faire attitude, that must not become so fixed that people would disregard another person's need and leave that person to stew in his or her own juices. While one silent person may talk when the right moment arrives, other people might need to be invited. Asking the person whether he or she feels OK about not talking is a quite understandable and empathic concern. Or telling the silent person that you are interested can be done without pressuring the person to say anything. People in groups are surely not infallible, but in my experience they commonly make good judgments about when to invite and when to leave well enough alone.

4. *Things Are What They Are*

Because the search for hidden meanings has been so important in the history of psychotherapy, we have become too wary about whether experiences may not be what they seem to be. Of course, there is merit to the belief that what one sees is not the whole story. Nevertheless, while such incomplete understandings must be faced, an innocent acceptance of the manifest is often a good beginning for finding a subsequently more complex reality.

Suppose, for example, we ask people to tell each other about two people who have had a large impact on their lives; many would tell about people who have helped them. But others may tell horror stories about a teacher or a bully or a parent, whose toxic imprints remain. While probing for the hidden details of such painful experiences would be a common process in office therapy, that would not be a priority in the Life Focus Community. Instead, the highest priority would be given to what people actually say, do, and feel about these experiences rather than to *probe* for unspoken undercurrents. Whatever deeper reports might come out would depend on the more innocent sweep of conversational momentum.

The absence of probing for the deeper story may seem to make the experience superficial, short on personal meaning. On the contrary, probing for meaning is only one way to reach it. I have previously described differences between vertical meaning and horizontal meaning (Polster 2006). Vertical meaning is what is achieved through digging down for specific meanings. However, this has two weaknesses for the Life Focus Community. First, such digging often stops the music, distracting us from simple, ongoing conversation. Second, it calls for greater expertise than is expected from the psychologically untrained members.

Horizontal meaning unfolds step by step, as people take each other pretty much as they are; it evolves through the *sequences* of personal exchanges. One does not have to know the whole story right away. Each moment is part of an ongoing sequence of personal experience, an innocent contributor to an evolving portrait. Each level of enlightenment, therefore, moves forward in spontaneous fragments, eventually contributing to the picture of a person. We move to a faith in continuity as the best assurance of deepening insight. Sometimes the markers of meaning are so small as to be apparent only with later realization or through repetition of similar experiences. At other times the effect of any vignette may be so large as to be a turning point in people's lives. The scent of gypsy or of kidnapping or of being a foreigner serves like a novelist's dream, inviting elaboration—not through probing but through the story's momentum in the continuing engagement in the Life Focus Community meetings.

5. *Addressing Themes of Everyday Life*

A further ground for this benign ethos will be the emphasis on themes of everyday life, such as family relationships, career, recreation, and competition. As I have said earlier in this book, the naming of such themes accentuates their commonality, creating a collective attention. Such a collective attention invites special excitatory effects. As Emil Durkheim has pointed out, "Collective life . . . brings about a state of effervescence which changes the conditions of psychic activity. Vital energies are over-excited; passions more active; sensations stronger; there are even some which are produced only at this moment" (1961, 469).

This recognition of the excitatory powers of the collective is a testament to the importance of this strange merger between a person's individual story line and knowing simultaneously that we are all in the same boat.

6. Contagion

Contagion is another key factor in the development of a group ethos. That may seem like an unfitting word for a fruitful atmosphere. "Contagion" usually refers to pathology, as in catching the measles from another person. It may also refer to the toxic spread of psychological conditions. As Yapko has noted in his documentation of the social contagion factor in depression, "Drugs may address some of the depression's symptoms, but they cannot change the social factors that cause and perpetuate it" (2009).

However, a more full view of contagion would be to recognize its healthful role in the creation of a collective frame of mind, where people gravitate toward each other's ideas and feelings. I am reminded of training groups I have conducted. I would tell the members at the start that we were forming a learning community in which the rightness or wrongness of behavior was not predefined; that, within certain limits, they should be faithful to their own ideas and behaviors. Yet, in spite of this invitation to freedom, some people, later in the process, would say they didn't cry, express warmth, or make critical observations because that's not how the group did things. Apart from being mistaken in their conclusions, we see that, for these people, the model of people's actual behavior was more influential than the abstract rules of the game.

While the reasons why groups behave as they do are very complex, the role of contagion itself must be taken into account. In some groups laughter is prominent, while in others people are more sober. In some groups looking to the leader for direction is the norm, while in others the members are inclined to go their own ways. In some groups agreement, benevolence, or happiness is suspect, while in others the ethos welcomes the positive, and members freely accept mutuality, patience, and helpfulness. With such contagion operative the leadership must be alert to the specifics of what any group imbibes, distinguishing between the self-negating influences and the enabling norms.

While such norms can represent a mindless conformity, they may also be part of a spontaneously formed dialect, resulting not from inculcation but from social familiarity. That is, whatever people are authentically saying to each other may well become recognized as a group characteristic, one that fittingly represents the group's mode of function. To call this a "dialect" has different implications than to call it "conformity." That differentiation is more than tricky semantics. "Dialect" reflects a group norm that does not sacrifice individuality. For example, the language we all speak is spoken in dialect: its tone grows out of New York City, the hills of Appalachia, or a country other than the United States. But none of those dialects interferes with people saying what they mean to say. Having a Scotch dialect or a southern American dialect does not identify one as conformist. When such harmony is achieved through conformity, individual needs are set aside. When it is simply a part of the group dialect, individuality remains intact. Just as individuals may differ in magnanimity, surprise, or rebelliousness, so also will groups differ in the way they address the ideas that come up. Some groups will work best if music is a part of the design, while others may prefer perspective-making lectures; some will be interested in social issues, others in family relationships; some will want to spend a lot of time on one exercise, and others will want the exercise to be short.

In summation, these illustrations of some of the conditions for a benign ethos in the Life Focus Community are built on a foundational belief that a benign ethos depends on benign requirements. It develops responsively within the group because of the shadowy good will that forms a large part of human priority.

Guidance

Freud tried to establish a dispassionate purity through his portrayal of the therapist as an ambiguous figure who encourages the free reign of his or her patients' minds. Large groups require a different form of leadership: one more open to designating themes; more open to giving instructions for exercises; and more open to playing inspirational music, reading illuminating poetry, and providing informative lectures. Consequently, there is a choice to be made between the undesigned style of the familiar therapeutic process and the Life Focus Community formats. The challenge for the leader, always, is to accept the author's role in the *design* of meetings, while always being mindful of each person's idiomatic participation.

Understandably, there is room for considerable variation in the strictness of guidance and even of the themes and exercises that would be of interest to different groups. There has, for example, been a long-standing wariness about highly authoritative guidance, exemplified in the controversy about Large Group Awareness Training vehicles. Werner Erhard introduced these intensive group experiences of self-examination under the name of EST, which was the forerunner for later groups, such as the Forum, Lifespring, and Landmark. The EST meetings were highly compacted into a short number of days. They were marathons of self-awareness procedures and highly charged activities, all directed by an insistent leadership. While the reaction of participants ranged from highly positive to highly negative, the research results have also been equivocal, showing neither clearly negative nor positive effects. Evaluating their results, however, is not the object of my focus here, especially as my Life Focus Community proposals call for a distinctly different format for exploration and relationship. Rather, I want to emphasize the light these groups shine on a public need, as they draw millions of people to their meetings (Gastil 2010).

It may already be clear throughout the reading of this book that the guidance I am proposing leaves plenty of room for personal self-determination. Chapter 5 gives extensive attention to details of designs that explore common experiences of people at large. If people are feeling celebratory about a promotion at work, they can spell out the experience; if they are faced with the geographical dislocations of their families, they can talk about it; if they are confused about the behavior of their adolescent children, they can explore it. If the leader asks them to tell the group about their ambitions or pivotal experiences or hopes for the future or any other thematic trigger, the freedom to speak idiomatically is encouraged. So is the freedom to be silent. This form of guidance—accepting people at face value—is a more indistinct form of guidance than a system of strict personal inculcation, but guidance it nevertheless is. Whatever the differences may be between the design of the Life Focus Community meetings and those that offer a stricter guidance, what is crucial is the need for communal guidance in exploring the landscape of living.

Section C

Social Implications of Life Focus

9

From the Supernatural to the Human: Part 1

If we want to understand what psychotherapy's versions of life focus mean to our society, the religions of the world help by providing context. They are predecessors in the orientation and guidance of people's lives. To examine the connection with them is not unlike looking at the lives of our parents to help get a reading on our own lives. Otherwise, we are overlooking a large progression of social influence from which we might differentiate ourselves but from which we cannot disconnect. The religious precedent is widely unwelcome in psychotherapy circles, but, nevertheless, its communal role as a life guide helps us to recognize psychotherapy as something quite larger than a medical instrument. Beyond its medical heritage psychotherapy's transformative set of ideas and procedures has become a communal heir to religion by fostering a spirited free enterprise of the mind. That is big, and it represents a freestanding entry into a whole new communal appreciation of what life focus is about.

A key part of this progression from religion to psychotherapy is the move from allegiance to supernatural authority into the exercise of human authority. Starting a few thousand years before Freud, the Judeo-Christian religious perspectives, under the authority of God, have been the great shaper of the western psyche. In churches and synagogues people have, in God's name, been taught how best to live their lives. Their behavior and feelings have been influenced by sermons and liturgy to obey such guidelines as the Ten Commandments and the Golden Rule. They have also received lessons through biblical stories about desired human qualities. In Matthew's Gospel, for example, Jesus Christ tells people that even the smallest acts of kindness, such as giving a person a drink of water, are done for God. David represents bravery in his conquest of Goliath; Esther reflects cunning in saving her people by influencing her husband, the king; Abraham's obedience to God is tested in his willingness to sacrifice his son; and Joseph offers forgiveness to his brothers, who had betrayed him.

People have been taught how to view death and an afterlife. They have been led to communal worship, in which they gather together to create a sense of belonging. They have been given the security of a ubiquitous *other*, a perpetual and altogether dependable relationship of the highest intimacy. As Jesus said, "Where two or three are gathered in my name, there am I in the midst of them" (Matthew 18:20, King James Version).

It is an old story now that the power invested in the emissaries of God has been huge but often corrupt, leading in the sixteenth century to Martin Luther's transformative rebellion. He rebelled not against God or the biblical teachings, but against the Roman hierarchy, which allowed no room for doubt. As Manchester points out in his *A World Lit Only by Fire* (1992), skepticism simply did not exist. The support for mindless acceptance suited the holistic requirement that the church be as one, undivided and infallible. The authority of God, administered through the church, served as an incontrovertible voice. It was, therefore, a defining power, dominating all walks of life. Facing this atmosphere of unbridled authority, Luther cracked through the wall of sacred exception, refusing to yield to the self-serving privilege and licentiousness of the presiding powers, and called out their usurpation of God's voice.

What was especially persuasive and an early precedent for psychotherapy was Luther's dethronement of *the priesthood*—by commissioning each person to have his or her own direct relationship to God. This single reformulation had unseen implications as a historically pivotal declaration of the ascendancy of the individual mind, as Luther guided each person toward becoming his or her own advocate. While continuing to experience God as supreme, Luther rode on the wave of the Renaissance, which freed people to experience their own direct relationships with God, and by so doing, he "broke the dam of medieval discipline" (Manchester 1992).

Freud's psychological ideas, arriving more than three hundred years later, echoed this release through radically different perspectives. He was also riding on the wave of a remarkable cultural effervescence that invited a distinctly new future. He helped to counter nineteenth-century religious discipline by looking with fresh eyes at the workings of the psyche, and incisively examining human conflicts and values, this time from an emphatically humanistic position. Freud set authority itself into a new dimension by enunciating the primacy of the self-defining forces of the person. Consequently, the slippery cultural foundation of western society began to shift more quickly away from familiar religious leadership, challenged by a spirited free enterprise of the mind.

The excitement of this exploratory rejuvenation was so compelling that few assumptions felt safe anymore. The freshness of new knowledge was not limited to Freud's psychoanalysis. It was breaking out everywhere at the turn of the twentieth century and overrode many fixed positions in science, literature, music, architecture, and psychology. Even though many of the new developments were cognitively opaque to the population at large, the zest and intuited validity felt by its avant-garde were enough for these developments to have transcendent influence. Few people fully understood what Einstein was talking about, or Picasso or Joyce or Freud. Yet their ideas became passwords for entry into a new enlightenment. The genie of unstructured living was released, and the unbounded individual mind was raised into ascendancy. In such an expanded landscape, could we ever set our individual lives back into recognizable context? How long would we be able to hang on to the context of dependable religious perspective in the face of a humanistically free-floating mind?

Indeed, in Freud's time the old precedent of Luther's rebellion against the priesthood seemed like a small increment of change when compared with the mushrooming of a new cultural renaissance. Science and art joined psychotherapy in fracturing set perspectives. Science contributed through the idea of relativity and its accompanying theoretical and technical surprises. Art invited people to a new recognition of what often seemed like incomprehensible tonal, visual, and verbal combinations. These all formed a cultural groundswell that opened the society to recalibration of our understanding of the way the world worked. The accompanying mindset went hand in hand with Freud's portrayal of the mysterious energy of the unconscious, the normalization of sexual diversity, and the relativity of morality.

However, some of his conceptual leaps were of such magnitude and were so unfamiliar in both principle and procedure to those of the Judeo-Christian religions that it was difficult to see Freud's proposals as revisions of their perspectives. *This giant leap into the wilderness of the individual mind did not seem like religion revised but religion crushed.*

Therefore, instead of being widely recognized as a drastic renovation of existing religious creeds and formats, psychoanalysis was seen as a total departure, a creature of science and academia, quite disparate from religion.

A number of Freud's dimly supported and inassimilable ideas received an outraged reception. What stood solidly underneath these controversial details, however, was an intriguing wedge into a new understanding of human experience, with a clear call to a humanly minted orientation and guidance. He replaced the certainty about how to live that was so prominent in the Judeo-Christian morality with an emphasis on the conflict-ridden nature of humankind and the individuation of personal guidelines. His psychic relativity contrasted sharply with the strict edicts and aphorisms of the western religions. For example, Freud would not have categorically advocated turning the other cheek or loving one's neighbor or honoring one's parents. Those behaviors are all surpassingly communal, culturally stabilizing, and fundamentally humane, but in the evolving morality one would also value the role of circumstance and a respect for appropriate independence of mind.

Though his contrast with the Judeo-Christian ethos did have large reformational implications, Sigmund Freud had no desire to be a Martin Luther (Noll 1994). He rejected all notions that his psychic insights might parallel those of religion in providing new orientation. Instead, he portrayed religion in the medical language of pathology: as a corruption of human needs. What he emphasized was the neurotic circumstances of religious reasoning as a conformist psychological dynamic that distorted natural human struggle: the collision between cultural norms and each person's ever-present drives. Equating the Judeo-Christian systems and their supernaturalism with religion itself, he saw religion as antithetical to his own contrasting ideas, which he draped with the medical imprimatur as the target of healing.

Psychotherapy was thus born as a new form of personal experience, at first largely outside the existing cultural stream, and was commissioned to pick up the pieces of a flawed system that was fueled by mistaken principles. Instead of recognizing the *generic* character of religion, which goes beyond the specifics of the Judeo-Christian systems, society took the *specifics* of Judeo-Christian orientation and guidance as the *definition* of religion itself. The primary specific was a dependence on the unquestioned authority of God, which was profoundly reassuring to many believers and provided them with a rich guidance and heritage.

What Freud did not recognize was that, irrespective of the question of God's actual existence, a number of crucial human needs converged in the creation of God's image. Among the overlooked needs was, *first, the religious precedent for orienting and guiding people in how to live their lives and, second, the formation of lifelong assemblages of people guided by these perspectives and procedures.*

Early Psychology

The struggle against the dominance of religion was also waged in scholarly circles. At about the same time as Freud sparked the evolution from supernatural guidance to the human, the field of academic psychology also took a giant step by exploring elemental human experience and using direct observation of perceptions, behavior, and emotion. These scientific explorations were conducted without behavioral advocacy, and with a carefulness of interpretation and a diligence never previously exercised in psychological inquiry. By examining each experience exactly as it manifested itself, these researchers undermined supernatural mystique by meticulously examining the details of what people felt and did. In contrast to the large canvass of images and lessons created by the stories of religion, the researchers searched instead for scientifically grounded laws guiding people's lives. Examples that are only the tip of the iceberg are the work of Wilhelm Wundt, who was the father of experimental psychology and made consciousness a secular cornerstone; of Gustav Fechner, who explored perceptual experience; of Hermann Ebbinghaus, who examined memory and the learning process; and of Isaac Galton, who experimented with word association (Boring 1950).

These men communicated zero concern with either religion or with psychotherapy. They were well-known in their day in psychological circles but rarely elsewhere. Nowadays they are hardly known even in psychological circles, and they themselves had no intention to open a passageway into an arena where religion had been the sole authority. They prided themselves in being "true" scientists in the sense of setting up hypotheses and testing them and of illuminating particular psychological phenomena; they were dedicated to learning how people functioned. They offered no advice or counsel concerning one or another form of behavior, and they bypassed any agenda for how people should live their lives, which was the essence of both religion and the yet-to-be developed psychotherapy.

However, even in this innocent stage of psychological research, a number of more culturally minded psychologists were already concerned that their profession might be taken—mistakenly, they thought—as a threat to religion and to the moral structure of society. G. Stanley Hall and other psychologists at the turn of the twentieth century felt obliged to explain that psychological research was not an instrument of godless materialism (Picken 2000, 1022–24). In fact, Hall saw the Bible as "man's great textbook in psychology" (Menand 2001, 283). Religion's concern with the person as a whole impressed Hall, and as a psychologist he was determined to aid in enhancing the Bible's social impact. This is the man who primed psychology's future by starting the first psychological laboratory in America, serving as the first president of the American Psychological Association, and bringing Freud to the United States for his now famous introductory lectures in psychoanalysis. Hall nevertheless did not see psychology as an alternative to the existing religions but rather as a new instrument to improve their function.

John Dewey, the great spark for progressive education, known for his antiestablishment ideas, also sought acceptance by religion as he wrote about it in *The New Psychology*: "As it [psychology] goes into the depths of man's nature it finds, as stone of its foundation, blood of its life, the instinctive tendencies of devotion, sacrifice, faith, and idealism which are the eternal substructure of all the struggles of the nations upon the altar stairs which slope up to God" (Dewey 1999).

These words clearly did not portray the psychology to which he was a key contributor as independent of the religious foundation of God. However, with some key shifts in language and perspective, he reflects enthusiasm for this new orienting format: that psychology could guide people in the eternals of everyday living, which was a short arc from new personal promise, comparable to what he saw as religion's "instinctive tendencies of devotion, sacrifice, faith, and idealism" (Dewey 1999).

William James, however, came closer than Dewey to a direct vision of psychology as a social force of its own. Even though in his day (the turn of the twentieth century) psychotherapy was only a dimly emerging reality, he was a step into this future when he exercised his foresight in lectures at the University of Edinburgh. He identified what he saw as a "religion of healthy mindedness," singling out, among other dynamic developments of his day, the "mind-cure" movement. These people believed in the "all saving power of healthy-minded attitudes as such in the conquering efficacy of courage, hope, and trust, and a correlative contempt for doubt, fear, worry, and all the nervously precautionary states of mind." James painted a visionary picture for the future of such groups, aware that he might be jarring an academic audience with tales about what seemed to be a fleeting, poorly grounded phenomenon. But he explained by saying, "The plain fact remains that the spread of the movement has been due to practical fruits, and the extremely practical turn of character of the American people has never been better shown than by the fact that this, their only decidedly original contribution to the systematic philosophy of life, should be so intimately knit up with concrete therapeutics" (Dewey 1999).

While this movement had some affinity to the familiar religions of the day, it was actually more heavily focused on what we would now recognize as the stuff of psychotherapy, though it neglected, as James observed, the darker sides of human experience. With visionary validity, he went on to say, "One is tempted to ask whether it may not be destined to play a part almost as great in the evolution of the popular religion of the future as did those earlier movements in their day" (Dewey 1999).

Jung's Voice

It was during this same period that Freud appeared on the scene with his watershed contrast to familiar religious perspective. Though denying the commonality of religion's concerns with his own concerns about human existence, Freud nevertheless was mightily drawn to examining the psychological motivations for adherents of religion, whose intrusions into healthy human function he emphasized (Freud 1985). Contrasting, however, with Freud's cleavage of religion and psychotherapy was the voice of Carl Jung, who accentuated the bond between the two. As Richard Noll describes (Noll 1994), Jung made a strong pitch for the religious nature of psychoanalysis, because he saw that religious symbolism could have a potentially enormous social impact if it were to be incorporated into the principles of the psychoanalytic repertoire. He was a major advocate for the inclusion within psychoanalysis of myth, symbol, shared beliefs, social cohesion, ecstatic experience, and salvation in what he saw as a communal process. In letters to Freud Jung said that he was concerned with much larger dimensions of living than psychoanalytic sessions addressed. Freud was not persuaded, and his response to Jung was: "But you mustn't regard me as a founder of religion. My intentions are not so far reaching. . . . I am not thinking of a substitute for religion: this need must be sublimated" (Noll 1994).

Jung gave a broad view to the meaning of religion. He recognized that its realm was the normal needs of humankind and that the psychoanalytic imprint was targeted to serve that same purpose. It is also true that as Jung's mythology and psychic archaeology pervaded his writings; his speculations became murkily poetic, difficult to understand even for many professionals, and entirely outside the range of the ordinary reader. His observations often required a strong faith in his own brand of antiquity, not all that different from the leap of faith required in many religious positions. Furthermore, and more applicable to the theme of this book, his early therapeutic procedures never complemented his religious thought with a pertinent activation of a communal format.

While his work did not reach this objective, Jung did, in his *Answer to Job*, exercise a certain poetic license that is intriguing in its implications. He portrayed Job as a step in the historical road to convergence between the role of God and the role of humans, a convergence that set the stage for the development of human prospects for self-authorization *and people guiding people.* For Jung, the story of Job showed that the superiority of God and his supposedly incontrovertible judgment were impaired. God had made an ego-laden bet with Satan that Job's faith could not be shaken. He then, as a test, allowed horrors to be inflicted on Job. Job was steadfast, while at the same time calling God to task for the outrageous injustice inflicted upon him. God brandished his power in the argument with the prosecutorial Job, but God nevertheless came to recognize the validity of Job's reproach.

Thus was Job exonerated and recognized for his own earthly virtue through his eloquent confrontation with God about the injustice of merciless tyranny. What Jung declares is that the rapprochement between God and Job—where Job measures up well to any standards of good judgment and devotion—opened the human psyche for its pathway toward human ascendancy and self-affirmation. While it is questionable whether the Job scenario was actually a key historical motif, it is a metaphor that complemented God's supremacy with human self-affirmation. Jung believed that this new dynamic of human advancement was animated later by the birth of Christ, who, as God's son, would also be a human representative, interceding and advocating justice from a God whose perspective might be unbalanced (Noll 1994).

Since the book of Job is variously said to have been written three hundred to six hundred years before the birth of Christ, Jung's account of its cause-and-effect relationship to the birth of Christ requires a considerable leap. Nevertheless, the book of Job, partly because of the epochal implications of its message and partly because of its literary excellence, illuminates the adversarial engagement between man and God. Man shows he can hold his own—in rationality, in justice, and in endurance—earning recognition for his raised authority. From Jung's sense of a historical sweep we may now also extrapolate from the metaphor of Job's superiority to see a glacially slow move toward the contemporary primacy of human beings, who have graduated from subservience to the supernatural into the capability to guide each other in their own lives.

Ascendancy of the Human

Indeed, in the ambiguous character of the dispassionate psychoanalyst, who is witness to the psyche, we may see such a historical consummation of the human authorization for guiding humanity's own behavior and feelings. It may seem grandiose to portray the analyst as a new god. Quite the contrary—such a portrayal actually shows a lowering of human ambition: no more were people to place their psychological bets with the monumental powers of the supernatural. Rather, they began to seek the merely sufficient power psychotherapists have invented—a power that provided new understandings of human experience and created an amplified human bonding. The enchantment so common to this newly sanctified engagement was the result of a humanly designed relational scenario—not a mystical exceptionality but a palpable representation of actual human bonding.

To stretch beyond the now familiar individual therapy scenario, we may see further that the Life Focus Community is an enlarged human entity, a multiple of the individual therapist, and that it serves its members as a relational rallying point. People relate not only to each other in these groups but also to the mass of people joined together, a psychologically compelling instrumentality with a character of its own. This community is a sensate "Being," directly accessible, individuated in character, and malleable in response to its constituency, and this Being lights the way to the future that lies ahead.

Such a community may seem a long shot from the power attributed to the supernatural. Yet, by its enhancement of each person's individual significance, the Life Focus Community creates symbolic dominion for an abidingly present, strongly felt mini-world. Since this relationship is not so everlasting or ubiquitous as God, let us look at how it may nevertheless serve as a parallel in continuity, as well as in relationship, affirmation, and direction.

First, the Life Focus Community operates through an extended succession of meetings. It is a continuing vehicle for individual people; it is dependably available for each person for recognition of his or her life experiences, and is joined with a lively responsiveness. This enduring opportunity helps to cross the line between fleeting observations that people commonly make to each other and elaboration of one's story line through the group's invitations to open-ended conversation.

Second, the group's *converging attention amplifies* everything people say to each other, making their stories count more than they would in ordinary conversation. When ten or a hundred or a thousand people are attending to the same theme, this attention deepens the importance of the theme. When all of these people are singing the same song or addressing a common topic, the group mind joins the individual by increasing the poignancy of the experience.

Third, the *microcosmic* quality of the community establishes a transcendent expectation. That is, this sense of the group as a representative world stretches the meaning of experiences beyond the individual immediacy into an appreciation of universal human experience. One person's problems are important, but they also commonly cross over into more generally felt concerns. For example, one person's dismay about being fired from his job would have common ground with another person's variation on the theme: for example, her own individuated examples of insecurity, anger, or unfairness. While such an aura of group commonality with any individual's life must not distract from that individuality, it does add gravitas to that person's own specific life experiences, as well as to life itself.

That is, the themes addressed would have communal importance, stretching beyond personal problem solving into a more broad human application. While the glory, ubiquity, and infinity of God are a prodigious precedent for amplifying these life themes, the community and its leadership can, independently, also produce a high level of importance. Indeed, the community's concentrated attention, thematic relevance, guided exercises, and special understanding of the psyche provide their own aptitude for nurturing this significance, as I have illustrated throughout this book. The Life Focus Community, as such a supervisory "Being," is, of course, not God, but it taps the human need for sharpening life focus and is well-placed as a parallel to God's amplification of each person's life.

The Poetic Humanity

While many people in psychotherapeutic circles scoff at believers in the supernatural, these beliefs are not trivial human creations. They are tributes to the malleable human mind, which can fashion an expanded reality, one that is more faithful to people's broad concerns than the reality given by everyday perceptions. Indeed, the creation of God may be the greatest poetic achievement of humankind, because it embraces supreme human ambition and satisfies a complex of basic human needs, some of which I will elaborate in the next chapter. But this poetic consolidation of the obvious and the implied comes with a vexing paradox. While the creation of God achieves a desired transcendence of materialistic perceptions, people generally look past the poetry of the psyche's achievement. Instead, they see a concrete reality of God, *devaluing the poetic as a lesser experience.* This victory of the concrete over poetry then elevates the supernatural over human ingenuity; it is a surrender to an advanced form of idol worship.

The basic idea of poetry is that what is manifest in our lives, every day, implies more than it seems to say. The idea of God achieves this by inviting imagination about eternity, about morality, about executive power. God is mysteriously intriguing. He is a connoisseur of existence. He beckons us to an only partially understood context. He adds direction, meaning, and fulfillment to the manifest through a deepened attention to what may otherwise pass casually through our consciousness. What is especially relevant here is that this poetic thrust—that energizes the popular image of God—can be a reminder to psychotherapists that our own methods and perspectives have a surprising commonality in satisfying many of the same human needs that have been embedded in the relationship with God.

Such a reverberation between the poetic and the concrete can be seen in a less controversial implication if we look at the phenomenon of Santa Claus. Children quickly accept that Santa Claus is "real," not poetry. Adults, however, have no difficulty recognizing Santa Claus as an honored vessel, which is poetically meaningful. While there is a lessening of devotion to Santa Claus among adults, they do continue to celebrate Santa Claus. They enjoy the pleasure his image gives their children. They are sentimental for the days when they believed in the reality of his existence. But there is also more than the nostalgia. They also smile at the symbolism he represents as a romantic figure who transcends the grim boundaries of actual everyday human beings, as he rides sleighs through the skies and bestows goodies. To see Santa Claus ringing bells on the streets of Manhattan, joined with the sale of chestnuts, draws adults into the festive spirit of the Christmas season. We see, therefore, that the meaning of the Santa Claus of childhood does not dissolve after adults have given up believing in his concrete reality and have accepted him as a poetic representative of the Christmas festivities.

But that form of meaningfulness is not commonly acceptable where God is concerned. Metaphorical skills notwithstanding, the supernatural God has greater value for most people. The strictest believers totally bypass their imaginative powers as the creators of the God experience. However, there are many others who can, indeed, pray devotedly to God, even when they don't believe in his concrete existence. For them this prayer is an amplification of the importance of the words they intone, and they are rapt in the poetry of it. They fuse the imaginative mind and the mundane reality, affirming a guiding human truth, that poetry and reality go hand in hand; such people effectively feeling the relationship to God, irrespective of God's concrete existence.

Close to this experience of the poetry of God are the observations of T. M. Luhrmann, who writes about an evangelical union of the supernatural and the wordly. She reports her explorations in the Vineyard Christian Fellowship, describing a process that, through special forms of concentration, teaches these worshipers how to hear the voice of God. They believe that God is ever-present but breaks into the mind only if one pays attention devotedly. The breakthrough is not abstract or misty. She says about these worshipers, "They speak as though God interacts with them like a friend. He speaks to them. He listens to them. He acts when they pray to him about little mundane things, because he cares." Through a period of learning how to pray, the person is guided to a deep concentration on the presence of God. When successful, the person actually hears the voice of God, which is not only felt as a belief but an acoustical reality.

Is this a hallucination? Not in the eyes of people praying. Luhrmann sees them to be in an altered state of mind, brought on by their deep concentration; God is *not created* by the concentration but *released* by it. The key to the achievement of this intimacy is the personal investiture of attention, a testament to the power of focusing the mind. She distinguishes between these altered states and psychosis and concludes that in these congregations, through hard work, effort, and training, "God will answer back through thoughts and mental images he places in your mind, and through sensations he causes in your body." She reports that the imagined conversation with God will increase the felt presence of God and that the explicit exchanges will intensify one's sense of the existence of an actual God. For them this is not poetry. God is actually there already. The method allows him to enter into an experienced actuality. Luhrmann concludes, "Everyone has the ability to treat what the mind imagines as more real than the world one knows." In a world of diverse approaches to the experience of God, such observations set a functional ground, illustrating how profound attention can fashion a sacred experience (Luhrmann 2012).

However, the advent of the psychotherapist has taken people on an unreservedly humanistic pathway by transposing supernatural authority into a poetic humanity. What I am calling a poetic humanity was achieved through the dramatization of the special meaning of the therapeutic engagement, at root a simple secular experience. The attribution of meaning to these ordinary events unified the things people said and did every day with the larger experiential vessel of the world with which we identify our lives (Freud 1914). This form of understanding was harmonious with the human impulse to converge the ordinary and the sublime, joining ordinary interpersonal conversation with a symbolic perspective that deepened personal experience.

Freud, however, failed to give the sublime aspects of his achievement the attention they deserve. Caught in the mindset of medical culture, he rejected the commonality between his ideas and those that had given religion its sentimental and cosmic implications. Nevertheless, while careful to stick to his version of science, he, in the face of disclaimers of a religious relevance, created a poetic environment within his professional setting. He invented a rationale for entering unobservable regions of the mind. This included not only a road map to the mysterious unconscious but also the meditation-like technique of free association, the recognition of transference, and the extended sequences of meeting. This placed him in the future of a sanctified human experience, extracted from conditions of ordinary conversation. In this respect he was actually more than the neuroscientist who had simply expanded his or her laboratory to the psychotherapy session. Indeed, Freud created a new level of enchantment with human experience, quite recognizably comparable to the exotic powers of the religious experience.

What is crucial is that no supernatural leverage was required for the exceptionality of his enlargement of the secular experience. Instead of miracles he tapped a literary bountifulness in the stories his patients told of their personal struggles and their personal enlightenment (Freud 1957). The singular personal narratives were as compelling as the so-called cures. Though more modest than the apocryphal stories of Christian, Jewish, Muslim, and Buddhist religions, they were nevertheless novel to the society at large, which was accustomed to the privacy of distress. Freud was able to give his patients' stories personalized meaning matching the drama of religious lore. He did so by skillfully integrating the enchantment of the unconscious with the ordinary life experiences of his patients.

It is not altogether surprising, given the outrage about some of his sensational—often mistaken—observations, that he would have been careful to emphasize the rationality underlying these exceptional experiences. Still, rationality notwithstanding, he was no stranger to the exceptional experience. He became immersed in the pansexuality of Charcot, the influential nineteenth-century French psychiatrist. Freud also incorporated hypnotism into his therapy. He experimented personally with cocaine. He went far beyond the medical interview when he induced the microcosmic sense of the therapy session by his recognition of transference. In further exceptionality, through the technique of free association, came his discovery of the fertility of the mind when released from ordinary standards, such as those of grammatical sentence structure, logical connections, or personal purpose. He had discovered a ritual so mind-opening that, when rightly practiced, must be held on a par with prayer and meditation for consciousness enhancement. Free association merged the concentration inherent to meditation with the syntactical, content-rich, talking-to-a-listening-being powers of prayer.

Surely these expansions of the psyche, packaged in psychoanalytic method, revealed an exorbitance of personal experience that could have jetted Freud into recognizing the enchantment of his special brand of personal exploration. Alas, rather than to accentuate the arousal powers of high focus and free mind, he kept one foot firmly in the mundane by rational explanation. He would provide artful logic to both free association and transference, overshadowing the creation of intimate bonding and rapt attention by the search for insight. As Freud bypassed the experiential embeddedness of his patients, he became guided by the rationality of explanation as the road to cure. Spirit, in the form of awareness and an exceptional inner life, took a back seat to understanding the causes and resolutions of specific problems.

Now history has gone beyond the rationality that blurred the more visceral roots of Freud's discoveries. While it is only natural for minds to gravitate to the supernatural, it is a significant mark in social progression to transcend the supernatural by incorporating human leadership in deepening relationship and in exploring the mysteries of the unknown. Freud's original impact aroused an appetite for the adventure of the mind, and for many people there is no turning back from this *humanistic* transcendence of ordinary secular existence.

People are driven to seek the ultimate, and the image of God satisfies the believer's version of the ultimate. However, there are also mundane ultimates: the Nobel Prize or being homecoming queen or the Super Bowl or the presidency. Ultimates can be useful as guiding images that direct people forward from their familiar state to an imagined enlargement. They serve as orienting and motivating images, reference points for growth, and are grounded in people acting as the agents of their own directions. While God is a great inspiration to many, so also is a communal value perspective and the imagery of self-affirmation. Such a foundation of actual experience excites the mind and belies the neutralizing observation that "I owe it all to God." While some reasons for success may not be entirely understood, it is nevertheless invigorating when people honor their own responsibility, clearly verifiable or not.

Daniel Dennet exemplifies the acknowledgement of such human initiative. Having survived life-threatening heart surgery, he was asked whether he had an after-life experience and whether he had changed his view of being atheistic. He gave the following testament to human determinism, saying,

> Yes, I did have an epiphany. I saw with greater clarity than ever before in my life that when I say "Thank goodness" this is not merely a euphemism for "Thank God!" ... There is a lot of goodness in this world, and more goodness every day, and this fantastic human-made fabric of excellence is genuinely responsible for the fact than I am alive today. It is a worthy recipient of the gratitude I feel today, and I want to celebrate that fact here and now. (Dennet 2007)

Dennet's celebratory perspective invites him to name many sources of his gratitude, including especially the work of his surgeon, but also a large range of specific workers as well as the entire field of medicine. For western religions the precedent of God's will steers many people away from themselves as the definer of the universe and the guide to acceptable behavior. For them "God's will" is the answer to understanding why they are the ones who broke a leg or won in a lottery. Such centrality of God's authority is magnified when human behavior is measured by his will instead of the strategies created by a community looking out for its well-being. When Cain killed Abel, for example, this act became enshrined as a warning. It was more than a simple murder. It was a lesson to humanity, giving sacred status to a biblical admonition.

The concept of God thus formed a scaffold onto an encompassing orientation and guidance, as though the immorality of murder would otherwise not have occurred to human beings. While God's judgment has been given a hugely enabling role in creating a system of morality, it bypasses the human initiative in making these judgments, which are grounded in people's own life experiences. These human perspectives are the foundation for a clarifying, arousing, and supervisory position in creating socially acceptable behavior. (I will present some observations about a humanistic version of morality in chapter 11.)

10

From the Supernatural to the Human: Part 2

While the role of the supernatural in western religion remains an abiding influence in addressing a number of fundamental human functions, I want to spell out Life Focus Community perspectives on some of the same functions. Beginning with Freud, psychotherapy redesigned the domain of the divine by raising the therapeutic relationship beyond practical conversational exchange into a symbolic message. That is, any bit of behavior or feeling was not only a moment's experience but also a signal pointing to a larger realm of anyone's life—or even of life itself. This transposed a key domain of God's role as the source and administrator of personal experiences into a new authority, offering the powers of humanistic agency. Now, instead of deferring to the supervision of God, we are invited to map the geography of the psyche, and to seek a pointedly human understanding about a human journey. I shall now provide a sample of these contributions by elaborating four basic human needs that are commonly satisfied by supernatural authority but that also can be satisfied by psychotherapy and by the Life Focus Community. These needs are:

1. Relational indivisibility: People need to feel interwoven with the world of otherness. This is especially evident in the specific mergers represented in belonging and in the experience of "we."
2. Sanctification: People need a communal opportunity for personal exploration, set apart from the pressures of everyday living.
3. Extrapolation: People need to lean forward into what will happen next in life's trajectory.
4. Anthropomorphism: People have a need to attribute human characteristics to nonhuman entities.

Relational Indivisibility

Relational indivisibility is one of the blessings many people feel in their relationship with God, who is said to reside in each person. Paul says to the Ephesians:

> He has made known to us His hidden purpose: namely, that the universe, all in heaven and on earth, might be brought into a unity in Christ.... And you too, when you heard the message of the truth, the good news of your salvation, and had believed it, became incorporate in Christ and received the seal of the promised Holy Spirit. (1:9, 13, New English Bible 1961)

Many people who live under this aura of union believe the divine oneness with God to be in a class by itself. This is one of the more dramatic phenomena of our western civilization, which has imprinted its recognition of the need for indivisibility. The religiously grounded marriage vow, to give another well-known example, commands people "to have and to hold, from this day forward, for better, for worse, for richer, for poorer, in sickness and in health, until death do us part." This is then followed by "What God has joined, men must not divide."

In secular contrast what is most dominant is the recognition that, no matter how intimate a relationship may be, the participants all retain their individual distinctiveness. From this position they do, however, show great loyalty to the family, church, political party, and sports team—affiliations that often create so strong a feeling of indivisibility that breaking from them may seem like a personal amputation. "Belonging," "intimacy," "togetherness," and "coordination" are more cool words, but they also point to an active merger among people more than to a predetermined unity. So also do the words "dedication," "loyalty," "mutuality," and "allegiance" attest to a created oneness. Furthermore, indivisibility from the universe, as distinct from God, is experienced by many spiritually minded people as a worldly harmony. These are all testaments to the intrinsic secular avenues for people to link their lives with a world of otherness, a world achieved without supernatural presence.

This fundamental incorporation of relational indivisibility is reflected in psychotherapy theories. I have already discussed a psychoanalytic version in chapter 2, where I showed how the concept of transference spotlighted the interwoven nature of patient and therapist. Therapy theories have since proliferated in describing the power of interpersonal bonding, exemplified in the mid-twentieth century by gestalt therapy's concept of the contact boundary (Polster 2006). As is true of all boundaries, there is an infinitely narrow point of demarcation, at which the bounded entities are jointly identified. While the human meeting point is not so fixed as geographical boundaries are, such a meeting point nevertheless provides both an enhancement and a threat to the identities of each party, as the two merge into a compelling "we."

As Miriam Polster and I have written,

> Contact can only happen between separate beings, always requiring independence and always risking capture in the union . . . although me and thee become we in name only, through this naming we gamble with the dissolution of either me or thee . . . when I meet you full eyed, full-bodied and full-minded, you may become irresistible and engulfing. (Polster and Polster 1974)

Of course, the differentiation between me and thee offers a distinct clarity. You are, indeed, another person, whom I *see* or *touch* or *talk to*. With this separateness so apparent, it is a large step to take indivisibility literally. Still, people can come to feel pretty close to feeling literal unity with otherness through meditation, drug experiences, the semiconsciousness experienced in illness, the mistiness of spiritual experience, and surely also where God is concerned.

However, the most common experiences of indivisibility are most likely to be felt in an allusional mode, which is loose enough in its meaning to include a number of forms of social connectedness. A significantly embedded relationship—usually a parent, a spouse, a wise friend, a charismatic leader, or the community itself—all may be felt by some as indivisible from one's self. While these human approximations of relational indivisibility are recognizable every day, the literally intended designation of the indivisibility of God contrasts with the approximations that are built into some very important human scale relationships.

Still, in spite of the predominance of differentiation, there are some signs of raw experiences of neurologically induced indivisibility in the experiments of Newberg and Waldman, whose brain scan studies showed that their subjects, at the height of meditation, did, indeed, literally lose a sense of boundaries. They report a decreased activity in the parietal lobe of these subjects and that the subjects' sense of self "begins to dissolve, allowing the person to feel *unified with the object of contemplation*" (Newberg and Waldman 2009, emphasis added). While the research on specialized brain functions is still in the early stages, these results suggest a familiar yet uncanny paradox: that while we live with a simple perception of separateness, we may, under the right circumstances, lose this distinctiveness. By implication it is only a short step to expect the experience of indivisibility with God to be reproducible through a humanly induced state of mind, created by absorbed relationship.

In seeking further precedent for such hospitality to indivisibility, the fetus comes readily to mind. We can easily imagine that the fetus does not make the differentiation between self and other. Self/object theorists have proposed this, saying that the infant continues what the fetus began: to experience mother as indivisible. This changes during the maturational process, where the differentiation becomes more and more marked. Still, residuals of this infant sense of union are said to survive even into adulthood. We are all embedded in this history of seeming indivisibility, even as our more individuated personhood evolves. We acknowledge this continuing indivisibility even in such hackneyed sayings as "You can take the boy out of the country, but you can't take the country out of the boy" and in the Jesuit claim "Give me the child for his first seven years, and I'll give you the man." When a large part of this background of embeddedness is in the intimate relationship with another person, this relationship between an observable you and a palpable me becomes transformed from the obvious you and me into the commonly felt approximation of indivisibility.

To reconcile this sense of merger with its counterpoint individuality, we have to transcend the obvious fact that people are manifestly far removed from *merging* with another. Even those who are captured or dominated or incorporated are always captured or dominated or incorporated by *someone else* and, except in the case of delusional perceptions, are never merged. I may belong devotedly to a certain group of people: family, country, business organization. I may even designate certain symbols, such as flags, logos, and slogans to be signs of that indivisibility. I may feel my interests to be seriously affected by what happens within that group. Still, I always know I am a member of that group, an identity that will never disappear. That sense of immersion is certainly a hugely important phenomenon, a representation of the psyche's insistence on feeling the context for what we do. But this relationship of experience to context is, after all, a fluid merger, not the immutable union that many believe the merger with God to be.

Therefore, the Life Focus Community must find special ways to serve this dual requirement: the attraction to indivisibility and the palpable

From the Supernatural to the Human: Part 2

reality of individual existence. To examine this interface, here is an example of a group exercise that will accentuate the coordination:

The group is asked to divide into pairs. Person A talks for only a minute or two, saying whatever he wants to say. Person B is to *listen* to the speaker with full concentration, drinking her partner in, focusing as deeply as she can on Person A's characteristics and on what he is saying.

After completing this short but sharply focused receptivity, Person B, the listening person, closes her eyes. She is asked to watch the screen of her closed eyes, looking at the images that appear to her, one after the other, as though she is watching a movie screen. She has no other obligation but to allow these images to come and to observe everything that enters her visual experience. Then, when the imaging time is completed, she tells Person A what she saw on the screen of her mind. Person A then responds by telling whether that imagery has any significance for him. Did it tap into any of his own actual experiences in his own lifetime?

Here is what happened in one pair:

Person B, the visualizing person, saw her partner in a farmhouse yard, swinging on a tire hanging from a tree. Then she saw a railroad track incongruously in the background. Then a train was seen whizzing by, the whistle sounded, and the boy became startled and fell to the ground.

Person A, the observed speaker, responded by telling whether any part of the imagery reminded him about anything from of his own life:

He said yes, not the exact imagery, but he remembered that one of the turning points in his life came when he visited his cousin on a farm and really did fall out of a tree. He was scolded because he had been warned against climbing into it. What he remembered even more poignantly was seeing his cousin milking cows. What a strange shift this was in his sense of normality. But there it was, and he remembered an exhilarating feeling. In seeing his cousin milk the cow, he didn't know why, but he suddenly saw the world beyond his home as a palpable reality—a new way of experiencing life. This world beyond his familiar experience came alive to him like a revelation. Telling this story led also to a rueful awareness of being too much in trouble growing up but also of being glad for the novel experiences he had.

While the rural scene was part of both scenarios, Person B's visual imagery was, not surprisingly, an inaccurate view of Person A's actual life experience. It was suggestive, however, fertilizing her partner's actual memory. They built off each other, and this approximation of unity accents mutuality, with each person moving forward through his or her related perceptions. The observed person catches the imagery, and it coalesces into the overlapping of their minds: the observed person extracted the partner's perceptions as a stimulus for his own actual story. The bonding between the two people was immediate and surprisingly strong, beyond that of casual conversation, almost as though the visualizing person had some intimate knowledge of the observed person's life. While it is intriguing to see such examples of felt synchronicity between the two people, it does not require a mystical perspective to recognize the basic commonality of humanity and the resulting cues we take from each other in telling our own stories.

Another exercise would be for people to break into subgroups of three and tell each other about groups with whom they feel their identity to be crucially joined—as though their lives would be unrecognizable should that identity be ruptured. Surely a marriage or one's children would come quickly to mind. For many it might be their country or their place of work or an organization to which they have long contributed and with whom a large personal investment had developed. I think of one woman whose husband had died, and she felt like he had taken her brain with him. I think of another who had a large executive job, but when he retired he felt empty of identity. I think of people who are driven to return to the home of their childhood. I think of Nathan Hale, the patriot in the American Revolution who said, just before being hanged by the British as a spy, "I regret that I have but one life to give to my country."

These examples all represent extreme loyalty, mutuality, and common sense of identity, but they are only the sharpest of the humanly grounded testaments to indivisibility. When we further stretch the meaning of indivisibility to include familiarity, habit, confidence, and comfort, we are extending the meaning to include all those activities where people feel securely joined with each other: the source of personal belonging. Such approximations to indivisibility are less romantic or psychologically insistent than the belief in indivisibility with God, but they are humanly grounded and, likely, are all that many people need.

Sanctification

To sanctify experiences is usually associated with making experience "sacred"—that which, as the *American Heritage Dictionary* tells us, is set apart for the worship of a deity. I want to modify such common understanding of sanctification to incorporate a basic characteristic of psychotherapy. One of its great innovations was to transform the doctor's office into a special environment, one where the freedom of conversation was set apart from the prohibitions and pressures of everyday living. This reprieve for people to say what they wanted to say created a situational Sabbath, a break from everyday rules of engagement. People need such an option for getting off the conveyor belt of everyday living to enter a place where nobody will fire them, ostracize them, or insult them. Accordingly, from its beginnings the psychotherapy session invited people to a sanctified setting: a special place positioned to discover new dimensions of awareness, new thresholds for safety, new stimulation for telling their own stories.

We see the ancestry for such sanctification in many aspects of religious experience. The majestic medieval Christian cathedrals are one. They served the purpose of sanctification by projecting their buildings into the heavens, beyond the boundaries of the earthly dimension. More relationally, the early Christians sanctified face-to-face group confessionals and provided a highly complex system of God's blessing and community support for all believers (Mowrer 1964).

That promise of unswerving acceptability of believers is a sanctified condition for overriding specific secular error and for being restored to one's fundamentally unspoiled nature. That view of unearthly purity has been echoed in well-known secular beliefs, such as those of Rousseau's noble savage, John Locke's tabula rasa, or Carl Rogers's unconditional love. This ideal of unspoiled existence sees past the societal effects to the basic person, who is as pure as electrical energy or the colors of a flower or the contours of a mountain.

God is the most famous example of such suprapersonal exceptionality. His example is more practically abetted by the religious community's more specific promise to provide many forms of kindness, and its willingness to see beyond the complexity of individual personhood. Under ideal management of the religion's requirements, the community offers assurance of benevolent relationships among its people. Those who correctly join with God will presumably be cushioned from the oppressive blows of secular forces, a safe place for security and guidance. They find this special dispensation not only through the eternal implications of God's supervision but also through the sanctified relationship and supervision of the religious community.

While Freud's creation of a safe haven in the therapeutic office also recognized the need for a sheltered space that would be impervious to the common social standards, the requirement to be a believer or the need to give up one's preference for this or that behavior was ideologically absent. Instead, the respite from the mistakes and confusions of everyday life was assured because all but the most heinous or criminal forms of behavior were contextualized. In this therapeutic setting there was a clear amnesty for the patient's thoughts and feelings. Of course, this was only a temporary relief from external reality, but these moments of high concentration shined a light on qualities otherwise blurred or distorted by everyday judgments. Even so temporary a glimpse of exoneration was inspirational and expanded the possibilities in the everyday world—a world where sin, frustration, and confusion had made their mark (Polster 2006).

In its own form of sanctification, the Life Focus Community goes a step further than private therapy by expanding this special ethos into the realm of communal relationship. A glimpse of this reprieve is evident in the words of one member of a Life Focus Community group, where people were telling each other what the group meant to them: "The first thing that came to my mind was sort of having a toothbrush for the soul. If we do daily life long enough with no reflection, things get gunky. It's important to have a way to clear out, so that you get to more of a sense of essence. What is truth for me below all this gunky stuff? That always refreshes me."

The group chimes in by asking whether the member is talking about some special essence of herself that gets lost. She says it is more like having sludge removed, and goes on to say:

> I think it has something to do with us being mutually committed to discovering the truth underneath. Not taking things entirely at face value but kind of pulling the rocks away a little bit and feeling that there is a mutual support for that, and even if we find a slug under there, it's not a big deal. There's something about a lack of concern that I will be found unacceptable. I'm not concerned about that here, and I think that is an invitation to take a chance on embarrassing myself in the service of discovering something. I think that that has something to do with longevity too. It's being known over a long time. I don't think I would have that sense of "no danger" in any group that was new to me. I don't think I'm wired like that.

One might wonder whether such human-scale engagements are only pale facsimiles, lacking the holy deference that is often reserved for God. Devotion to him is commonly experienced as a unique reprieve, but God is not in a class by himself. While the exceptionality of his special dispensations sets aside worldly pressures, the human option also provides its own forms of relief, the feelings of affirmation more powerful than is commonly recognized—for many, more powerful than the relationship to God. How can this human leverage develop?

A primary vehicle is the induction of concentration. This recognition mushroomed with the mid-twentieth-century flowering of interest in gestalt therapy's newly accented attention to the basics of personal awareness and in an expanded interest in meditation. The high focus represented in these methods amplified specific experiences, ratcheting up attention to a simple reality, reducing the complications of a lifetime of contradiction and debasement. This reality, released from hackneyed meanings but valid in its own narrow awareness, was formed by spotlighting simple experience, independent of a lifetime of complexity. Gestalt therapy's accentuated concentration on immediate experience went beyond the limits of meditation's mantra to arouse fresh themes that evoked the defining stories and feelings of a lifetime. This heightened attention enlivened each moment to a surprising flow of detail, inspiring a new appreciation of the simple flow of life and its novel directions.

Furthermore, as we move beyond the therapy setting into the Life Focus Community, the designs of the meetings augment each person's readiness with inspirational music or reading a literary gem or showing a film. For example, let us say the theme for the meeting is neighborliness. A group design might highlight neighborliness by reading a poem about it. Robert Frost's poem about the "Mending Wall" and his famous observation that good fences make good neighbors would be a stimulating beginning for telling one's own stories about neighborly experiences. While the Frost poem itself would induce sharp concentration on his own words, it does more by evoking individual stories about neighbors. These may include personal arguments or exchanges of funny experiences or taking care of each other's children. People need such a special world, one in which they have the sanctified introduction of themes that may otherwise slip into a neutered region of the mind.

Still, notwithstanding the value of such *arranged* social opportunity, it must be recognized that the phenomenon of sanctification is also spontaneously operative in everyday life. Certain families accept people unconditionally, irrespective of their successes or failures, irrespective of their dissonant ideas, irrespective of choices of friends, and irrespective of the jobs they have. People may also find the benefits of sanctification outside the family when they experience dependable acceptance from friends or business associates, whom they can trust to understand them, stimulate them, and further their purposes. Yet, the reality is that many people do not find acceptance in either their families or other groups of people. Instead of serving as a haven, these places may be a source of condemnation at worst, and of lukewarm acceptance and failure to understand at best. Furthermore, even those who do have assured acceptance in the everyday world often get it only in passing, as a meager and fleeting attention to matters of such key importance.

While the relationship with the Life Focus Community is not as almighty as the relationship with God, it doesn't have to be in order to be felt as both respite and stimulation. Indeed, there is much to favor in the lowering of ambition from the supernatural to the human, such as incorporating humility about human powers and keeping expectation within the range of the available. Such acceptance of human limits is, paradoxically, open sesame for the enchantment of storytelling because it transposes each person's natural flow into its equally natural dramatic dimensions.

A key condition of this sanctified openness is that these experiences must not be cloistered from the everyday world; its messages must be applicable in the larger world. As Miriam Polster and I wrote long ago:

> Though retreats from the toxicity of the general culture are useful—almost indispensable for recouping the losses people sustain in their everyday lives—integrity requires that what one practices in a therapy situation be practiced there primarily so as to make one more skillful in engaging generally, not merely marking time in everyday life until one may retreat and be "real" again. (Polster and Polster 1974)

The design of the meetings and the outlook of the leaders, therefore, must be directed not only to *leaving* the confines of the secular world but also to *building bridges back into it*. The special setting must not be so colloquial as to represent a quasi-secret society, excessively removed from the way people normally talk to each other. Whatever themes are explored in the group have their representation outside the group. Group friendship highlights friendship itself, even exploring how it may also be developed elsewhere. Honesty or uniqueness or liveliness—valued in the group—are transposed into life outside the group. People want to be nourished in their work, to laugh more or rest more or read more, to worry less or squander less or ignore problems less. A most surprising phenomenon is that when people can be *freed of preset standards and narrow conclusions*, they can often see past these into what is already available to them. Indeed, they often discover that they already are much of what they hope to be. They may realize that they are more intelligent than their self-images allowed, that they are more interesting than their self-images allowed, or that they are more generous than their self-images allowed.

The Hallowed Relationship

A complement to sanctification is to hallow relationships, to add depth to what might otherwise be taken for granted. Such hallowing is obviously represented in the worshipful relationship with God, enunciated through prayer, chanting, and obedience to religious guidelines. The ubiquity, omniscience, and perfection of God are a tough act to follow. But the oft-repeated theme of this book is that the human-scale alternatives are compelling. In the human scale the potential for hallowing the Life Focus Community relationships is foreshadowed by the psychotherapy relationship. This relationship set the stage for humanistic hallowing by its focus on intimate subject matter, its sharp attention to the mind's process, and its guidance on people's journeys through their lives. Especially pertinent to the hallowing process was the idea of transference, which turned a practical problem-solving engagement into a microcosmic experience. (See chapter 3 for a fuller description.)

Most directly comparable to the therapist are the priest, minister, and rabbi, who also have long been given hallowed status, in that they have been authenticated as intermediaries of the supernatural. Such conferring of hallowed status to a Life Focus Community leader should not be interpreted as a testimonial to that person's individual skills. Clearly, some would be better at exercising their communal role than others. The hallowing function is so basic, though, that, in spite of some disappointments, it survives beyond the uneven skills of its human practitioners. The prescribed mission, the training, and the personal characteristics of these leaders all help, though, to provide confidence that they will provide life-defining attention. The fact that these people may sometimes talk too much, hear the wrong message, or have favorite forms of response irrespective of individual differences must not distract from the more-than-ordinarily-acute sensitivity and broad humanity these leaders exercise. To lower ambition from the perfection of God to the human range of personal skills is quite realistic and should not discolor the hallowing function. While the social hallowing process is real, there are surely individual differences in whom to hallow and to what extent. Hallowing a role does not imply that the hallowed individual can do no wrong, but it gives emotional affirmation to a serious relationship. The landscape of the psychotherapist, for over a century, has been dotted with a wide range of capabilities, but hallowing it has been supported by a respected, though not untarnished, track record.

Of further relevance to the hallowing process is that it may apply also to the aggregation of people, such as those in the Life Focus Community. Their continuing togetherness attains identity as an entity of its own, honored and engaged as a unit. One member reflected this unified identity when he said,

> The group has a family feeling. It has a special place. Actually we call ourselves The Special Group. In this capacity the group is like a sacred vessel that holds the member in a kind of emotionally soothing amniotic fluid. In this special place we "hang out" in every imaginable way and we tell our stories, tales about our points of passage to our trusted loved ones. I think most us would say we relate to each other with more honesty and intimacy than we do to the people we are related to.

This humanly grounded gravitas of awe and devotion is common among people engaged together in deep relational probing. While the hallowing of the relationship to God is a key to much of religious experience, the Life Focus Community members are moved to appreciate their identity through the congregational attention to their lives. Psychotherapy's historic induction of amplified human experience, applied independently of any supernatural leverage, becomes the core for this manifestation of sanctification.

Extrapolation

People innately stretch to see what is going on beyond their actual experiences. Starting with what is happening now, they infer this experience's origins and its consequences. To project into this unknown possibility, they have imagined gods, myths, history, and eternity, the starring characters in a world of wonder. This is a crafted world, constructed in an artful psyche, undaunted by the absence of hands-on knowledge.

Among all these ventures into the realm of worldly mystery, the most dogged and dramatic search imagines life after death, the ultimate threat to the extrapolative reflex. Many studies show that for a huge number of God's believers, this stretches them to believe in a heaven, a place where there is everlasting existence; death becomes only a new step, harmonious with humanoid continuity.

Psychotherapy's management of death is less ambitious than that. It starts innocently with a smaller extrapolative arc, concentrating sharply on the unfolding life, dramatizing the sequences of one moment and the next, one year and the next, one phase of life and the next (Polster 1995; Polster 1987). The end of the year, the end of a job, the end of a thunderstorm, the end of a relationship, the end of a ball game, and the end of any felt unit of experience—all are recognized as examples of closure, a natural goal of the psyche. This sense of completion is satisfying in its own right; it is a momentary complement to the need for extrapolation, which soon resumes the person's search beyond immediacy.

Such endings do not end continuity, of course. Being fired from a job, getting divorced, or losing the use of an arm—these endings are commonly followed by new beginnings. We can get new jobs, relationships, ballgames, years, and functions. We go to the movies *again*. We go home *again*. We eat *again*. Thus, discontinuity is moderated by a paradoxical truth: while there are specific endings, *the process never ends*. Life does flow on, *except for the individual's death, where that particular life is over, period*. The mind's relentless insistence finds that verdict hard to incorporate, however, and will try to cheat nature out of its starkness.

Undaunted, people may fill the mysteriously vacant space with ambiguity, a compromise between the mind's extrapolative reflex and the reality of ignorance. People then become free to live with their ignorance about life after death, letting the psyche make up for the blankness of the future. Among these potentials is the invention of an imaginative scenario that sidesteps the unknown facts of the future. People can do this by *identifying themselves—still alive*—with the continuity of an enduring family, group, nation, personal contribution, or life itself. These are psychologically endowed affiliations based on the great likelihood of the continuation of these entities. They are not ordained or adjudicated. Without resort to the supernatural, while alive, I project that my son will live on beyond me. I have no assurance that my point of view will continue to be heard or that my religion or my company will continue. Perhaps I will have been mistaken in my expectation, as we see when people say their father would turn over in his grave. But, having died, I will no longer have the extrapolative need (Csikszentmihalyi 1991).

The bearing of children and membership in a community in particular provide an extended future for those using humanistically grounded imagination, much as they do for those who bank on a future in heaven. Such poetics reflect the reality that "life" does truthfully continue after one's own death, while offering a measure of meaningful continuity and personal implication. This form of extrapolation may seem like small consolation. Perhaps so. Death is not built to be a fun ride, but the affiliative psyche gives people a personal stake in the future, *without necessarily subordinating themselves to the supernatural*. For all practical psychological purposes, I believe that is about as much extrapolation as dependable knowledge will allow.

While such saving graces soften the starkness of death, they are a tough sell compared to the supernatural option, and they are not enough for most people. Neither is the supernatural outlet, where the dread of death remains very much alive. In either case, anxiety reigns in the face of a possible auto accident or childhood illness, the threat of which will leave little relief from either the poetry of heaven or affiliated continuity. While ameliorative beliefs matter, what remains is ambiguity. It is, however, more than trivial to notice that death is an enlarged version of the mini-ambiguities people live with every day. Will the traffic prevent us from being on time? Will our daughter get the scholarship she depends on? Will the stress test show my heart is OK?

Yes, compared to death, these are minor ambiguities, but what they tell us is that *we practice at managing ambiguity all our lives.* Some of us learn the management of ambiguity better than others, and when we do, ambiguity is a lessened dread; often it is even a welcome adventure. In creating a proportional place for the ambiguity of death's future, it is worth noting a paradoxical reality: under many circumstances, people love ambiguity. We see it in our attraction to mystery stories, unsolved crimes, conflict-ridden politics, sports events, and family planning. There is no lack of ambiguity in anyone's life, and the Life Focus Community will contain ample opportunity to examine and face these ambiguities. People tell each other suspenseful stories about career, marriage, children, and the whole range of events that color the ambiguities of a lifetime. To feel this phenomenon continuingly and confidently, as it unfolds, provides a precedent for a flowing lifetime. While I offer no data in support, we may reasonably conjecture that the more we successfully practice the management of ambiguities, the more open-minded would we become to death's ultimate arrival.

Accordingly, a secular *faith* may enter the scene. The faith is this: that if we stay tuned into the sequences of life experience, enduringly and skillfully, we will be propelled forward to a surprising capability;

at the right time we will be able to manage what would previously have seemed unmanageable. What can be heartening to recognize in life's complex set of demands is that *what seems impossible to handle at one time in a person's life may be quite manageable at a later time.* Eight-year-old children feel altogether incapable of learning algebra, but when they are older, they do learn it. An entry worker cannot do the work of the executive because he or she is not ready, but later he or she may well become ready. One lives a lifetime in which the succession of new experiences has prepared us for a previously unimaginable capability. Accordingly, a person who believes he or she can't handle dying may temper the threat with a faith that an unknown readiness will appear when the time comes, a readiness that is unreal until that moment arrives. Of course, such a confidence-creating flow is easier said than done.

The main point to be made here is that building confidence in extrapolation is a lifetime process, with each successful step a preparation for the next challenge. Csikszentmihalyi has been one of the writers who have been especially effective in popularizing the concept of "flow," which elaborates the many ways to dissolve the barriers to a smooth sequence of personal experience. He highlights a graceful momentum that is confident and rises beyond the interruptions of everyday existence (Csikszentmihalyi 1991). He portrays a psychological momentum that thrives on sharp attention to what is going on and moves forward continuingly. He shows how this flow helps people do their work, play their games, think their thoughts, use their bodies, and understand their perspective on life. In his words,

> Because attention determines what will or will not appear in consciousness and because it is also required to make any other mental events—such as remembering, thinking, feeling, and making decisions—happen there, it is useful to think of it as psychic energy. . . . And it is an energy under our control, to do with as we please; hence, attention is our most important tool in the task of improving the quality of experience. (Csikszentmihalyi 1991)

In the same philosophical perspective, the gestalt therapist has long emphasized the importance of immediacy and its movement into individualized story line (Polster 1995; Polster 1987). The importance of the move into the *next* experience may be as elemental as the expectation that if you jump off a diving board, you will fall into the pool; or, with more uncertainty and complexity, that if you enroll in an architecture department, you will become an architect. This extrapolative sequence is so natural that it may escape attention in everyday living, but the implicit meaningfulness of this trajectory is amplified by the sharp focus of the therapy process. The relationship of each moment to the next receives a special focus that is nowhere else so pronounced. This phenomenon of "nextness" is the stimulus for building a conversational momentum. As I have previously written,

> Therapy in its greatest moments provides masterful examples of a sequential imperative, the sense of the irresistible sweep into nextness. Experiences appear to be seamlessly and inevitably interconnected, forming a sequential fit.... The seeming inevitability of events has a quasi-hypnotic effect and offers relief from the vexing questions and contradictions that...immobilize the mind. (Polster 1995)

To achieve this goal of a smooth movement from experience to experience, people must coordinate their large perspectives with the small steps in life. There is, indeed, a greater attraction to the more glamorous events, like graduation, marriage, a new job, bearing children, an anticipated visit, or, alas, death. However, such standards of interest often overshadow many of the simpler experiences that contribute to life's continuity. The vital flow that is composed of getting a drink of water when thirsty or laughing at a funny story or stumbling in the darkness going to the bathroom—these are the stuff of everyday living. They offer direct awareness of experience, often dwarfed by preoccupation about extrapolations into larger realms of experience. Listening to a friend who tells about a visit from his family may be more absorbing than Dostoevsky. These ordinary experiences grow in momentum and implication, leading us to assimilate experiences of larger dimension. All too often, death has been so prominent as the major human catastrophe that it has dominated life's story line. A counterforce is to keep its place in our lives proportional to the huge range of extrapolative experiences that guide our minds. No grand solutions, like the assumption of the after life or an affiliated life after death, will replace the urgency of living well in a continuing immediacy.

Anthropomorphism

Human beings see human characteristics in nonhuman entities. A most daring and far-reaching example of these anthropomorphic attributions is the image of God, a supernatural being with humanoid characteristics.

However, while dramatically apparent in the humanized image of God, anthropomorphic attribution is just what people do all the time. We do it in describing an "angry" sky or a "smiling" sun or a "forbidding" mountain pass (Polster 1995). We speak of earthquakes as the earth grumbling, of houses welcoming us, and of bee colonies having a queen. We also see a special level of trust and enchantment when we humanize animals, as we do, for example, in the age-old *Aesop's Fables* and in certain Hollywood icons: Mickey Mouse, Rin Tin Tin, or Donald Duck; and in *Sesame Street*'s Big Bird and the Cookie Monster.

A current example of this anthropomorphic influence is *Henry's World*, a story written in the voice of a three-legged cat. Because of Henry's heroic adaptation to the amputation, the author, Catherine Conheim, has ballooned the voice of Henry into a communal message, one that she calls the Just Me Project. Henry's experience is that of an indomitable cat who won't let his handicap lower his spirit. For those living with chronic illness and disability, especially for wounded soldiers, this humanly relevant cat cuts through the rigid images of human possibility, inviting an unsullied look into life's prospects. The human barriers of self-image and its implications for normality fade into the background for Henry, who is a fresh spirit, free of human fixity. Conheim has turned this book into an educational outreach that has received over thirty-three thousand e-mail responses and distributed over thirty thousand books to people, including military families, families of sick children, and children displaced by Hurricane Katrina. Conheim says, "The Just Me Project initiates conversations about recovery, resilience and the recognition of existing strengths and skills despite the wounds and trauma of disability, illness or stress. These conversations help to reinforce adaptability, to reframe the experience and to improve capacity for recovery" (Conheim 2005).

In a larger intellectual dimension, we see the anthropomorphic aspects of T. S. Eliot's famous commentary about the still point of the turning world where "the dance is." The still point doesn't really accommodate a dance; humans dance. Many would say the anthropomorphic humanizes the fusion between past and present; others would say it clarifies the options at pivotal moments in life; others would say life is grounded in an undercurrent of stillness, and only through feeling this stillness does meaning arrive. Whatever interpretation one might offer, the anthropomorphic is a poetic invitation for a fresh look at life.

Popular songs may also utilize anthropomorphic attribution to make a point. "We Are the World" is a song that accentuates the quasi-individual personhood of the "world," attributing to this vast entity the characteristics of the individual, and exercising potentiality, mutuality, and lyricism. The "dance" and the "world" are only a hint of the range of anthropomorphism in our literature and our music, a graphic tool in highlighting personal awareness.

I-Thou

This interface between the metaphorical and the concrete is also evident in Martin Buber's famous portrayal of the I-Thou relationship, which he portrays as the quintessential intimacy. Buber names God as the ultimate Thou, but he also applies the term "Thou" to more earthbound experience. From this perspective, if one looks at the contour of a mountain with full absorption, one fuses mind and mountain, reaching a depth of personal experience that transforms the mountain into a *Thou*. Accordingly, Buber's Thou may also be experienced in a devoted visit to a gravesite, viewing a sculpture of David, or a sunset. These entities may, therefore, be as compelling as if they were all actual human intimates. We see, therefore, that the absorbed attention to the "other" is the key to entering the kingdom of I-Thou (Buber 1952).

From this perspective, the Life Focus Community may be seen to represent the "Thou" status when this created entity is fully engaged. Though these groups surely do not have the infinite duration of God, one group I meet with has been meeting for twenty-five years and still keeps on meeting, having outlasted the ordinary disruptions so familiar in individual relationship. While unable to measure up to the grandeur of God, the group itself nevertheless serves as an anthropomorphic entity, much as God does. While not having the supernatural powers of God, the Life Focus Community will, nevertheless, derive great leverage as a quasi-personhood from its relational importance to its members. The group develops a character of its own by the way the members dialogue with it, within it, and about it. They think about the group, they talk to the group, they visualize the group, they belong to the group.

Everyone knows that the group, at bottom, is a collection of individual people. It has no other concrete actuality. Still, it has a special psychological existence, an anthropomorphic image offering continuity, cohesion, personality, and purpose. The group is responsive, it is supervisory, it is stimulating, it creates the feeling of belonging. It takes on the qualities of a supra individual. The only voice it has is through the *aggregate* of people who comprise it, relate to it, honor it, and love it.

In this sense it is an enlarged person, not dissimilar from how people speak of God. Mind transcends literal truth when the anthropomorphic attribution creates the group as a humanoid individual. This poetic statement trumps literality, providing an amplified identity of the group and with the accompanying enchantment of its members, parallel to the relationship with God. Such anthropomorphic attribution to the group transcends relational casualness; it personalizes the community and enhances both its importance and its familiarity. It must not be overlooked as a fundamental contribution, parallel to the attractions of the supernatural.

Empty Chair Dialogue

I am reminded of teaching a class of theological graduate students. The subject was "worship and human relations." I asked a few of them to speak, one at a time, to the class membership about any subject. After each student finished speaking to these real people, I asked him or her to turn their backs to the class and speak to God. There was a large difference in how the students spoke to God. They were more emotional, more fluent, more straightforward, less self-conscious, and altogether more engaged. What was evident in this exercise was what has long been apparent in gestalt therapy's use of the "empty chair" exercise: talking to an imagined entity stretches the communication beyond the ordinarily permissible.

To illustrate this phenomenon, let us look at an anthropomorphic scenario as it may activate an insightful dialogue. Ray says he is troubled by the idea of love and characteristically keeps his distance from people. The leader tells Ray to place "Love" in the "empty chair," which makes "Love" a quasi-person. In the ensuing dialogue Ray speaks from both positions, alternately playing Love and himself. As Love, he says to the literal Ray, sitting in the other chair, "You keep me away, and I don't know why."

Ray then says to Love, "I want to let you in, but you always get me into trouble."

Love says, "Of course you think I'm trouble, because you feel embarrassed about me. You think I make you soft and weak."

Ray is surprised and, after a few more exchanges, tells about being six years old and remembering his father shoving him away when he wanted to sit on his lap. Then he remembers that, just the other day, he felt the return of a strange edginess he had not felt for a long time. His nephew had said something especially funny, and he began to feel a hilarity that felt out of proportion, like he might get out control. He knew that edgy feeling was actually a larger level of pleasure than he could let in.

Love then says in response, "There you are. You almost let me in."

Ray says, "OK, OK, I got it."

This type of personification of a characteristic gives color to the alienated "love," inviting it back into the person's experience. The value of anthropomorphic accent is broadly evident in other kinds of experiences as well, such as giving a nickname to a trip to a strange city or an auto accident or a ride in an amusement park. There is a considerable satisfaction in these animations, a satisfaction gained through the fundamentals of humanizing the nonhuman. Such highlighting of personal experience is only a small version of the anthropomorphic leverage derived from the relationship with God, human in image but free of human limits of wisdom and relationship.

Conclusion

The story I have been telling about these four human needs has been throbbing for a long time in human enterprise. They are familiarly associated with the role of God, but I believe are also recognizable within the psychotherapy ethos. While the relationship with God has been the guiding force for life focus in western society, it is timely to see the parallel pathways of psychotherapy in guiding attention to the lives people are living. While many familiar religious practices have created large social benefits over the centuries, it is important to see that these contributions are not in a class by themselves; that the psychotherapy ethos, including a large religious constituency, is heir to the traditional western religions and is incorporating the orientation and guidance of people into its life-attending domain.

11

A Psychotherapeutic Morality

Psychotherapy and morality both guide people in how best to live with each other. However, the therapist is only the *client's* agent, trying to help to improve relationships that are important for the client's psychological well-being. The therapist is responsive only to the client's best interests, not those of the *community*.

In contrast, society's moral guidelines represent the community's interests, instilling social values that help people at large to live well together. Whether you take your place in line at ticket windows, whether you respect the privacy of your friends, whether you keep promises—all belong in the province of morality. More socially complex aspects of morality would include standing up for yourself in a cutthroat workplace or making sacrifices for someone in need or confronting a school authority about unfair treatment of your child. While these same behaviors are also important to explore in therapy, they are addressed there only as they may contribute to solving the client's problem.

There are good reasons for this split. Leaving aside the common clash between legitimate individual and communal interests, morality has a reputation among many therapists of setting up inappropriately oppressive standards. Excessive punishment for disobedience, pigeon-holing people as cowards or ne'er-do-wells, creating guilt about sexuality, shaming those with unpopular political positions, demonizing atheists, imprisoning scientists who threaten religious beliefs—all of these excessive pressures have marked our history. Though most therapists have steered clear of telling people how they "should" behave, they have actually created an ethos of distinct preferences. They foster empathy by listening with a welcoming mind, reciprocating good deeds, giving people the benefit of the doubt, telling a story honestly, and accepting one's own responsibility. We see, therefore, in spite of psychotherapy's wariness about the inculcation of behavior, the quiet truth is that many of its moral preferences are quite evident, even though these preferences seem like relational wisdom. That insinuation of the psychotherapy ethos into society's moral positions is reflected by Hunter when he tells us (Hunter 2000) about the paradoxically large impact of psychology, even within religious circles. He speaks of a "psychological regime," saying, "The vocabulary of the psychologist frames virtually all public discussion." While psychotherapy-influenced changes in morality are far from unanimously accepted, they are well-known: loosened sexual prohibitions, lowered self-recrimination, heightened accessibility among races and classes, increased attention to personal self determination, and freer interplay with established authority. These variations on the existing moral code have created a backlash in some religious circles, where the loosening of familiar moral standards alarms many people.

Differences in content notwithstanding, it is clear that both psychotherapy and morality are charged with guiding people's relationships. If, for example, therapy leads a person to forgive a parent, this may not only be a resolution of this alienated relationship, it may also raise the moral standing of forgiveness. If a patient stops badgering a spouse to go to church, that not only reduces friction in the household, it is a moral statement about freedom of choice. Let us imagine, therefore, the story of Alice and her husband, Franklin, who came to therapy because Alice caught him looking at computer porn. She became furious because she felt personally betrayed. From a problem-solving perspective, there may be many explorations of the context for each of their behaviors. Possibly, the porn was an isolated experience and does not have to interfere with their normal relationships; possibly Franklin was addicted, watches porn at work, and is in danger of losing his job; possibly Alice was unknowingly turning him away sexually; possibly Franklin was expressing hostility indirectly; possibly he likes to take the easy way to satisfaction; possibly this, possibly that. Together, therapist and clients head toward an improvement in this troublesome relationship.

As the exploration evolves Alice tells her therapist what she had never said before—that Franklin presses so hard against her when they are having sex that she feels invaded. Then she stiffens and becomes otherwise unresponsive. That is her practical response to feeling invaded. It is surely a relational mistake. She needs to discover a better way for them to integrate their bodies, even in the face of his failure to do it well. What is relevant here is that she not only took the wrong relational step from a therapeutic standpoint, she also took the wrong moral step, by rejecting rather than connecting. At the same time, from Franklin's position, he just finally gave up on her, let her stew in her own juice, and took the porn route. Again, turning to his computer instead of turning to Alice was not only a relational failure but also a moral one, assuming a morality that frowned upon letting one's wife stew in her own juice.

However, from a therapeutic standpoint, morality is not the point and may even be a distraction from the problem-solving mission for these two distinctly individual people. It may shift attention from each of their own sharply felt personal interests into a broader, socially preferable standard. Suppose Franklin needs to rescue his individuality from the demands of marriage. That only complicates his therapeutic agenda, but in the final analysis, he will have to accommodate his needs for freedom with the need for better relationship with his wife. That is a therapeutic complexity.

The moral challenge, however, can't take every individual into account and must satisfy the communal need. From the standpoint of currently common morality, one can read serial moral considerations into Alice and Franklin's behavior that are relevant to the society, irrespective of their personal need. Such considerations include telling the truth, forgiveness of those who have erred, moderation of criticism of vulnerable people, filling in generously to make up for the weaknesses of others, willingness to change one's own characteristic behavior in the service of others, and kindness to those in trouble. All of these considerations were crucial in the therapy, but they are also important guidelines for the communal morality. That is, these behaviors not only carry implications for Alice and Franklin and their personal well-being but they are important planks in a social system that strives for people at large to live well with each other—the realm of morality.

It is, of course, true that the therapeutic attention to each person's needs has been an effective therapeutic guideline. It has been practically useful as a vehicle for personal problem-solving, and this may justify selectively sidestepping the broader concern with cultural standards. Private therapy is, after all, contractually arranged for the well-being of the individual client, especially so when there have already been substantially harmful effects of the strict moral codes. Therefore, even though the moral implications for the society are actually indivisible from the psychotherapeutic domain, therapists have often concentrated their energy on the practical mission to improve the lives of specific people. *Nevertheless, the mission I am describing for the Life Focus Community is broader than that of private therapy, and it is explicitly designed to go beyond attention to troubled lives into examining how people at large live with each other.* A natural step to be taken, therefore, is to create a new resonance between what psychotherapy has learned about relationships and its relevance for the moral guidance required by the society. This expansion of purpose must counter a historical wariness about the guilt created by violating moral generalizations. It may well be a sad reminder that a one-size-fits-all pathway to socially acceptable behavior will be booby-trapped, because life is too untidy for social fixities.

As I have previously said,

> Our fate as morality bearing creatures is a key part of civilized living.... With the advent of psychology, guilt and shame have been profoundly studied and recognized for both its corrective effects in people seeing the error of their ways and the destructive effects in immobilizing and torturing transgressors. However, in psychological circles, resignation to guilt and shame has been replaced by the urgency of doing something about moral dilemmas, which has become as great as the need to recognize them. (Polster 2006)

Should We Have "Shoulds"?

The idea of telling people what they "should" do has a bad name in psychological circles. We know that many people will mindlessly obey authority, and others will use authority as a power base to control people's behavior. However, even though the establishment of a system of "shoulds" has had poor consequences for many people, "should" is an altogether natural phenomenon and guides much of what people do. Obviously, with some notable exceptions, most people "should" study in college if they want to be physicists, they "should" exercise if they want to increase their muscularity, and they "should" respect other people's point of view if they want them to listen to theirs.

We also know that none of these "shoulds" is a *must*. To satisfy the standards for "should" is not the insistent requirement represented in the idea of *must*. It leaves an open space for sensitivity, wisdom, experience, and humility. However, the need for good sense is unavoidable in the development of any but a robotic morality, which will inevitably bump up hard against the complexity of choice-making. Instead, the "shoulds" of morality must provide a communal light for the unfolding demands of everyday living. Indeed, there will be loopholes and potholes in any system, including the strict one, which has also created social and individual contradictions.

Let's look, therefore, at an example of a few "shoulds" that deserve recognition in a psychotherapy-driven morality. We start with the fundamental reality that we, as a society, do not know everything we need to know about what people "should" do. But we do know a lot. And so do individual people. In the Life Focus Community groups, issues of fairness, justice, compassion, dependability, dedication, sacrifice, and a whole range of other "shoulds" are a sample of the concerns that people face. In addressing such themes the conversational exchanges provide story lines that reflect existing and potential forms of human morality, feeding experiences and perspectives into a *forming and viable morality*.

Here is a small sample of moral issues that would be addressed:

1. Looking Anew at an Old Morality

Steve, a participant in a Life Focus Community group session, is gay and has grown up seeing this as a moral perversion. For him the self-image as a "disgusting sissy" was his deeply implanted moral delinquency. In telling the group about it, Steve replays these feelings, and in the telling he breaks up his abstractions about his weakness and ineffectiveness with his own life details. He then affirms himself as an idiomatic person, rising above his distorted self-image. That is, he tells us about his work as a computer expert, spelling out some of the intricate problems he has solved. That brightens his energy and fleshes out his productivity. Before he is done, he also tells us about the value of his femininity. Now femininity gets a halo. With high self-regard, he spells out his femininity by telling how he is dependably kind in that he gives free help to friends who need his computer savvy. He takes care of his neighbors' children when they need his help. He behaves with sweetness and patience with his friends, and they enjoy being with him.

He is sophisticated enough already to have known that his self-image was distorted by an antigay morality. That is an old story for him, and he knows that he is not a freak. The knowledge becomes more real, though, when he tells his story, and it gives the rest of us details about his life; not just once, but whenever he still needs to remind himself that the stale abstractions are no longer the navigational coordinates of his existence.

While Steve is personally affirmed as a viable, desirable person and the group is moved to hear this happy ending to a tortured beginning, there is also an enlivened morality that registers in them. His story is only a tiny contribution, like one person's vote in a national election. But it registers as part of the accumulative understanding that forms society's morality. While this process starts with Steve's personal acceptability, it enters its perspectives into a growing social ethos about being homosexual. Just such small steps create an evolution of morality, rebalancing existing perspectives on how people "should" behave.

2. Expressing and Receiving Gratitude

To feel gratitude is a greater part of the mutuality that colors our moral perspective than most people realize. We say "thank you" many times per day, most of the time honestly felt but at such a casual level that the phrase is often unregistered. When, for example, I say "thank you" to the waiter who just brought me a refill of my drink, I may hardly think about it. However, adding up the thousands of such honestly felt "thank you"s reflects a mutuality of relationship that deserves recognition.

Many other, more vital experiences call for stronger individual expressions of gratitude, but even those often receive inadequate attention. Some are lifelong contributions by parents, friends, employers, teachers, and physicians. These people do things over and over that are just part of everyday living. People are grateful to see the way a friend smiles at them, or they may be grateful for an insight they got from a teacher or a helping hand from a doctor. Many people have no idea how important they have been to others. Only under special circumstances may some people reveal the key benefits they have received. These experiences may be so much a part of the natural flow of events that they are taken for granted, silently appreciated.

While it is true that there is plenty of room for improvement in expressing gratitude, to do so may be an interference with just living with it, with letting it soak in and reciprocating with never a mention of it. Too much acknowledgment may upstage the naturalness of the act. For example, it may be better for a person to tell a friend years later about the importance of the walks they had together after a divorce than for the first person to feel self-conscious about just walking together. Clearly, there is no formula for the best timing or frequency of expressing gratitude. Therefore, the institutionalization of opportunity and stimulation serves a good purpose: filling in the gaps in everyday living. In the Life Focus Community groups, the design of meetings may invite recognition of both the everyday "thank you" and the highly significant experiences, memorializing all these events with communal affirmations, sometimes in the subgroup conversations, sometimes in song, sometimes in the recitation of poetry, sometimes in the stories told by people who have special reasons for gratitude.

What is important to coordinate is the reverberation between the individual experiences of gratitude, told by each person, and the communal recognition of a large range of personal reasons to be grateful, celebrated through the attention of the entire community. To savor each experience of gratitude every day, to be continually and consciously grateful, would upstage the spontaneous happenings for which we are indeed grateful. The designed opportunity adds up those passing experiences with a culminating gratefulness that speaks for a multitude of "thank you"s.

3. Accepting Moral Dilemmas

Everyone faces the call for difficult moral judgments. For example, Arthur is about to go off to college when he is confronted with the sudden death of his father. Should he go on to college anyway and leave his mother and siblings to take care of themselves? Should he transfer to a local college? Should he get a job and delay going to college? Should he get married as he had intended to? Can he become self-educated while working to support the family? It is quite clear that there is no systematic morality that can take full account of the practical and moral clashes that complicate Arthur's management of a vexing situation. Where no norms may apply, the moral system should have room for a special empathy for the rightfully conflicted person.

4. The Moral Effect of Key People

Our lives are dotted with people whose morality has influenced our own. Sometimes the morality is not so much explicated as it is just lived. A teacher who treats all her students with respect is, without ever saying so, demonstrating her own brand of morality. A person who works when sick because his family needs the income, a person who smiles at you after you have made a mistake, a person who stands up against a boss who is bullying a colleague—they are all just living a life of a high-quality morality, reflected in their own behaviors.

To acknowledge these nonverbal representations of morality by talking about them in the Life Focus Community group accentuates the nonverbal morality. This gives people a chance to frame their own moral guidelines and to find a place for them within the group's sense of how to live with others. At best, this offers the security of mutuality when it exists, but the free conversation also allows for a diversity of understandings about the best way for people to live with each other.

Suppose, for example, that one person believes that insulting people is an acceptable form of honesty. Many people would find this a flawed morality, but such dissonance can often be assimilated by the group.

Of course, there are limits. If someone insults people frequently, he or she will have to face his or her compatibility with the group, which from its own moral needs may or may not be able to accept this behavior. At some point a crisis of compatibility may arise and require resolution. The group morality may be quite able to live with the differences, or it may not. This struggle may be the engine for what may become a recognizable morality, where exceptions to the common perspective are usually, but not always, assimilated.

5. Righting a Wrong

Suppose that I spoke to a friend about a person who was recently driven to suicide by his parents' cruelty; this was just a conversational recognition of the life of a person we both knew. Unfortunately, what I did not take into account—because it happened years ago—was that my friend's son had committed suicide. I cringe to think of what I said, but it was not an immoral thing for me to do; it was quite accidental, with no reference to his son's suicide intended. Nevertheless, the potential harm was done, and I did it. What moral issue am I now facing? Do I apologize and explain that there was no connection implied? Do I just ignore it, letting the coincidence slide by in a continuing relationship? Do I ignore this but make more than ordinarily sure that my friend knows of my high regard for him—perhaps through a special invitation to some event, perhaps through a gift with the motives for the gift only to be surmised, or perhaps through more frequent phone calls than before? Perhaps, perhaps. What is clear in full moral flavor is that I owe some form of restitution for the wound I may have created. This is a scenario that would evoke many stories from people in the Life Focus Community groups, giving the members a chance to air out some of their own moral gaffes.

6. Responsibility for One's Own Behavior

Suppose you always leave conversations abruptly, come late for appointments, don't send Christmas messages, dominate conversations, and don't return calls. All of these are just part of your normal behavior. You are unaware of any disregard for the people who are the recipients of your habitual neglect of normal kindnesses. Are these merely peculiarities of yours with no moral implication, or are they moral deficiencies? You have never even thought about it until one day someone talked to you about it. Though surprised, you began to wonder about the morality of your repeated disregard for the mutuality of timing or mutuality, period.

The need to be idiosyncratic, according to the dictates of your own personal way of life, is fundamental. But there are questions that pop up. Do you believe that you, in your relationships with others, owe people more personal consideration than you are accustomed to giving? While you have a right to your idiosyncrasies, do you have a free pass as you enter into and out of the minds of others? Would you want to change your ways to synchronize with others, or would you choose to live as you already authentically live and take your chances with the world around you? Furthermore, might you not feel quite satisfied with your moral character if you recognize how much more responsively you behave in many other situations? Can you place your neglectfulness in proportion to the fact that you help your students long past your professional obligation, give money anonymously to support morally important community services, make breakfast so your wife can sleep late, and pick up your neighbor's kids when your neighbor has conflicting commitments?

In sum, thematically framed conversations in the Life Focus Community groups would cover the complexity in people's moral concerns. Rather than offering authoritarian indoctrination, these relational messages would tap the diversity of individuated style. Unanimity of perspective would not be expected, and the group continuity would provide a developmental sense of the lessons learned. The recurrent messages over time, more or less integrated, would replace the fast track of moral clarity, so that the group would live with differences in circumstance and values. Further, this open mindedness would energize a creative evolution of the community's perspective, providing human scale to moral consciousness.

Moral Relativity

What is evident in my description of the "should" phenomenon is the interface between moral relativity and moral absolutism. To incorporate moral relativity, so basic to the psychotherapy ethos, is a daunting objective because absolutist morality has a strong foothold in the public mind, which has long been dominated by a sharp definition of acceptable behavior. A lie is a lie, cheating on your spouse is cheating on your spouse, and being late is being late—no ifs, ands, or buts. The raw truth is that, while the sharp definition of moral absolutism has its merits, there are some equally important and innate reasons for moral relativism.

One is the need for *context*. There is no choice about that, except as we may temporarily ignore this or that part of the context. It is altogether clear that no behavior occurs only by itself, embedded, as it is, in the world that houses it. The development of morality is no exception. We know societies where polygamy was morally acceptable. We know that killing in a wartime battle is morally acceptable. We know that it is morally acceptable to miss a meeting to take care of a parent's health emergency. In less clear circumstances it may be morally acceptable or not to be a whistle-blower or to take a planned vacation instead of going to a friend's wedding. Such a range of contexts is basic and is a challenge to absolutism.

The second innate need is the experience of *proportion*. Much as the number two has a proportional relationship to the number four, stealing bread has a proportional relationship to murder. We see, therefore, that the need for absolutist thinking must take its place with the equally imperative awareness of *proportion*. For example, a man on his deathbed, in order to satisfy an absolutist principle of honesty, tells his wife the full truth: he has been seeing another woman for the last ten years. How does this square morally with the importance of compassion for his wife, who suffers from the confession? For him the need for truthfulness seemed more important than his wife's well-being. Which principle has the greater importance: his absolutist need for honesty or his wife's need for a harmonious ending? While there is no one answer, I believe there is a contemporary social momentum toward moral relativity. The proportionality of this man's need for truthfulness on his deathbed and the quality of his wife's continuing life would weigh heavily in favor of his keeping his mouth shut.

Plainly, there is no absolute blueprint for how people should live their lives. In spite of the widespread belief in moral absolutism, people exercise moral relativity, not as a cop-out from the severity of absolutism but because a sense of context and proportion is deeply embedded in the human psyche. In spite of the apparent dominance of absolutist morality, especially in conservative religious circles, we see moral relativity every day. People offer a rationale for errant behavior, love their roguish friends, forgive their prejudiced parents, make allowance for people under duress, humanize their own moral unevenness, and cheer movie heroes who had temporarily gone bad. People who are appalled about moral relativity because of its ambiguity are failing to notice that it is a common part of living.

However, because of the flexibility of such standards, many people believe that moral relativity provides a weak foundation for a moral society. Worse, moral relativity is often mistakenly seen as the *absence* of morality. Critics will say that society can't live with approximate perspective on relational basics. Actually, it does so every day. Many people are hospitable with each other, even when their views conflict; they keep their appointments even when other morally compelling interests call; and they let gauche remarks pass by without rancor.

Perhaps such loose standards are less supportable when we address issues with larger social consequence, like getting drunk in a bar when you are supposed to be at home or getting money on false pretense or spreading vicious rumors. The standards within any community— whether it is a Life Focus Community group or a neighborhood or a nation—may be quite strict, as needed, but they may also be lenient when circumstance warrants it. Murder, robbery, rape, extortion, and other morally abhorrent behaviors are so toxic that law prohibits them. But these gross moral violations, which arouse our strongest absolutist need for prevention, must not be the decisive vote for absolutism.

Therefore, we may see that creative judgment is not just an excuse for social violations. It is a testament to the nature of being human. Still, because of the inescapable complexity of moral relativity, the management of it is a challenge to interpersonal skill. Psychotherapy's methods have been grounded in the idea that people can be taught how to correct for mistaken context and proportion. These lessons have been only a step toward shaping morality to the human dimension, both by introducing new perspectives on the nature of people and communities and by enlarging opportunity for exploring the best ways to live together. This influence of relativity harmonizes well with the various types of pluralism that are so widely recognized: religious pluralism, national pluralism, gender pluralism, and political pluralism. However, the growing face-to-face confrontation of the diversity among people has become all too familiar. The adversarial splits breach individual context and proportion and are a growing concern in trying to resolve seemingly intractable political and international differences.

Plainly, such problems exist, but this should not be disenfranchising. Indeed, governing with fixed morality would not be so troublesome as it has been if it were not also seriously flawed. Take, for example, the biblical prohibition of eating the apple, the Ten Commandments, and Abraham's obedience—only a few examples of the absolutist moral behavior. Most people take this absolutism with a grain of salt. They know that curiosity is desirable, that honoring father and mother may be rightfully breached where there has been severe parental abuse, and that a person obediently killing his son is an awful precedent. Nevertheless, the supremacy of biblical teachings is so deeply embedded in the culture of western civilization that much of it has become sacred and set apart from personal opinion. Over the ages we have been warned, commanded, and moralized into and out of particular behavior and feelings. Over the centuries these perspectives have offered an aura of a mystical but dependable validity that is unwarranted.

I conclude, therefore, that clear standards must be joined by proportion and context. If your child violates morality by skipping school and you find out about it, you might not even want to mention it. That does not necessarily mean you are dismissing it. Perhaps you quietly recognize that he needs some disobedience or daring and that a mild transgression is not likely to turn into a major problem. With other children that would not be the case, and some serious talk and mutual strategizing about how to solve the problem may well be in order, perhaps including one or another form of punishment.

This calls for sensitive judgment, a major requirement of any system of morality. That is what happens anyway, even in our existing priority for absolutism. People commonly ponder whether this or that behavior is right or wrong and change these standards over time. These judgments are part of a communal evolution where people's minds play off each other over time. The Life Focus Community group and its explorations of the world of relationship would be one of those social activities that feed their messages into the developing communal mind.

12

Dependable Identity

Who am I? Why is this question so difficult for people to answer?

One reason is that there is no single answer. We may have had bouts of screaming as a child and been burned into thinking that we are screamers. Or we may have won prizes in the fifth grade and think we have to have some exceptional reward. We may see ourselves as shy when in full truth we are just introspective or careful or uninterested. In various moments, under changing moods and circumstances, we may, alternately, be infantile, cunning, kindly, and silly. To know one's self as a great student may lose out to the time we backed down from a street fight. Thus, we often see that, complexity notwithstanding, the allure of simplicity often raises single events into self-definition. Simplicity makes our experience brighter, more assured, more unified. Simplicity may, indeed, be so dominating that all the other characteristics remain obscured. We are then captive, contained in a small segment of who we actually are.

The Life Focus Community is designed to counteract such narrowing by introducing life themes, the stories behind which awaken the spark of versatility. One example of such an awakening is the man in a Life Focus Community group who told us about growing up devotedly identified with his traditional Greek family. However, his own life went far beyond this Greek background. When he became a sociologist and a political activist, there was no denying that he was an educated man with friends and opportunities that stretched far beyond his family. Yet, in spite of his contributions in a more complex society, in a dominant corner of his mind, he remained simply a working-class Greek man. In actual fact, he had merged his empathy for these people with his new skills by becoming a social advocate. But his fixed identity with his past kept him blind to his progress: he pugnaciously hallowed his past, wandering in and out of his new world, but never feeling like a member of it.

His story is the story of growth, the flow past the past. He eventually spoke of his experiences of love, fear, surprise, disappointment, and laughter, all of which contained the seeds of an adventurous existence. These absorbing conversations were held in harmony with the present, side-by-side with his clash of the old and the new, which had distracted him from incorporating the Greek in him with the breadth of what he *really* was. In his words, "I broke my rationality and cut through with something that was true but that I wasn't paying attention to. And that has carried me many times in my life, and it's a guide to action on my part. Oh yeah, that's the Greek in me, and that's a pretty powerful force in me, and I like it instead of being embarrassed by it."

A person's lifetime is, indeed, made up of an inclusive range of such identities that are the building blocks of the person's psyche. Anyone's identity is a psychologically embedded agent of a many-sided existence, one that must take account of a population of the selves within. As I have previously written,

> With the naming of each Self, the Self becomes brightly organized, a spotlight on otherwise ephemeral existence, a banner, so to speak, around which the person rallies his psychological energies. . . . The therapist uses the device of the Self to give life to his patient's experiences, registering them so vividly that the abandoned aspects may be more fully re-experienced and the fragmented person made whole." (Polster 1995)

The Life Focus Community taps this need for knowing both the whole story and its parts by inviting conversations that feature contrasting personal characteristics, such as exuberant and steady, gregarious and private, conversationally fluent and awkward. People may be asked, for example, to tell each other about something that was characteristic at one time but not now. A thoughtfully quiet man might tell about the days in high school when he was a terror on the debating team. A professional athlete might tell about his pleasure in reading *The Decline and Fall of the Roman Empire*. A history professor might tell about his collection of clocks. Or group members might tell about the opposite change, that is, characteristics they have now that they never used to have: perhaps a thirst for learning, perhaps standing up for one's self in an argument, perhaps a new level of enterprise and leadership. These exercises help to reconcile their sense of simple identity with their vital versatility.

Fluidity and Constancy

Not only does identity contend with the integration of the narrow and the complex, but there is another pair of conflicting phenomena: *fluidity* and *constancy*. That is, we live in a *fluid, ever-changing* world while, at the same time, our minds crave a dependable and recognizable *constancy* (Polster 2012). While we can't just choose constancy or fluidity as a single guideline, we can play favorites, and we do. To give one pivotal example, the seminal existentialists of the twentieth century made fluidity of life a philosophical priority. That is, the actual *flow* of experiences, one after another, was given primacy over the *classification* of life experiences. Jean-Paul Sartre (7) long ago proclaimed a still-common attitude when he said, "Man is nothing else but that which he makes of himself," reminding people of their full responsibility as agents of their effervescent existence. It was exhilarating for people to be reminded that they are not wedded to the lives of their ancestors or geography or cultural priorities or even biology. People in the United States often proudly say, "Anybody can be and do anything they want to." Obviously, slogans don't tell the whole story, but the image of dissolved boundaries was exhilarating. It raised attention to the excesses of social pigeon-holing. Whether you were a professor or a laborer or a gambler did not say who you were. This boost for individuality was open sesame for the future, a reinforcement of psychotherapy's mission for change (Polster 1995).

The artists of our society at the turn of the twentieth century influenced this aura of fluidity by introducing new perspectives on music, literature, and painting. Their mysterious, chaotic interrelationships of the pictorial, the verbal, and the tonal enchanted people even though many of these people had little understanding of what the artists were doing. We are now familiar with parts of a face strangely arranged, dream-like combinations of animal and human characters joined together, flashbacks that fracture linear time lines in novels, and atonal music that thwarts melodic expectations. This elasticity gave center stage to disconnection itself, highlighting the task of seeing beyond fixed expectations. People were no longer so clearly identified as before by wearing a tie or working an eight-hour day or being married or living in a certain neighborhood. Pharmacists could be painters, university faculty could work out in gyms, and it became common for Americans to buy foreign cars.

Still, enthralled though the artists became with a fractured sense of reality, and rebellious as they were about the tyranny of frozen reality, paradoxically, they created a freshened understanding of the commonplace. For example, an incongruity of sequences in novelistic story line prevented the reader from taking continuity for granted. It called for concentrated satisfaction with what one was reading right now. Disconnected musical sequences opened listeners to the excitement of new combinations of sound, as well as to sound itself. Surprising psychoanalytic interpretations of old understandings put experience itself in the center of attention.

With such revamping, the familiar was no longer the routine. Whether it be a face, a house, or a childhood, the observer was called to have a raised threshold of individuated awareness. The accomplishment of these new ways of hearing, seeing, thinking, and imagining promised that the new vision of the world would sharpen our attention to it and expand our understanding of it. When a person's existing circumstance is habitually engaged, whether it be dinner with the family or reading a novel, the experience is easily taken for granted. The scrambling process and its invitation for the observer to reconstruct the picture invite people to an active role in completing the incomplete picture. By the recognition of this need to finish what is left indeterminate, we can see that the diversity of human experience is a challenge that dares people to put together discordant elements into a harmonious portrait. Such experimentation with fluidity lit people up, a fact that was timely for a society in which many were changing jobs, moving to new cities, inventing personal opportunities, practicing meditation, seeking pointedness in conversation, and embracing an expanded sexuality.

However, while these developments invited people to increased originality, there were unintended consequences: an impatience with the obscure and a blurring of identity. Cracking through packaged existence, the emphasis on fluidity seemed incompatible to many with the familiarity of life. As for personal identity, in featuring fluidity there was little room left for what a person is "really" like, continuingly and recognizably. Misguided though many such classifications of people have often been, there is, nevertheless, a human imperative for a dependable identity. Nowadays, while fluidity remains a key characteristic of contemporary living, its counterpoint condition, constancy, is calling out more strongly than it has for a long time.

Obviously, to have a clear sense of our personal identity, we need to know we are the same people we have previously been and will likely continue to be. Such dependability is thwarted when new things are always happening, overshadowing the familiar and dependable.

Dependable Identity

Someone close to you dies, you read an eye-opening book, or you strike up a conversation with someone from India. These are the barest suggestions, taken out of the millions of new happenings that, in their multiplicity, challenge the sense of constancy, each contributing to a perpetually changing scene. Restoring a sense of constancy from such an irrepressible fluidity is partly satisfied by the quiet constancies of human existence: that we are flesh and blood, reactive to experience, mortal, searchers for understanding. More individually, we may be dependably compassionate, physically strong, effervescent, and enduring. Whatever these constancies may be felt to be, they provide a primary lesson in dependability. This dependability is a takeoff point for carving out an identity so confidently that the ever-changing, even chaotic happenings with which people are also faced will become more exciting than threatening, freshening identity rather than obliterating it.

We see how compelling this need for constancy is when we identify ourselves with national, religious, professional, or social groupings. We recognize ourselves as American, Catholic, pharmacist, or Rotarian. We also identify with personal characteristics: our IQs, the color of our hair, the major sins we commit, the awards we receive, the books we read. These are relatively constant and dependable sources of identity, though none of them reflects the range of who we actually are.

Still, even with such clear personal markings, the question of constancy remains. It is only natural to wonder, "If I am what I am, will I still be what I was as I move through this ever-changing world?" Change is especially prominent in modern society, which has been informed by evolutionary theory, quantum theory, and cultural theory. Even my recognizably constant desk, sitting fixedly in my office, is composed of atomic movement. Does this evidence for perpetual fluidity from the world of science not belie the human experience of constancy? No. Indeed, the experience of constancy is grounded not so much in its literal meaning as in the *functions of the human mind*. We find our own sense of constancy in what we experience as a *dependably constant approximation* of the world, and we find it even in the face of universal fluidity. Let's look at how the human mind does this.

From a literal perspective, it is true that a person can't catch bus number 22 twice. Yes, I call bus 22 by the same name, and I take it to work every day, and I see some of the same people every day, but it is not really the same bus; even the color of the paint would be microscopically dimmed every moment. Still, people will rightfully insist that bus number 22 is "my bus," and it will, indeed, get me to work every day. So, in my humanoid psyche, the constancy of that bus exists, *approximation* though it may be. So also, irrespective of ever-present change, my sense of a constant identity keeps me clear that I am a person who does the same job every day, or who is characteristically kind, or devotedly studious, or easily confused, or all the other personal approximations that I feel to be "me."

A recent memoir written by Lucette Lagnado tells the story of the migratory struggles of her Middle Eastern Jewish family, which had long ago settled in Aleppo, Syria. Then, in more recent years, the author passed through Egypt and France before arriving in the United States (Lagnado 2000). In the face of these huge changes, she portrays the power of constancy when she recalls, "Though Aleppo was long ago, its culture still exerted a powerful, almost mystical hold on all those who traced their origins there, and always would, whether they lived in nearby Cairo or settled in far more distant cities." This "mystical hold" made its mark in the background of everything the elders in her family did after immigrating to New York. The pull of familiar identity trumped those greater prospects for well-being that accompanied the changes. In spite of the new world and its promise, the old and the constant remained firmly entrenched.

Constancy in the Life Focus Community

Now I want to show how the experience of constancy and the accompanying sense of dependable personal identity will be enhanced in the Life Focus Community groups.

1. Familiarity of Format

Each meeting would have certain recurring experiences: approximately the same people coming continuingly, the same meeting place, a familiar design of meetings, music and dancing, and rituals of beginning and ending. This familiarity reminds me of many common experiences in everyday living that are pleasurably recurrent: neighborhood greetings, salespeople, regular walks. Other familiar experiences include going back to school after summer vacations, going to familiar restaurants or the theater, and coming home after a stay in the hospital. Though the familiarity of Life Focus Community meetings would create such a sense of constancy, it is important to say that, always, each meeting would nevertheless have its own uniqueness, the constancy colored by the freshness of the experiences. Lifelong hospitality and familiarity would live side by side with the fluidity of all that we do.

2. The Focus on Life As It Is

Emphasizing the importance of life as it is already being lived rather than pressing for change will also accentuate constancy. This will be achieved through exercises that highlight themes that familiarly affect people's lives. People would talk to each other about their favorite recreations, the way they tell stories to their children, their continuing friendships, and their career experiences. Change would be portrayed as a natural partner to the acceptance of one's own life experiences, the novelty refreshing the familiar but not obscuring it. In one group a member spoke of constancy in this way:

> One of the things that came out of our group was that one of our members works with suicidal people, and she said she tried helping them feel at home with their feelings and I thought, *Wow, that's a great name to a group, "feeling at home with your feelings."* I thought, *What a wonderful entrée into doing this with a group in my community.*

Being at home with one's feelings is a time-honored therapeutic principle, not exactly a novel observation. Yet, feeling at home felt novel to this person, not because she had never thought of it but because the group reminders raised it to a special centrality. Such high focus on familiarity not only serves to highlight the feeling but is a grounding agent, a dependable stimulus for moving the person's story line forward. What might be classified as stagnant or bromidic becomes enlightening and fluid when it is distinctly received and registered in lively conversation. The group experience itself helps to create this; its continuity provides a strong aura of dependability, wedded to freedom of expression. One curious manifestation of this constancy is the common discovery that certain characteristics, when freshly revisited, may show people how they may already *be* what they were hoping to *become*. This look at the *refreshed constant* is a beacon for letting the present inform the future. As T. S. Eliot has said,

> We shall not cease from exploration
> And the end of all our exploring
> Will be to arrive where we started
> And know the place for the first time.
>   (Eliot 2014)

3. Communal Idioms

While communal idioms may be created deliberately, they are also a part of the spontaneous developments in any group. This communal idiom might include special styles of humor, familiar language, marking of endings with a special song or dance, commonality of the life themes people are interested in, and celebrating group experiences. All of these and many other idiomatic characteristics serve as points of familiarity.

In one group that has been meeting for twenty-five years, for example, there are special themes that are recurrently addressed. One person is raising a grandson, and people always want to know the new developments in her unusual parenting experiences; another who is repeatedly late receives good-natured razzing about it, especially when he surprisingly comes on time. Another is normally the last one to speak, but when he speaks earlier he gets various forms of applause. Everybody is familiar with everyone else, knowing each other's foibles and virtues, and each feels warmly known by all the others. They would not have it otherwise; each point of familiarity adds to rather than subtracts from the experience of fluidity.

4. Portrayal of Lives

Since the guiding ethos of the Life Focus Community group is a major shift from changing people into knowing other people as they are, this points people toward feeling the constancy of experience. Furthermore, the recognition that our likenesses are as important as our differences is another source of dependability. This is reflected in the generalized truths that cross individual boundaries. Parenthood, mortality, ambition, truth-seeking, storytelling—these are all commonly shared phenomena, individuated though their content is. Add to these the individualized characteristics that may be dependably recognized in any particular person: compassionate, physically strong, effervescent, wise (Polster 1995). The lesson about identity, therefore, is that its fluidity and its constancy must each be incorporated into one's self picture. To trust the enduring quality of our identity confidently is a boost rather than a barrier for the more fluid happenings. These happenings serve as a solid foundation for life as it evolves, as the union between constancy and fluidity becomes more exciting than threatening, and freshens identity rather than obliterating it. The lesson for the Life Focus Community group is that we can create a user-friendly pathway to *dependability* of identity as the welcoming ground for an assimilable novelty.

13

Belonging and Indivisibility

Hopeful as people may be about finding their own individual identity, the contrasting need to belong is so powerful that many people are overmatched. While the United States and western civilization have been the messengers of individual empowerment, conformity is everywhere. In the mid-twentieth century Erich Fromm's *Escape from Freedom* influenced a generation of people to see how conformity, a common adjunct to belonging, was swallowing up individuality (Fromm 1941). Many other twentieth-century social observers felt the same way. The novelist John Marquand characterized a style of life that would now be a caricature of the need to belong (Marquand 2004). His fictional George Apley wrote this letter to his young adult son:

> I am quite well known around the Club, you know, and your first object must be to "make" the Club. I believe that everything else, even including your studies, should be secondary to this. . . . The best people are always in it, the sort that you will understand and like. I once tried to understand a number of other people, but I am not so sure now that it was not a waste of time. Your own sort are the best friends and you will do well not to forget it. (Marquand 2004, 17)

The characters and scenarios have changed, but the conformity remains, everywhere evident, especially in the inculcation of values of the people who belong to political parties, races, economic classes, gangs, and professional affiliations. In each of these prominent hosts for belonging, those who think differently from the defining positions no longer are secure in their sense of belonging. Conformity is a price to be paid. Nevertheless, such conformity notwithstanding, our society still treasures a self-image of individuality, which is adopted in many circles almost as a social mantra. The resulting duality of motivations is so interwoven that people spend a lifetime seeking proportionality between them.

This challenge is natural, evident in everyday functions. If we look, for example, at a particular student who is learning how to play tennis, we see that the student should indeed yield some of his individuality in order to drink in the teacher's lessons, perhaps even doing the teacher's bidding. This recognition of the teacher as a distinct otherness, differentiated from the student himself, must absorb the mind of the teacher, creating a sense of an identifiable union. You and me become we, even while you and me must remain just you and me. Whether to yield is a good idea or not is a judgment call, but the benefits are there if the lessons improve the learner's ability to hit the ball—a key to his self-sufficiency and ultimate independence. Still, both the teacher and the student should know that a person can't maximize his or her tennis skills by becoming a carbon copy. More and more, the teacher should fade into the background, stepping aside, providing less and less leadership. What remains is a strong feeling of belonging within a valued dyad of relationship.

There is, of course, no assurance of this happy move into individuality. If, for example, the student becomes obligated to do the will of the teacher—to play, for example, in tournaments in which he would prefer not to play or hit the ball in a way that fits the teacher's image better than the learner's personal ability—his individuality is endangered. The common risk is that conformity will make his experience more of a sacrifice than it will maximize his own sense of self. Because of the frequency of such sacrifice, joining up meets a significant measure of skepticism in American society, where individuality has been its guiding image. Still, notwithstanding the risks of conformity, there is no escape from the fundamental imperative to belong. In the next section I will explain why this is the case.

Two Principles of Belonging

There are some obvious historical reasons why it has been strategically important that people band together. Clearly, there is safety in numbers. Joining together protects against danger, whether it be from predatory animals, earthquakes, or human competitors. Furthermore, many ordinary tasks can best be handled by cooperative endeavor, such as the setting of moral standards, the building of complex structures, and the expansion of knowledge. However, at a more primitive level, I want to name two fundamentals that go beyond strategy: *generic* sparks for the need to belong. The first is represented in the idea of the *contact boundary*; the second is the intrinsic nature of *figure/ground* interrelationship (Perls, Hefferline, Goodman 1951).

Contact Boundary

The contact boundary is a pivotal concept in gestalt therapy theory, and it is a foundational condition for belonging. (See chapter 10.) This boundary is the point at which each person meets otherness (otherness being a phenomenon so basic that a world without it would be unimaginable).

Yet, we do not experience this indivisibility. The separation is more obvious than the union. What is always clearest is that I am I and you are you. The truth that "you and me become we" is not so immediately clear. John and Jane have married, but what is most manifest is that they are still John and Jane. There is a dramatic novelty in their marriage because they now "belong" to each other. There is social recognition that they "belong" to each other because of the implied contract for a union of their lives. People like this feeling of belonging when it doesn't cost too much of their individual satisfactions. We know, however, that there are many painful aspects of this union. Still, the experience of *we*, especially when magnified by communal affirmation, not only provides dependability, sharing, and other practical and emotional advantages but can also be a great personal pleasure, common to the satisfaction of innate needs. Such belonging sparks life, much as one log burning in the fireplace plays off the others, which, isolated, would burn out.

The union of you and me is, therefore, more than personal strategy; it is a force of nature. This relationship with otherness happens inescapably through the operation of contact's major functions. To see, for example, is a natural absorption of "otherness"—a person, a tree, or a shopping mall. To hear, to touch, to talk, to smell, to taste, to imagine—each of these merges us with otherness. We converse with each other, we play games with each other, we paint the walls of our houses, and we send flowers to a friend. Moreover, the raw meetings are emotionally enlarged into love, enthusiasm, dismay, fear, and wonderment. In sum, all of our relationships and the accompanying feelings go on every day, and they are the stuff of which belonging is made; they keep us joined with the world we live in, from each moment to the next.

The Life Focus Community joins in this quest by creating an ethos and procedures that heighten the sense of congregation. This union of people is felt through the convergence of attention on commonly important themes, fleshed out by personal stories. The Life Focus Community group, in evoking the often dramatic details of members' lives, creates a strong personal registration that is often absent in many people's lives.

The mutuality of this experience gives people a common ground that *belonging* requires. While this feeling jeopardizes one's sense of individuality, it is reassuring to discover that a belonging formed of respect for individual experience has a special freedom. When John and Jane tell each other about key incidents that have helped define their lives, they do become joined, but they are still John and Jane.

People are commonly aware of making choices about who or what they will join. However, the possibly terrifying reality is that they have *no choice about joining itself.* That is a generic fate, where, at the point of contact with the "other," there is an ever-present measure of indivisibility. The saving grace is that, insistent though the experience of contact is, each moment or each day or each year has only a fleeting effect on a flexible continuity, leaving much freedom for whatever may happen next. Therefore, in spite of the insistent biology of connection, each person retains his or her own shaping powers; he or she creates his or her own proportional allegiance and future experience. Each person never *becomes* fixed into the other. Whatever connection any moment of contact creates, the moment is enveloped in an undefined flow of life. While joined momentarily with the other, each person nevertheless may develop his or her own views about child discipline, the attractions of travel, choice of music, sexual preference, or loyalty to the family.

The creation of contact is most clearly transformed into belonging when a group connectedness is involved. A person's family, for example, is an obvious source of belonging, one that is easily identifiable as an object of my thoughts, feelings, and intentions. That is also true of my neighborhood, book club, religion, or corporation. When I meet such an aggregate otherness only casually, as in walking through an unfamiliar neighborhood, the sense of belonging is absent. When, however, I dedicate myself to my religion, when I sign a ten-year contract as a corporate executive, or when I attend a book club for fifteen years of absorbing discussions, the feeling of belonging is vivid. This reverberation between individuality and indivisibility is pivotal in the intrapsychic machinery that harmonizes person and otherness. It calls for incorporating vast neurological interconnections and the countless events through which people live. For some this process toward belonging comes with the diminution of individuality; such people sacrifice their own needs to guard against the pain of disapproval. For many, however, the feeling of belonging is among life's dearest sources of both security and stimulation. The Life Focus Community group is an attempt to create such a communal "other," trying to form an exceptional humanity—one that attracts the feeling of belonging but looks beyond itself toward a universe that is a relational marvel of people reverberating with each other.

Figure/Ground Relationship

This move beyond the person-to-person union brings us to the second innate basis for belonging: the figure/ground relationship. This concept tells us that nothing can be experienced by itself. I can't see a tree, period. If I see a tree, it is on a lawn or in a park. The tree or the lawn is a simple background for the tree: where it *belongs*. However, if we delve more deeply, the background could be grander than is immediately apparent. I may see the tree in the context of all the things I already know about other trees. Or I may remember my life as a lumberjack. I might even explore the origins of life itself. That tree "belongs" in all of that contextual complexity.

The implication for people is clear: we are all embedded in the world in which we live. That is inescapable. However, I may or may not *know* I belong or *feel* like I belong or *want* to belong in any particular host entity. I may enjoy it or not, participate actively or not. I may be confident about belonging. I may sacrifice much to belong or make little sacrifice. I may be invited to belong, or I may be rejected. How this dynamic plays out is complex, but it is always a reverberation between the experience of the individual and the nature of the composite host.

Psychotherapy has flourished in individuality-oriented countries and has itself commonly accentuated the importance of the individual. Yet, it has always recognized the indivisibility of the person from the environment in which he or she is enveloped. The same is true of even the iconic messenger of individuality, Adam Smith. What he said was that the aggregate of individual activity, exercised without regard for communal interest, would best serve the needs of the community. The individual, acting spontaneously in his or her own interests, would, in almost mystical purposiveness, be guided, as Smith famously said, "by an invisible hand to promote an end which was no part of his intention. Nor is it always the worse for society that it was no part of it. By pursuing his own interest he frequently promotes that of the society more effectually than when he really intends to promote it" (Smith 1776).

Surprisingly holistic in seeing the individual's communal destiny, Smith's theory about the integrative momentum of individual experience suggests that nature has a built-in coalescence between individual need and the common good. That is, even this quintessential protagonist of individuality recognized the community as a vital collaborator, the host whose benefactor is the mysterious constituency of its individuals living together. This means that, without intending to help the community, individuals will, like metal filings around a magnet, come together to the mutual benefit of all. Without directly taking the community into account, Smith believed that nature would see to it that the well-being of individuals was basically the best assurance of the well-being of the community.

Of course, the practical problem is this: though there is obvious merit to the idea of an innate impulse to merge individual interests, there is also, equally obviously, much interference to the merger. The perverse truth is that it is just as natural for things to fly apart as for them to hold together or to coalesce only around certain dominant agents of communal power. Some years ago the premier of China, Wen Jiabao, in an interview with Charlie Rose, applauded Adam Smith's "invisible hand," which he has imported into an otherwise Communist scenario. Wen said it was important to have all hands functioning well for optimal results, and he pointed to China's efforts to better accommodate the needs of the huge numbers of people who were otherwise not contributing to the communal well-being. He concluded that the "invisible hand" must be coordinated with the "visible hand." For him the individual, the community, and their skills were to be interwoven in their purposes and their results.

The psychologist Michael J. Mahoney contributed to the measured psychological corrective of its accent on individuality when he pointed out that, as late as the eighteenth century, French thinkers were warning that individualism would block progress, drawing people away from public life and eroding the social order (Mahoney 1991). This view contrasts with the common American reverence for individuality that was built early into the political and social system, and that is represented by the writings of Emerson, Thoreau, and Whitman. Each of these writers' testaments to individuality resonated powerfully with the American psyche. A more recent contrast to this perspective is that of Wallace Stegner, a literary witness of the American experience. He ruefully recognized the losses created by these freedoms and lamented the absence of belonging. He said,

> Not only is the American home a launching pad, as Margaret Mead said; the American community, especially in the West, is an overnight

camp. American individualism, much celebrated and cherished, has developed without its essential corrective, which is *belonging* [emphasis mine]. Freedom, when found, can turn out to be airless and unsustaining. Especially in the West, what we have instead of place is space. Place is more than half memory, shared memory. Rarely do Westerners stay long enough at one stop to share much of anything. (Stegner 1993)

Ironically, this individuality has not always created the intended freedom in a society where hero worship often fills the blank spaces of identity. Stegner goes on to portray the American West's homage to individuality as a mythic enlargement, evident in the common imitation of society's idols. He says, "Plenty of authentic ranch hands have read pulp Westerns in the shade of the bunkhouse and got up walking, talking, and thinking like Buck Duane or Hopalong Cassidy" (Stegner 1993). Alas, Stegner's view of the American West is no longer geographically bounded, and it is hard nowadays to live a single day without hearing reports of the diminishing sense of belonging, or of the reduced accessibility of such honored hosts as families and neighborhoods. There have been many observers of the disconnections between our government and various classes of the population, but perhaps it is enough to note here that the well-being of constituent people often depends on the will of existing authority, the economic circumstances, the limits of geographical conditions, or the pressures of geopolitical strife. Nowadays, and perhaps always, the agonies of isolated individuality and failure to belong fruitfully in one's milieu are insinuating themselves into the lives of alarming numbers of people (Schlesinger 1992).

Let us look, for example, at Robert Kennedy's statement of a social need, a statement remarkable for an active political figure: "Even if we act to erase material poverty, there is another greater task. It is to confront the poverty of satisfaction . . . that afflicts us all" (Sandel 2010). Kennedy goes on to say,

> Our Gross National Product now is over 800 billion dollars a year. . . . But that Gross National Product counts air pollution and cigarette advertising and ambulances to clear our highways of carnage. It counts special locks for our doors and the jails for the people who break them. It counts the destruction of the redwood and the loss of our natural wonder in chaotic sprawl. It counts napalm and counts nuclear warheads and armored cars for the police to fight the riots in our cities. It counts . . . the television programs that glorify violence in order to sell toys to our children.

> Yet the Gross National Product does not allow for the health of our children, the quality of their education or the joy of their play. It does not include the beauty of our poetry or the strength of our marriages, the intelligence of our public debate or the integrity of our public officials. It measures neither our wit nor our courage, neither our wisdom nor our learning, neither our compassion nor our devotion to our country. It measures everything, in short, except that which makes life worthwhile. And it can tell us everything about America except why we are proud to be Americans. (Sandel 2010)

This concern with being proud to be an American may seem like political sentimentality. However, it resides within a fundamental human need for a hospitable context, one that offers a benevolent home base. While all of Kennedy's concerns are focused on the executive role of the government, his observations also point to the psychological struggle between practical public priorities and the relational concerns about living well with each other. While the answers are not clear, the skewing of priority for individuality or community is a barrier to the required union of the two.

The Psychological Response

The lesson learned long ago by psychologists about the disabling effect of conventionality caught on too compellingly, as many people became excessively vigilant about losing themselves. Some samples of this vigilance are the responses received by Dr. Caroline Paltin, a psychologist, when she was forming a Life Focus Community group (personal communication 2014). Though there were many heartily welcoming responses to her announcement, here are a few that reflect the threat to individuality. One person said, "I don't like the idea of a group, and especially an ongoing group, because my experience in church or organizations is that the organization takes control and the individuals are lost. Dissent is a crime. It becomes all about group think."

Another one said, "I like my individuality. I've never really enjoyed watered-down group activity. I always leave feeling glad to be able to think my own thoughts."

A third person said, "I don't like the feeling of losing myself in a crowd of other people's ideas. I like to think my own thoughts."

In contradistinction, when the group of fifty people actually met, the tone of the group's meeting was represented in such words as these:

> It achieved what I am hoping for: moments of sadness and laughter, thoughtfulness, and a deeper connection with a community of people

who are also searching for connection, as well as a moment to ... just be alive and be reflective in a different way from any other way.... I'm so motivated to feel a part of a positive community, both to meet my own needs for connection and support, and also just as a reminder that there are so many good and caring people and authentic people in this world and I am not alone in that.

Of course, none of these spokespeople has been elected as a representative, and I am not quoting them as scientific evidence. Rather, they are illustrative of the dangers of stereotype and can remind us to examine individuality and community in a more-than-dichotomous dimension. The Life Focus Community group is a cheering section for individuality, a fact that rarely threatens its communal function. There is no incompatibility, for example, between everybody in the group simultaneously examining their ambitions and the unique role that ambition plays in each person's life. The people who are too vigilant about their individuality look past the many communal influences that provide support for individual enterprise. There is surely a societal support for individuality in business through its loan guarantees, and for individual safety in society's police force, in its encouragement of ingenuity, and in its better educational systems. Contrastingly, there are, of course, also so many examples of social pressures to conform about sexual choice, religious beliefs, and occupational priorities. The difference between society's affirmation of belonging and its pressures to conform is murky, but the assumption of its negative role must be balanced by the recognition that the communal receptacle is the container for individuality. Whatever failures the community creates are failures of a necessary integration, not a sign of incompatibility. Every community must balance its existence as a communal entity with its service as a support for its individual constituents.

The Life Focus Community group contributes to the union of individuality and belonging through the high focus and personal drama induced by its exercises. These are offered in a setting where everyone is telling his or her individual story while addressing common themes. Here are three examples of the kind of interpersonal exercises that would accentuate the individuality of belonging:

1. People in three-person subgroups are asked to tell each other about the first time they consciously recognized themselves as members of a group: perhaps their first days in school, perhaps a team they played on, perhaps a group dance performance, perhaps a gathering of family, perhaps when they became members of a church. They are

to tell each other whether they would have been able to think of this or articulate this group feeling at the time the experience happened. Did they get any feeling of joint existence with these other people, of coordination with them? Did they want to repeat this group membership, or did they look forward to it? Did they feel any sense of this communal aspect when they were away from the community, as when they were reading, playing, daydreaming, or doing their chores?
2. Members tell each other whether they have had an effect on anyone in their community so that they that might have modified that person's view of himself or herself. Then they tell about how someone from the community has affected their own sense of self. Furthermore, does it make any difference to be telling this to each other, as contrasted with the memory remaining in their private awareness?
3. Finally, members tell each other about any experience they have had with changing the sense of their own identity. Are there points at which they became newly aware of being intelligent or being conversationally attractive or finding an occupational direction they may not have expected? Wherever these changes happened, did the new view arise from a new feeling of belonging, or did it affect their feelings of belonging?

The role of such communal exercises is remindful of the role of prayer in the religious format. Prayer is a special brand of communication, one that imagines God as a common listener whose attention is available to the entire community. While this relationship is of one person expressing himself or herself, others join this person in common activity, a unifying force for all those who pray. So also the Life Focus Community group exercise places people into a position of common purpose, a shared experience that accents the togetherness that is the essence of belonging. Furthermore, the function of religion includes its powers to bind people together in a common belief system, one that helps to understand life's meanings, practices, and purposes. Psychotherapists have shunned this role for a complex set of reasons, high among which is an implied diminishment of individuality. In the exercises of the Life Focus Community group, however, the *individual* story lines of its participants would be pivotal. These story lines, told in community, rather than diluting individuality, would give it a home, and would highlight the merger of communal and individual experience.

14

A Social Trust

This final chapter is a summation statement about the rightful place of psychotherapy and its social offspring, the Life Focus Community group. I have already pointed to religion as a dominant precedent for psychotherapy in society's historical progression. (See chapters 9 and 10.) For many this is a troublesome connection. They identify religion with supernatural guidance and its incontrovertible standards for rightful living. These are often associated with illusion, bigotry, authoritarianism, gullibility, and a distorted view of the needs that drive people's lives (Dawkins 2006). Yet, if we look beyond specific objections to religion's points of view, we see a large realm of social influence from which psychotherapy may take some important lessons. Chief among these lessons is religion's recognition of the vital, lifelong public need for personal enlightenment and guidance in how people may best live their lives, both independently and jointly.

Psychotherapy has already achieved a large measure of its own social influence. Nevertheless, much of the widespread effect is taken for granted. (See chapters 1 and 4.) Many psychological ideas are so well-known that they testify to a general awakening to the workings of the mind. Included among these ideas are sibling rivalry, the unconscious, post-traumatic stress, child abuse, and compulsive behavior. Nowadays, when a friend or a family member tells a person that he or she should "talk to someone," the "someone" is understood to provide therapeutic guidance. The indirect use of "someone" is both a general recognition of the need for guidance and a wish to soften the implication that there is something damningly "wrong." It is also commonplace for people to speak openly about the influence of others in their lives: a mentoring uncle, an eye-opening teacher, a civic hero. They tell each other about their conflicts, their celebrations, their ambitions, their disappointments, and their reluctance to see their mothers. Each of these is part of a large realm of people who quietly affirm the broad scope of psychology's populist presence.

However, the silent momentum of this century-old expansion appears in the wake of the continuingly dominant role of religion, whose hold on the cultural mind remains unarguably huge. In spite of a gnawing image that religion spoils the joy of living and sponsors a number of archaic beliefs, the influence of religion continues to be strong. A major voice in exploring the evolution of religion is the highly regarded neuroscientist Scott Atran. In his exceptional neuroscientific explorations, he observes that there is a halo around religion's image (Atran 2002). He maintains that science and secular ideology, within which I include psychotherapy and its offspring, the Life Focus Community group, are poor competitors with religious belief in attracting the *trust* of the population.

That is a pivotal observation and will be my center point now as I examine the role of trust in the expansion of public interest in psychotherapy's offerings. Atran's observation is a call to examine the role of trust in the future of psychotherapy. He believes that supernaturalism is not extinguishable and, further, that it is a major source of this trust. For him the belief in God helps people to transcend the ordinary struggles for supremacy of one idea or another, and provides assurance against the competition of these ideas and cultural behaviors. When God speaks the message is both infinite and universal. Atran says, "People apparently infer that explicit professions of faith carry the implicit message that trustworthiness matters—in the unblinking and ever watchful eyes of God—and commitments will be met even at great cost and even when there is no hope of reward."

There is good reason to recognize the enduring powers of the belief in an everlasting supernatural guidance. There are, indeed, some innate characteristics of people that are well-served by a belief in the supernatural. (See chapter 10.) In such a projected permanence, the supernatural will continue to exercise its influence on the society. However, the perpetuity of religion's existence is not the question I am addressing. What is more pertinent is to recognize that religion is not the only game in town. (See chapters 9 and 10.)

Psychotherapy's palette of ideas represents an alternative system of orientation and guidance, a system more explicitly awakened to the *integration* of diverse human experiences than to a universalist credo. Rather than to advocate sameness of behavior, psychotherapy sees the successful merger of anyone's individuated personal circumstance with communally prescribed priorities as a hallmark of an inclusive mind. Such recognition of compatibility of the idiomatic and the universal is so fundamental to a beckoning society that a successful management of the two merits a high level of social trust.

It must be said that belief in the supernatural will surely exist in the Life Focus Community groups. After all, secularity notwithstanding, it is humanly compelling, perhaps irresistible, for people to want to understand a universe through speculations and beliefs that rise beyond the missing facts. As I have already said (see chapter 10), people have a natural extrapolative function that strives to tease out beliefs about an invisible world or about the ultimate nature of existence. That is common, even among those who are dedicated to the perspectives of psychotherapy. Many people in the Life Focus Community groups will have such spiritual interests, and these represent their legitimate need. Indeed, this reach into the seemingly unknowable is often quite exciting and illuminating. However, it is not standard dogma. It is only one part of human interest that does not replace that broader landscape of more directly observed aspects of the lives of its members and of society itself.

Psychotherapy's prospects for establishing a social trust in its explorations, while hospitable to the supernatural beliefs of some of its members, must be achieved in its own thematic and procedural vehicles. To expand the communal impact of this distinctive style and repertoire, I suggest that such trust, so vital to its social application, can be expanded by the satisfaction of a triad of conditions. The triad is composed of *conceptualization, continuity, and community*. I believe psychotherapy has historically made prodigious contributions to the *conceptualization* of the human existence but has fallen short on the other components of this triad: *continuity* and *community*. Let's make an overview.

Conceptualization

When I speak of conceptualization, I am referring to the large body of perspectives and procedures that affect the way people live their lives. I have already enunciated ten illustrative themes that serve as a sample of these conceptualizations, but there are many more themes that flesh out the content of our lives. (See chapter 7.) In the large picture much of psychotherapy's accumulation of concepts has been disseminated in writings, teachings, and clinical practice that were pointed to the professional in the mental health fields, not the public. However, there is also much of its conceptualization that has crossed over into the population at large. Newspapers, magazines, movies, and widespread conversational exchanges have contributed psychological ideas that have expanded the cultural interest in understanding the nature of our lives.

Still, these conceptualizations have not been so widely received as the poetically resonant and age-old homilies of religion's Beatitudes, its Ten Commandments, its Psalms, its 613 mitzvot, its heroes, or its political struggles. Psychotherapy's communication style has been to enter reservedly into the realm of pithy communication, the kind that lights up people's minds. When it has exceeded these cautions, the results have often been mixed, getting across simple messages but losing proportionality and accuracy. For example, gestalt therapy's widely influential advisory to live our lives in the "here and now" caught the attention of the populace, reminding us that the moment-to-moment experience should be recovered from the befuddling complexities of past and present, there and then. While the aphoristic here and now represented a necessary emphasis on immediacy, the larger theoretical gestalt picture included the entire background of anyone's immediate existence. It is this coordination of immediacy and context that is crucial for good living.

Another popularly recognized observation was created during the heyday of transactional analysis, which coined the concept of "I'm OK, you're OK." This represented an affirmation of the acceptability of people as they are. This was an important message, but it left out obvious exceptions, where people were clearly not at all OK (Berne 1964).

Another more recent example is that of the team of Harville Hendrix and Helen Hunt. In advising marital couples, they make three lively points: (1) conflict is growth trying to happen; (2) it's not him, it's you; and (3) a laugh a day keeps the divorce lawyer away. Those are sharp guides, which bring clarity to many people, but of course the contradictions are also there. Conflicts don't only lead to growth, they also may squash it. It may not be as much you as it is him. A laugh a day may not keep the lawyer away, and it may cause you to ignore what should be faced. Hendrix and Hunt, of course, elaborate these maxims with detailed illustration, and their short and easily assimilated aphorisms have turned out to be a safe stimulant for public understanding. The beauty of successful slogans is that, while they are all plagued with contradiction, they may hit the social communication mark by getting the intended message across while the contradictions remain inactive in the background. That is what is often felt about the beatitude that tells us that the meek shall inherit the earth. It gets across the equality of people, whatever their social status, but it may not be seen as an advocacy for meekness. What the successful slogan will do is provide a general perspective that sweeps into the public mind as a rallying point around which people may organize their lives.

Still, though psychotherapists have not generally encapsulated their ideas in commonly understood terms, the material for wise prescription has been there since the beginning. Some of the observations contributed by major theoretical contributors have expressed perspectives quite comparable to the homilies of religion, providing distinct social potential, if reframed only slightly. For example, Freud said, "We are so made, that we can only derive intense enjoyment from a contrast and only very little from a state of things." He is implying that we should pay attention to life as it is rather than to compare ours with other people. Pavlov said, "Don't become a mere recorder of facts, but try to penetrate the mystery of their origin." This tells us not to narrow ourselves with simple facts but to welcome mystery. Erik Erikson said, "There is in every child at every stage a new miracle of vigorous unfolding." He is telling us to recognize the exceptional flow of life, one miracle after another. William James said, "The greatest discovery of my generation is that human beings can alter their lives by altering their attitudes of mind." This is a reminder that if we think anew and feel anew, we invite the new. These were all wise observations that were read by many, especially in the professional ranks, but they were stated for rational rather than inspirational purpose. Though people did not leave whistling the tunes, the music is there. While these psychological assertions don't ring bells, they do reveal key aspects of the human condition, parallel to the illuminations provided by religious maxims.

Psychotherapy has created its own pathways to public understanding, and its future expansions will come in its own forms. As I have said, much of this has already happened and will continue to unfold as psychotherapy attends more pointedly beyond its clinical purpose by addressing such quintessentially common issues as conflict, personal desires, relationship, imagination, and loyalty. The Life Focus Community groups personalize these messages by evoking individualized stories about basic themes of living, aiming the arrow of implication at the actual lives people live. With sharply focused realization, therapy's conceptual abstractions are boiled down to detailed concerns, such as mercy, mourning, brutality, love, empathy, and all the rest of the abundant and individualized subject matter of psychology (Miller 1995; Jacobs and Hecman 2009; Polster 1987). Furthermore, while such merger of individuality with commonly important themes is in itself a step in the populist direction, the explorations are also fertile ground for the appearance of colorful messages that may ring bells of easy recognition.

While this summary recognition of psychotherapy conceptualizations is no more than a hint of their range, I believe it is enough to illustrate a conceptual reach that is very much up to what Atran says is religion's exclusive domain: the "moral and existential dilemmas." However, while offering its extraordinary conceptual contributions to the orientation and guidance of people in their human dilemmas, psychotherapy has fallen short on providing *continuity and community*, each of which is assured in most religious experience and is pivotal for public trust.

Continuity

Psychotherapy's relationship to continuity was bounded by its concept of "terminated therapy" and by its limited mission to solve acute problems. It is true that during the flush of long-term therapy, the process often lasted a few years. However, even then, people had one foot out of the door, because the sign of a successful therapy was that it would become finished. Nowadays even the original long-term therapy has been dramatically reduced by insurance-oriented time limits. (See also chapter 3.) The Life Focus Community group changes that time limit by its indefinite extension of the group's duration, as group members may potentially meet for a lifetime. This expansion makes sense, given a change in purpose from solving specific problems to the more general and everlasting need for orientation and guidance. Many groups nowadays already meet for indefinite periods of time, including the generic therapy groups, religion's relational groups, seniors' groups, men's and women's groups, self-help groups, meditation groups, and compassion groups.

Two life focus groups that I lead have been meeting for twenty-five years, though their membership has changed during those years. Not surprisingly, when the people speak about the trust they experience, it is based not only on the content of the meetings but also on the enduring nature of both the setting and the relationships. The longer people are together, the more chances they have to show their trustworthiness. Furthermore, they are more likely to be there when needed in the future. It simply takes time for ideas, empathy, and familiarity to get full registration.

While the trust in these groups increases with continuity, one must also ask whether this increased level of trust creates a risk of dependency. Therapy, after all, has commonly been seen only as a way station to living well. The capability to be independent has been measured by freedom from continued guidance. Indeed, it is true that dependency is a risk that faces the trusting person. However, packaging of such potentially contradictory characteristics as trust and dependency is common, perhaps inevitable. For example, if people are forthright, they may also become insensitive. If people are kind, they may also be gullible. If they are inventive, they may also be chaotic. Plainly, there is a natural downside to any desirable characteristic, which is to say that anything that can be done can be overdone.

Differentiating between trust and dependency can therefore only be achieved through individual circumstance. In an enduring Life Focus Community group, this differentiation could be explored, just as many other life themes are. The group design circumscribes a vigilant attention to the role of any theme in any member's life. Surely, it would be absurd to exclude a continuity of life exploration because it encourages trust. This would be a caricature of shortsighted interference with life's inevitable complexities, where the good and the bad often come intertwined. Given the benevolent effects of trust, it is better to deal with the potential errors in trusting than to wipe out the continuity that fosters it. It is a good bet that continuity is an important basis of trust and that this trust can help create further favorable experience and further trust.

Community

The *communal* option for psychotherapy has been blunted by psychotherapy's historical emphasis on privacy. Religion, especially the western religions, have shown the way to communal viability though the creation of the congregation, large or small, a fundamental vehicle for the gathering of people. (See chapter 8.) Each congregation has a life of its own, and functions beyond the attendance of any specific members. The housing for the congregation is usually a familiar edifice, with which the practices of the group are identified. Indeed, when one walks into a church or a synagogue or a mosque, one often enters a communal sanctuary, and is invited by its exemplary design to leave the ordinary stream of life and reach out for the eternal and mysterious. Sometimes the housing serves as a vehicle of glorification, symbolized by a monumental architecture that helps to enlarge people's experiences and gives them a head start in communal dedication and inspiration. However, this communal ethos of dedication and inspiration is also felt in the greater intimacy of small-scale settings. In either case the communal sensibility is grounded in a combination of people joining together with each other to face God, a strong presence that converges the minds of the congregants. Though God is a guiding force, the people gathered together are much aware of their union with others. This communal awareness is further amplified with music, historically important stories, and a universal affirmation of personal acceptability.

The Life Focus Community groups contrast the centrality of a vertical relationship to God with horizontal conversational engagements, where people talk to each other about key aspects of their lives. The design draws everybody's attention to targeted themes, and the simultaneity of responses amplifies individual personal awareness. Furthermore, the largeness of the community fosters microcosmic implications that what happens in the group is a model of the larger society, lighting up not only individual experiences but life itself. Music and its companions—visual and verbal art forms—add entertainment value for the community, and they also arouse a united attention to such broad experiences as beauty, peace, sensuality, and deep caring.

Nowadays the communal exploration of such intimate experiences is no longer so widely prohibited by the society's privacy orientation. Long ago, in 1953, one of the stunning novelties of my first attendance at a gestalt therapy workshop was the experience of people becoming engaged in personal revelation in front of the entire training group. Subsequently, over many years of conducting therapy sessions in front of large conferences, many of the people I have worked with have been more inspired than inhibited by the presence of a benign and lively audience. Daniel Siegel's observations are suggestive of a neurological enhancement of the communal experience. He says that brain studies show a "re-entry process," a reciprocal impact that any two people's brains have on each other. He says that this fosters a feeling of connection where "the self is both fully present and lost within the flow of a vibrant, unpredictable, and yet reliable dyadic connection" (Siegel 1999). The exploratory atmosphere of the Life Focus Community group is designed to keep such interpersonal reciprocation open. The resulting resonance encourages a high level of trust when these engagements are safely experienced and when they help to connect us to each other's lives. The engagement also provides the widely overlooked benefits of *witnessing*, which fosters the appreciation of others and heightens the value of their experiences.

Since people are naturally interwoven with each other, they cannot cut out their communal existence. Nevertheless, psychotherapy's emphasis has always been on how the individual would manage this complexity. In contrast, religion has over the centuries been highly focused on the generality of human need. It has offered a morality, a communal togetherness, an intimate relationship with an ubiquitous otherness, a leadership for the masses of people in how to live one's life and a story to live by. In recognition of this universality, Scott Atran says,

> Religion is here to stay. With it comes trust in deities good and bad, songs of fellowship, and drums of war, promises to allay our worst fears and achieve our most fervent hopes, and heartfelt communion in costly homage to the absurd. . . . No other seems to compete for very long. And so spirituality looms as humankind's provisional evolutionary destiny. (2002)

It is within this enlarged and lyrical landscape that a contemporary public momentum can move psychotherapy beyond the clinical remediation of what has gone wrong in individual lives. Throughout this book the purpose has been to present a contemporary idiom that characterizes the functions and relationships that are inherent to the creation of trust within the Life Focus Community groups. People must also be directed to the commonalities and wonders of what actually happens in their lives, which are as vital as what has gone wrong in their lives. Thus, the mission becomes less a matter of correcting people than orienting and guiding them in facing the inevitable challenges of everyday living. This trust has two faces offering interwoven standards: one is a symbolic trust, and the other is a practical trust.

From the symbolic position trust is grounded in a powerful belief system, which is sometimes mistily defined. Trust is attained not only because of benefits but by dedication to a general belief system. A symbolic trust about family, for example, may override the actual facts about whether the family's behavior is desirable or not. For many people the family symbolizes a special mindset for intimacy, and this is not up for continued assessment. Family is family, and to know it allows its desirability to survive beyond specific conflict or disappointment or personal violation. For many people this is also the case—multiplied exponentially—with the concept of God, in whom symbolic trust is supreme.

Whether psychotherapy can induce a symbolic trust that measures up to the symbolic trust of religion is not the primary question to ask. We see that people historically have been masters of the symbol. They create symbols quite generously, giving abstract importance to political parties, famous corporations, and heroic persons, just as they create trust in such emotional attachments as mother or flag. So it is within simple expectation that a movement such as the life focus movement may develop symbolic powers of its own, symbols associated with practical trust of receiving enlightening perspective, nourishing procedures, and vitality of relationship. However, Atran says about the supernatural that "no other mode of thought and behavior deals routinely and comprehensively with the moral and existential dilemmas that panhuman emotions and cognitions force upon human awareness."

Although Atran recognizes the unique trustworthiness of the supernatural, many people may not actually need such a supreme level of trust. They experience considerable trust along many streams of living, even though the trust may incorporate a measure of uncertainty. They live well with a supportable confidence: in their spouses, their financial managers, their doctors. This human scale trust has, indeed, been experienced in psychotherapy circles, where people have been receiving realistic benefits for over one hundred years (Cambell et al. 2013; Lebow 2007).

In fact, the everlasting trust accorded to the supernatural influence invites a blurring of human complexity. For example, in the Judeo-Christian religions, one of God's commandments is an instruction to "honor thy father and thy mother." This has considerable social merit, but there are many circumstances where the honor is unmerited. The unruly reality is that certain fathers and mothers are brutal or otherwise alien to the needs of their children. Religion softens the mandate by offering the wisdom of clerical leadership or the humanity of a congregation's supportive understanding or the availability of forgiveness, all of which serve as counterpoints to the universal hallowing. It must be recognized, therefore, that, while the belief in God creates trust, it does not have a monopoly on it. Even within the religious community itself, we see many reasons beyond the supernatural that account for trust.

From the practical position, the trust in religion is based not only on God's guidance but on actual benefits to its members. Can religious believers trust that the community and its authorities will accept them if they have deviated from the norm? Can members of the community trust the wisdom of the lessons taught? Can they trust religious leaders to be wise and unbiased in their relationships with members of the congregation? Are promises kept? Does the religious community take care of its needy people? From such practical considerations it is everybody's business to assess trustworthiness based on the benefits provided. We find the answer in our actual experiences.

In conclusion, my belief is that society's trust in psychotherapy can measure up to the trust religion enjoys. We may see that the expansion of continuity and community from psychotherapy's already potent understandings and procedures would raise the level of this societal trust. What I have tried to show is that there is now ample precedence for this to happen, for trust and connection to grow and to thrive among the members of Life Focus Community groups and the movement within which they are embedded. These perspectives and activities are on the edge of a new ethos. They can transform what has been a privately secular experience, and can kindle a new level of public awareness and accessibility. The guiding momentum is for the growth of a leadership and infrastructure in the life focus milieu that would be dependably available on a lifelong basis.

Bibliography

African Methodist Episcopal Church. 2004. "Connectional Lay Organization Lay Study Guide Supplement." Retrieved Online.
Alda, Alan. 2006. Quoted in Taylor Willingham "Listening is Key to Acting" http://texasforums.wordpress.com/author/texas forums.
Alexander, Ronald. 2008. *Wise Mind, Open Mind*. Oakland, CA: New Harbinger.
Amini, Fari, Thomas Lewis, and Richard Lannon. 2000. *A General Theory of Love*. New York: Vintage Books.
Atran, Scott. 2002. *In Gods We Trust*. New York: Oxford University Press.
Back, Kurt. 1972. *Beyond Words: The Story of Sensitivity Training and the Encounter Movement*. New York: Russell Sage Foundation.
Berne, Eric. 1964. *The Games People Play: The Psychology of Human Relationships*. New York: Ballantine Books.
Bessier, Arnold. 1970. "The Paradoxical Theory of Change." In *Gestalt Therapy Now*, edited by Irma Shepherd and Joen Fagan. Palo Alto, CA: Science and Behavior Books.
Blake, William. 1946. "The Laughing Song." In *The Portable Blake*. New York: Viking.
Borges, Jorge Luis. 1963. "The Other Tiger." Austin, TX: University of Texas Press.
Boring, E. G. 1950. *A History of Experimental Psychology*. Englewood Cliffs, NJ: Prentice-Hall.
Buber, Martin. 1952. *Eclipse of God*. Trenton: New Jersey: Humanities Press.
Cambell, Linda F., John Narcross, Melba Vasquez, and Nadine Kaslow. 2013. "Recognition of Psychotherapy Effectiveness: The APA Resolution." *Psychotherapy* 50, no. 1: 98–101.
Conheim, Catherine. 2005. *Henry's World*. Traverse City, MI: Breakthrough Press.
Csikszentmihalyi, Mihaly. 1991. *Flow: The Psychology of Optimal Experience*. New York: HarperCollins.
Dawkins, Richard. 2006. *The God Delusion*. New York: Bantam Books.
———. 2009. *The Greatest Show on Earth*. New York: Free Press.
Dennet, Daniel. 2007. "Thank Goodness." In *Philosophers without Gods*, edited by Louise Antony. Oxford and New York: Oxford University Press.
Dewey, John. 2000. "A Whisper of Salvation." *American Psychologist*, 55, no. 9: 1022–1024.

Donahue, Bill. 1996. *The Willow Creek Guide to Life Changing Small Groups.* Grand Rapids: Zondervan Publishing.
Donald, Ben. 2009. "A Social (Networking) Phenomenon." *Academic Perspective.* http://www.academicperspective.com/category/topics/social-issues/
Eliot, T. S. 2014. *Four Quartets.* New York: Houghton Mifflin Harcourt.
Estrup, Liv. 2010. *Flying without Wings: Life with Arnold Bessier.* Film available through LivEstrup.com.
Freud, Sigmund. 1914. *Psychopathology of Everyday Life.* New York: MacMillan Company.
———. 1957. *Collected Papers*, vol. 1. London: Hogarth Press.
———. 1985. *The Origins of Religion: Totem & Taboo/Moses & Monotheism.* Oxford: Penguin Books.
Fromm, Erich. 1941. *Escape from Freedom.* New York: Farrar & Rinehart.
Galloway, Steven. 2008. *The Cellist of Sarajevo.* New York: Penguin Books.
Gastil, John. 2010. *The Group in Society.* Los Angeles: Sage.
Goldstein, Rebecca. 2009. *36 Arguments for the Existence of God.* New York: Vintage Books.
Hadaway, Kirk, and Penny Marler. 2005. "How Many Americans Attend Worship Each Week?" *Journal for the Scientific Study of Religion* 4, no. 3: 698–712.
Hendrix, Harville, and Helen Hunt. 2013. *Making Marriage Simple.* Nevada City: Harmony Books.
Hunter, James Davison. 2000. *The Death of Character.* New York: Basic Books.
Jacobs, Lynne, and Rich Hycner. 2009. *Relational Approaches in Gestalt Therapy.* New York: Taylor & Francis Group.
Johnson, Deborah Liv. 1995. "Tanzania." *Across the White Plains.* Compact Disc: Mojave Sun Records.
Kabat-Zinn, Jon. 2004. *Wherever You Go, There You Are.* New York: Hyperion.
Kingsolver, Barbara. 2012. *Flight Behavior.* New York: HarperCollins.
Lagnado, Lucette. 2008. *The Man in the White Sharkskin Suit.* New York: Harper Perennial.
Lebow, Jay. 2007. "A Look at Evidence: Top Ten Research Findings of the Last 25 Years." *Psychotherapy Networker.* https://www.psychotherapynetworker.org/magazine/recentissues/2007-marapr/item/224-a-look-at-the-evidence
Lee, Amy. 2011. "FACT CHECK: Is Facebook Really Losing Users?" *Huffington Post,* May 30, 2011
Luhrmann, T. M. 2014. "When God Talks Back: Understanding the American Evangelical Relationship with God." *New York Times,* April 27, 2012.
Lukensmeyer, Carolyn. 2007. "Large-Scale Citizen Engagement and the Rebuilding of New Orleans: A Case Study." *National Civic Review* 96, no. 3: 3–15.
———. 2013. "Bringing Citizen Voices to the Table." *A Guide for Public Managers.* San Francisco: Jossey-Bass.
Mack, Mike. 1992. "Internet. Restoring the Relational Church-part 1." In *A World Lit Only by Fire.* New York: Brown Little.
Mahoney, Michael J. 1991. *Human Change Processes.* New York: Basic Books.

Marquand, John. 2004. "Quotes from Marquand." In *The Late George Apley*, 217. New York: Back Bay Books.
Merkin, Daphne. 2010. "My Life in Therapy." *New York Times Magazine*, August 4, 2010.
Miller, Michael V. 1995. *Intimate Terrorism: The Deterioration of Love*. New York: W. W. Norton & Co.
Mowrer, O. H. 1964. *The New Group Therapy*. Princeton, NJ: Van Nostrand.
Nabokov, Vladimir. 2009. "But Always Meeting Ourselves." Cited by Colum McCann. *New York Times*, A19, June 6, 2009.
Newberg, Andrew, and Mark Waldman. 2009. *How God Changes Your Brain: Breakthrough Findings from a Leading Neuroscientist*. New York: Ballantine Books.
Noll, Richard. 1994. *The Jung Cult: Origins of a Charismatic Movement*. Princeton, NJ: Princeton University Press.
Paltin, Caroline 2014. Personal communication with the author.
Perls, Frederick. 1992. *Ego, Hunger, and Aggression*. The Gestalt Journal Press.
Perls, Frederick, Ralph Hefferline, and Paul Goodmam. 1951. *Gestalt Therapy*. New York: Julian Press.
Polster, Erving. 1969. *Encounter in Community*. San Francisco: Jossey-Bass.
———. 1972. *Stolen by Gypsies in Twelve Therapists*. San Francisco: Jossey-Bass.
———. 1987. *Every Person's Life Is Worth a Novel*. New York: W. W. Norton.
———. 1995. *A Population of Selves: A Therapeutic Exploration of Personal Diversity*. San Francisco: Jossey-Bass.
———. 2006. *Uncommon Ground*. Phoenix, AZ: Zeig, Tucker, & Theisen.
———. 2009. Introduction to *Community, Psychotherapy and Life Focus* by Brian O'Neil. Mount Keira, Australia: Ravenwood Press.
———. 2012. "Flexibility in Theory Formation: Point and Counterpoint." In *Gestalt Therapy: Advances in Theory and Practice*, edited by Talia Bar-Yoseph Levine. London: Routledge.
Polster, Erving, and Miriam Polster. 1974. *Gestalt Therapy Integrated*. New York: Vintage Books.
Proust, Marcel. 1934. *Swann's Way*. New York: Random House.
Rank, Otto. 1941. *Beyond Psychology*. New York: Dover.
Reivich, Karen J., Martin Seligman, and Sharon McBride. 2011. "Master Resilience Training in the U.S. Army." *American Psychologist* 66, no. 1: 10–18.
Rogers, Carl. 1980. *A Way of Being*. New York: Houghton Mifflin.
———. 1970. *Encounter Groups*. New York: Harper.
Rowling, J. K. 2012. *Harry Potter and the Chamber of Secrets*. London: Bloomsbury: 254.
Sandel, Michael. 2010. *Justice*. New York: Farrar, Straus, & Giroux.
Schlesinger, Arthur. 1992. *The Disuniting of America*. New York: W. W. Norton.
Seligman, Martin. 2002. *Authentic Happiness*. New York: Free Press.
———. 2011. "Helping American Soldiers in Time of War." *American Psychologist* 66, no. 7: 646–647.
Seligman, M., M. Matthews, and R. Corman. 2011. "Comprehensive Soldier Fitness: Building Resilience in a Challenging Institutional Context." *American Psychologist* 66, no. 1: 4–9.

Siegel, Daniel. 1999. *The Developing Mind*. New York: Guilford.
Smith, Adam. 1965. *Wealth of Nations*. New York: Modern Library.
Stegner, Wallace. 1993. *Where the Bluebird Sings in the Lemonade Springs*. New York: Penguin Books.
Taylor, Anne. 2009. *Noah's Compass*. New York: Alfred A. Knopf
Weinberg, Haim. 2014. *The Paradox of Interest Groups: Alone in the Presence of Others*. London: Karnac Books.
Wordsworth, William. 1807. *Poems in Two Volumes*. London: Longman, Hurst, Rees & Orme.
———. 1950. *The World Is Too Much with Us in George Benjamin Woods: English Prose and Poetry*. New York: Foresman and Company.
Yalom, Ervin. 1995. *The Theory and Practice of Group Psychotherapy*. New York: Basic Books.
Yapko, Michael. 2009. *Depression Is Contagious*. New York: Free Press.
———. 2003. *Trancework: An Introduction to the Practice of Clinical Hypothesis*. New York: Brunner-Routledge.
Zauderer, Donald. In *Community Psychotherapy and Life Focus*, edited by Brian O'Neil. Mount Keira, Australia: Ravenwood Press, 2009.

Index

A
absolutism. *See* Moral absolutism
academic psychology, 131
accessibly hidden, 24–25, 76
Aesop's Fables, 159
African Methodist Episcopal Church, 66
Alcoholics Anonymous (AA), 61–62
Alexander, Ronald, 55–56
American Psychological Association, 132
American Revolution, 148
America Speaks, 60–61
amplifying reality, 91–93
anger, ethos and, 117–118
Answer to Job (Jung), 134
anthropomorphism, 158–162. *See also* Human needs
    concept, 143
    empty chair dialogue, 161–162
    I-Thou relationship, 160–161
36 Arguments for the Existence of God (Rebecca Goldstein), 92
art and science, 129
artful authenticity, 95–96
artistic experience, 85–86
artistic quality, domain of, 19
artists, fluidity and, 177–178
arts, life focus in, 17–20
arts and psychotherapy, 85–96
    artful authenticity, 95–96
    difference between, 88–89
    paralleling the role of art, 89–94
aspiration, 110
Atran, Scott, 194, 198, 201–202
attention
    communal, expansion of, 7
    and mental events, 157
    personal, 13
    psychotherapeutic, 13
authorship, 109–110
awareness, 50–51

B
Back, Kurt, 40–41
Bandura, Albert, 44
behavioral symptomatology, 20–21
belonging
    communal worship and, 128
    conformity and, 183
    contact boundary, 185–187
    feeling of, 37
    figure/ground relationship, 187–190
    overview, 183–184
    principles of, 184–190
    psychological response, 190–192
benign ethos. *See* Ethos
Bible, 132
biological purposes of life focus, 12
Blake, William, 105
blogging, 63
Book of Job, 133–134
Borges, Jorge Luis, 89–90
Buber, Martin, 160
bullying, 94

C
career logistics, 46–48
Catcher in the Rye (Salinger), 17
The Cellist of Sarajevo (Steven Galloway), 18–19
ceremonial affirmation, 10
Charcot, Jean-Martin 140
chemical mutuality. *See* Mutuality
children, violence in social learning of, 44
China, 188
Chopra, Deepak, 54
Christian cathedrals, sanctification by, 149

Christmas, 137–138
church, 128
church-going, reasons for, 20
cocaine, 140
commercial organizations, 58–60
common life themes, 35–36
communal accessibility, 7
communal affirmation
  from private therapy, 36–37
communal attention, expansion of, 7. See also Attention
communal conversational vitality, 34
communal formats, 48, 54
communal idioms, 182
communally desirable orientations, 66
communal relevance, 55
communal sensibility, 200
communal worship, 128
community, 113–114
Comprehensive Soldier Fitness program, 52
concentration, 50–51
conceptualization, 195–198
conflicts, 196
conformity, 122
  dialect and, 122–123
  and individuality, 183
congregation, 113–117
  housing for, 199–200
  therapy group vs., 113
Conheim, Catherine, 159
Connectional Lay Organization, 66
constancy, 177, 179–182. See also Identity
  communal idioms, 182
  focus on life, 181
  format familiarity, 180
  portrayal of lives, 182
contact boundary, 185–187. See also Belonging
contagion, 122–123. See also Ethos
conversation, piggybacking, 118–119
conversational engagement, 56
conversational exchange, 65
conversational opportunity, 60
conversational relationship, 99
Crime and Punishment (Dostoevsky), 28–29
critiquing reality, 93–94
Csikszentmihalyi, Mihalyi, 54, 157

D
Dalí, Salvador, 92
Dawkins, Richard, 115

death, 154, 155, 156. *See also* Extrapolation
Dennet, Daniel, 141
dependability, 109
dependable identity, 175–182. See also Identity
dependency, 199
depression and social contagion, 122
Dewey, John, 132
dialects, 122–123
Dickens, Charles, 92
Donahue, Bill, 64
Dostoevsky, 28–29
Durkheim, Emil, 121

E
Eastern practices of meditation, 54–55
Ebbinghaus, Hermann, 131
Eliot, T. S., 159
empathy, 99–101
employee productivity, 59
encounter group, 38–42. *See also* Microcosm
Erhard, Werner, 123
Erikson, Erik, 197
Escape from Freedom (Fromm), 183
EST, 123–124
ethos, 117–123
  addressing themes of everyday life, 121
  anger and, 117–118
  contagion, 122–123
  individual pacing, 119–120
  language of positivity, 119
  piggybacking conversation, 118–119
  probing meaning, 120–121
experimental psychology, 131
extrapolation, 143, 154–158. *See also* Human needs

F
Facebook, 7, 63
faith, 155–156
family, symbolic trust about, 201
Fechner, Gustav, 131
figure/ground relationship, 187–190. *See also* Belonging
films, 78–79
financial aspects of group psychotherapy, 48
fluidity, 177–182. *See also* Identity
Flying without Wings, 78
focus, sharpened, 50–52
free association, 140

Index

freedom, 110–111
Freud, Sigmund, 8, 44, 127–131, 139–140, 197
   on Americans accepting psychoanalysis, 13
   hypnotism and, 140
   Judeo-Christian ethos and, 129, 130
   Jung's letters to, 133
   personal exploration, 139–140
   poetic environment of, 139
   portrayal of therapist, 123
   psychological ideas, 128–130
   on religion, 45, 130
Fromm, Erich, 183
Frost, Robert, 151
full neutrality, 72

G

Galloway, Steven, 18
Galton, Isaac, 131
Gestalt therapy, 50–52, 196
   contact boundary. *See* Contact boundary
   meditation and, 151
God
   authority of, 128–131
   creation of, 137
   human needs and. *See* Human needs
   poetic humanity and, 136–142
   prayer to. *See* Prayer
Golden Rule, 66, 127
Goldstein, Rebecca, 92
Goleman, Daniel, 54
gratitude, 111, 168–169
group therapy, 36–38. *See also* Microcosm
guidance, 123–124. *See also* Ethos

H

Hale, Nathan, 148
Hall, G. Stanley, 132
hallowed relationship, 153–154
Hartford Institute for Religion Research, 20
healing
   professions, 9
   in religious congregations, 20
Heller, Joseph, 92
Hendrix, Harville, 196
Henry's World (Conheim), 159
horizontal meaning, 121
housing, for congregation, 199–200
Houston, Jean, 54
human determinism, 141

human individuality, 35
human needs, 143–162
   anthropomorphism, 143, 158–162
   extrapolation, 143, 154–158
   relational indivisibility, 143, 144–148
   sanctification, 143, 148–154
human needs, overview, 143
humor, 101–104
Hunt, Helen, 196
Hunter, James Davison, 164
hypnosis theory, 56–57
hypnotism, 140

I

identity
   constancy phenomena of, 177, 179–182
   fluidity phenomena of, 177–182
   overview, 175–176
   personal characteristics and, 179
individuality. *See also* Belonging
   American reverence for, 188–189
   conformity and, 183
   contact boundary, 185–187
   in groups, 116–117
   Mahoney on, 188
   self-actualization, 117
   Smith on, 187–188
   Stegner on, 188–189
individual pacing, in speaking, 119–120
individual therapy, 90–91
   in presence of group, 76–78
indivisibility, 185. *See also* Belonging
   in allusional mode, 145
   common experiences of, 145
   neurologically induced, 145–146
   relational, 144–148
induction processes, Yapko's, 57
insight, 50
Internet
   communicating relationships through, 48
   conversations, 62–64
invisible hand, 188
Irving, John, 88–89
Ishiguro, Kazuo, 93–94
I-Thou relationship, 160–161

J

James, William, 132–133, 197
Jesus Christ
   in Matthew's Gospel, 127–128
Judeo-Christian mind, 66

Judeo-Christian religions, 21, 43. *See also* Religions
Judeo-Christian system. *See also* Freud, Sigmund
　Freud on, 129, 130
Jung, Carl, 133–135

K
Kabat-Zinn, Jon, 55
Kennedy, Robert, 189–190
Key Executive Leadership program, 59
kindness, group orientation towards, 80

L
laboratory, psychological, 132
Lagnado, Lucette, 180
language of positivity, 119
leadership, 123–124. *See also* Guidance
life, themes of, 121
life-clarifying awareness, 56–57
life focus
　awakening to, 10–15
　excess of, 12–13
　as fundamental function, 13
Life Focus Community group, working of, 69–83
　consolidation of theme, 75–76
　design options, 76–83
　introduction, 70
　report to plenary group, 74–75
　subgroup demonstration, 70–73
　subgroups, 73
Life Focus Community groups
　arts as precedent of, 17–20
　benign ethos. *See* Ethos
　communal harmony, 114–115
　congregation. *See* Congregation
　constancy in, 179–182
　converging attention, 136
　conversational explorations in, 24–32
　effects of sharp focus, 51–52
　enchantment with life process, 8–12
　in everyday conversation, 15–17
　guidance, 123–124
　meetings, 135–136
　microcosmic quality, 136
　modernity of, 8–15
　naming life-defining themes, 92–93
　paralleling the role of art, 89–94
　religion as precedent of, 20–21
　sanctification in, 150

social setting, 6–8
worldview, 117
life focus practices
　in commercial organizations, 6
life orientation, 82–83
life scenario, 8–9
limbic resonance, 115–116
listening, 97–99
Locke, John, 149
long-term therapy, 198
Luhrmann, T. M., 21, 138–39
Lukensmeyer, Carolyn, 60–61
Luther, Martin, 128

M
Mack, Mike, 64
Mahoney, Michael J., 188
Manchester, William, 128
marital couples, guides to, 196
Marketdata Enterprises, 62
Marquand, John, 183
Matthew's Gospel, 127–128
meaning
　hidden, 120
　markers, 121
　probing, 120–121
　vertical *vs.* horizontal, 121
meditation, 79–80, 151
　eastern practices of, 54–55
meetings. *See* Congregation
"Me Generation," 12–13
Meichenbaum, Donald, 47–48, 54
"Mending Wall" (Frost), 151
mental health professions, 46
Merkin, Daphne, 13–14
microcosm, 33–48
　characteristics of Life Focus Community group and, 34–35
　encounter group, 38–42
　group therapy, 36–38
　structural logistics, 42–48
microcosmic effect, 35. *See also* Microcosm
Miller, Arthur, 29
mind
　guided tour of, 8, 15
　multiplicity of, 10
　tapping the mystery of, 10
mind, manifest aspect of, 24–32
　arousal of hidden, 26–28
　manifest/hidden split, 24–26
　observer/observed split, 29–32

Index

outward focus, 32
scaling down, 28–29
MindBody Stress Reduction program, 55
mindfulness, 53–56
mind-shaping conflicts, 36
mirror neurons, 115
Moby Dick, 17–18
moral absolutism, 171, 172, 173
moral dilemmas, accepting, 169
morality, 163–174
    communal, 165
    issues/concerns, 166–171
    oppressive standards, 163
    overview, 163–166
    private therapy and, 165
    problem-solving perspective, 164–165
    relationships and, 164–165
    responsibility for one's own behavior, 170–171
    righting a wrong, 170
    "shoulds" phenomenon and, 166–171
    therapeutic perspective, 165
moral relativity, 171–174
    context, 171–172
    innate reasons for, 171–172
    proportion, 172
Mowrer, O. H., 64
mutuality, 59, 114
    interrelational, 115
    limbic resonance, 115–116
    neurological studies, 115

N
Nabokov, Vladimir, 91
National Center for Complementary and Alternative Medicine, 53–54
needs. *See* Human needs
networking, 62–64
neutrality, full, 72
Newberg, Andrew, 145
The New Psychology (Dewey), 132
New York Times, 17
Noah's Compass (Anne Tyler), 18
Noll, Richard, 133

O
organizational context, personal explorations in, 58
organizational effectiveness, 6
Otherness, 185

P
Paltin, Caroline, 190
Pavlov, Ivan, 197
peak experiences, 41
Penn Resiliency Program, 52–53
Perls, Frederick, 50
personal attention, 13. *See also* Attention
personal awareness, 58
personal disability, sense of, 12
personal expansion, 10
personal explorations in organizational context, 58
personal heroes, 21
personal improvement, 12
personal well-being, 46
person-to-person exploration, 6–7
piggybacking conversation, 118–119
poetic humanity, 136–142
poetry, 8
    basic idea of, 137
    creation of God, 137
Polonius (Shakespeare), 29
Polster, Miriam, 80, 145, 152
Pope, Alexander, 29
practice, forms of, 79–81
prayer, 79–80, 119, 138, 192
privacy, 36
private therapy, 36–37
probing meaning, 120–121
problem-solving, 9
Protestant churches, 20
Proust, Marcel, 29–30
pscyhotherapy
    therapy theories, 144–145
psychoanalysis, 129
    criticisms of, 43
    Jung on, 133–135
    religious nature of, 133
psychology
    academic, 131
    early, 131–133
    religion and, 131–133
psychotherapeutic attention, 13
psychotherapeutic cure, 20
psychotherapeutic intention, 9, 20–21
psychotherapists
    ascendancy of human and, 135
    as cultural agent, 9
    Freud on, 13, 71–72, 197
    inspirational music and, 82
    office, atmosphere of, 9

privacy and, 36–37
relationship with, 33
role, 192
structural logistics and. *See* Structural logistics
psychotherapy. *See also* Life Focus Community group; *specific* entries
associated with office practice, 14
community and, 199–203
conceptualizations, 195–198
continuity and, 198–199
groups. *See* Therapy group
human needs satisfied by. *See* Human needs
in individuality-oriented countries, 187–190
morality and. *See* Morality
poetic humanity and, 136–142
priority of, 45
religion and. *See* Religion(s)
science and art in, 129
searching hidden meanings, 120
social influence of, 193
therapy sessions, importance of, 9
public enchantment, 9–10

Q
quasi-secret society, 152

R
Rank, Otto, 45
reasons for going to church, 20–21
recreating reality, 89–91
re-entry process, brain studies, 200
relational groups, 64–65
religious restoration of, 65
relational indivisibility, 144–148. *See also* Human needs
concept, 143
differentiation between me and thee, 145
differentiation between self and other, 146
relational networking, 62–64
religion(s), 64–65, 127–131, 193–194
communal format and psychotherapy's individual orientation, 45–46
Jung on, 133–135
leaders, 20
psychologists on, 131–133
religious behavior, 20
religious experience, evaluation, 21
religious relational groups, examples of, 65–66
symbolism, 133
Remains of the Day (Kazuo Ishiguro), 93–94
remedial purposes, 9
Renaissance, 128
Rogers, Carl, 39, 100, 149
Roman hierarchy, 128
Rose, Charlie, 188
Rousseau, 149

S
Sabbath, 149
sacrifice, 106–107
sanctification, 148–154. *See also* Human needs
concentration and, 151
concept, 143
hallowed relationship, 153–154
Santa Claus, phenomenon of, 137–138
Sartre, Jean-Paul, 177
savoring experience, 104–106
science
art and, 129
secular ideology and, 194
secular ideology, science and, 194
seekers of enlightenment, 15
self-actualization, 117
self-awareness, 55
self-centered thinking, 12–13
self-examination, 31
affirming, 38
self-exploratory process, 12–13
self-generosity, 55
self-identity, 89
self-improvement market, 62
self-help books, 6
self-help groups, 61–62
self-help orientations, 54
self-realization, 9
state of, 55
Seligman, Martin, 47–48, 52–53
sensitivity training groups, 58
sharpened focus, 50–52
Siegel, Daniel, 200
simplicity, 175
situational Sabbath. *See* Sabbath
Smith, Adam, 187–188
social control, absence of, 41

Index

social media, 63
social trust. *See* Trust
societal reverberations, 9
society's well-being, 75
Socrates, 29
space-bound therapy, 43–46
speaking, individual pacing in, 119–120
spirit, 140
spirited enlightenment, 9
Stegner, Wallace, 188–189
structural logistics, 42–48. *See also* Microcosm
supernaturalism
   belief in, 194
   social influence of, 194
Swann's Way (Marcel Proust), 29–30
symbols, 202

T
talking cure, 8
Ten Commandments, 20, 66, 127
themes for people's psychological existence, 97–112
   aspiration, 110
   freedom, 110–111
   gratitude, 111
   recovering what one already has, 108–110
themes of everyday life, 121
therapy group. *See also* Psychotherapy
   "group" designation, 113
   vs. congregation, 113
Thou, 160. *See also* I-Thou relationship
time-bound therapy, 42–43
transactional analysis, 196
transference, 33, 144
   hallowing and, 153
trust. *See also* Psychotherapy
   community, 199–203
   conceptualization, 195–198
   continuity, 198–199
   dependency and, 199
   overview, 193–195
   psychotherapy and, 193–202
   public interest and, 194
   symbolic, 201–202
Tyler, Anne, 18

U
unity, 114
   limbic resonance and, 115–116
University of Massachusetts Medical School, 55

V
vertical meaning, 121
Vineyard Christian Fellowship, 138
violence in social learning of children, 44

W
Waldman, Mark, 145
"We Are the World" (song), 159–160
Weinberg, Haim, 47–48
well-being, 89
   society's, 75
Wen Jiabao, 188
Western psyche, 127
Western religions, 45, 66. *See also* Religions
Wilbur, Ken, 54
Willow Creek Community Church, 64, 66
A World Lit Only by Fire (Manchester), 128
worldly themes, 35
Wundt, Wilhelm, 131

Y
Yalom, 65
Yapko, Michael, 47–48, 56–57, 122

Z
Zauderer, Donald, 59